BRITISH AND COMMONWEALTH MILITARY KNIVES

BRITISH AND COMMONWEALTH MILITARY KNIVES

Ron Flook

Airlife
England

This book is dedicated to my wife Margaret and
my sons Robert and Andrew for their forbearance
during the preparation of this book and during my
trips to arms fairs far and wide.

Copyright © 1999 R.E. Flook
First published in the UK in 1999
by Airlife Publishing Ltd

British Library Cataloguing-in-Publication Data
A catalogue record for this book
is available from the British Library

ISBN 1 85310 986 X

Typeset by Servis Filmsetting Ltd, Manchester
Printed in England by the Bath Press Ltd, Bath.

Airlife Publishing Ltd
101 Longden Road, Shrewsbury, SY3 9EB, England
E-mail: airlife@airlifebooks.com
Website: www.airlifebooks.com

PREFACE

Besides the normal introduction, I felt that some comment on the book, its structure and contents was warranted.

In attempting to put this book together the major problem was that of obtaining reliable information. Trying to locate relevant historical data has been an extremely difficult task. The loss by take-over or liquidation of many of the Sheffield cutlery manufacturers and the consequential disappearance of historical records proved a major stumbling block.

Very little information is available from museums, the Public Record Office – while holding information in respect of those knives subject to Registered Designs – has no information on official issue military knives, and even information on current or recent issue knives has been extremely difficult to obtain. To illustrate the latter problem, in one letter from a Ministry of Defence department staff stated they were unable to help because all historical data had been destroyed due to lack of storage space, and I was enquiring about a knife that is still an issue item.

These problems, coupled with the difficulties of locating actual specimens, have made the production of this book drag on a lot longer than I originally anticipated. However, I now feel that enough material is available to make this a reasonably authoritative book.

I have as far as possible tried to be accurate with descriptions and information, and I have also corrected some misinformation which has appeared in other books. None of us is, however, infallible and any errors are accepted as my own.

The photographs, taken in the main by myself, are not in the professional class. Some specimens were photographed under adverse conditions and vary in quality. However, the practicalities of employing a professional and getting the knives together under studio conditions forced a do-it-yourself approach. Though they could be better, I hope the photos are of sufficient clarity to illustrate the major feature of each knife. Where I have had to resort to drawings it was because the actual knife was unavailable for study and photographing.

The contents of the book are restricted to official issue items and those private purchase knives with known or obvious military use, e.g. the knives of Robbins of Dudley. Layout and classification of pieces, and what to actually include, obviously posed some problems. I have tried to follow some form of chronological order under various countries and knife types, and except for a few isolated examples have identified knives by the country in which they were issued. There is however obviously some 'blurring of the edges' when it comes to this latter aspect and not all pieces fall into neat categories. A section with knives of likely British or Commonwealth origins has also been included. As none of these knives has yet been properly identified, I would appreciate hearing from any reader who has any evidence or information which would aid identification.

I decided against providing any material on nomenclature as details of the various knife parts and terminology are well documented in other sources. Measurements have been given in imperial units rather than metric. I chose this approach as virtually all British and Commonwealth knives up until, in historical terms, quite recently were manufactured using such measurements. However, for the benefit of those more used to metric dimensions, help with conversion is given in Appendix Five at the end of the book.

While measurements are in general self-explanatory, I should explain the method used to measure pocket-knives and kukris. The length of pocket-knife blades was taken from blade tip to bolster, with overall length not including staple or lanyard ring. The correct method for measuring a kukri blade has not been established, but the method I adopted was to measure from blade tip to hilt by the shortest possible line.

The problem posed by fakes is not ignored.

Unfortunately, as in most fields of collecting, when prices rise in relation to demand the fakers make an appearance, and knives have not escaped their attention. Some fakes are quite crude and do not readily fool even novice collectors, but there are some excellent copies of Robbins' knives around, for instance, which are difficult to detect. Fantasy pieces can also be a problem. Many spurious knives were produced in the 1960s, 1970s and 1980s, and these still occasionally make a reappearance, ready to deceive a new generation of collectors. Notes on fakes are given in a special section at the end of the book, and I can only reiterate the warning of *caveat emptor* — let the buyer beware.

I hope you enjoy the book, and I am always interested in hearing from other collectors with details of knives not included in this volume.

Finally, I must mention that the purpose of this book is not to glorify knives as weapons but to place them in an historical context in relation to their use by the military of Britain and the Commonwealth.

ACKNOWLEDGEMENTS

There is absolutely no doubt that this book would be a much poorer effort but for the help and support of fellow collectors and museums who allowed me to examine and photograph knives in their collections, and/or provided information from their files. The assistance of all who helped in some way, either directly or indirectly, is gratefully acknowledged.

I should particularly like to thank the following for their help and assistance: Renzo Jardella, for his help in my early days of collecting; likewise Gordon Hughes, and for permission to use some illustrations from his *Primers*; Harry Jones; John Grottick; John Pidgeon; John Ensor; Gary Tucker; Fred Stephens, for allowing me to use photographs from his book *Fighting Knives*; David Hayden-Wright; Richard Craddock; Homer Brett; Jim Lang; Alan Simpson; Jeff Cossum; Ian Rasmusen; Don Lawrence; Leonard and Guy West for their assistance in turning some of my rough sketches into more acceptable illustrations; the staff at the Imperial War Museum; Herb Woodend and Carl Wood of the Pattern Room; and the staffs of various Ministry of Defence departments who were very helpful and patient in answering my many letters and questions.

CONTENTS

Photo credits

Imperial War Museum – 49, 74, 78, 131, 197, 251, 278, 279.
Australian War Memorial – 403, 409, 421.
Author's collection – 56, 157, 171, 241, 262, 524
Fred Stephens – 12, 68, 274.
Pattern Room – 69, 70, 71, 256, 257, 258, 342.
Jeff Cossum – 387.
Jim Lang – 449.
Peter Taylor – 497.
Andy Stevens – 242.
Crown Copyright – 90

Every effort has been made to contact and acknowledge owners of the copyright of illustrative material used in this book. In the case of any omissions, holders of copyright are invited to contact the Publisher.

INTRODUCTION

Over the last several decades or so the collecting of military knives has become increasingly popular. At one time the field was restricted to a small number of enthusiasts, but today the speed with which good specimens are snapped up reflects an increased interest.

With this interest in military knives there have come several books on the subject, but a field which has not received much attention in these publications is that of British and Commonwealth military knives. Unlike US military knives, which have received scholarly attention in the books written and published by M. H. Cole, British and Commonwealth knives have only been dealt with in general terms. This book endeavours to fill the gap by specifically dealing with the knives used by the British and Commonwealth military (including air force and naval) personnel from about 1850 to the present day.

PART ONE

BRITAIN

With the exception of pocket-knives virtually nothing is known about the issue of British Military Knives prior to the World War 1 period. Whilst the Scottish Piper's Dirk was issued during the Victorian era for Dress purposes those troops who required a knife for more warlike purposes supplied their own or had them supplied on a Regimental basis. Wilkinson-Latham bears out this latter point in his book *British Cut and Thrust Weapons* (1) in which he states that certain Regiments during the Boer War carried Bowie knives and some evidence exists (2) that in the 1790s certain Regiments carried Dirks rather than swords.[1] Even the trench warfare of World War 1 does not seem to have prompted the British Military into issuing a fighting knife. Official issue machetes from the period are known, a useful tool in the Colonies, but the troops in the trenches generally had to rely on private purchase knives, modified bayonets or trench knives captured from the Germans. In the interwar years some knives were introduced but these were primarily for survival or working roles. It was not until World War 2 that the British took the fighting and survival knife seriously. After years of neglect, a profusion of designs were officially produced, e.g. Commando and knuckle knives, the Smatchet, survival and other specialist knives for the RAF and the SOE.

The lessons of World War 2 have in general not been lost with several varieties of knife presently available to the British Forces. Whilst most of these are tools or survival weapons the Commando knife is still available for more warlike roles should the need arise.

This section illustrates and describes some of the knives used by British Forces from around 1850 in the case of pocket-knives through the private purchase knives of the Victorian and World War 1 periods, the Commando and other knives of World War 2 to the issue knives of today.

VICTORIAN PERIOD

Most of the knives from this period tend to be of very high quality and for the most part almost certainly weapons purchased by Officers prior to a posting in India or other parts of the Empire.

1. First illustrated by Hughes in his Primer Part 2 this extremely interesting knife possibly dates from around the 1850s.[2] The hilt is reminiscent of that found on the British 1853 Pattern Cavalry sword but as the piece is unmarked a positive dating is not possible. It is however the case that this style of hilt was used extensively on British swords and bayonets up until the late 1800s. Whilst obviously designed as a fighting weapon, whether it was an official issue item is open to speculation. Considering however the period from which it dates and the lack of marks I believe the knife is almost certainly private purchase. The knife has a single edged spear point blade some 9.25 inches in length. The hilt has a steel bolster which partially covers the ricasso and a steel pommel. The grips are of pressed chequered leather secured by five steel rivets. The sheath is of leather with a steel locket, the chape is missing and the frog is a later addition. Overall length 15.25 inches.

2. This very well made piece in the style of a Khyber knife

represents a typical example of a knife purchased by an Officer for service in India. The knife has a finely chequered green horn with the 11.5 inch blade marked

V R
THORNHILL
LONDON

This marking would place the date of this knife between 1837 and 1901. Another similar example of this style of knife was illustrated by Hughes.[3] Overall length 17.125 inches.

---

3. Dating from the same period as the previous knife this high quality knife in the form of the Kukri was again almost certainly a Officer's purchase prior to Indian service. The blade is marked

HILL & SON
4 HAYMARKET
LONDON

The piece is accompanied by a good quality sheath and the blade length is 5.375 inches; overall length 9.5 inches.

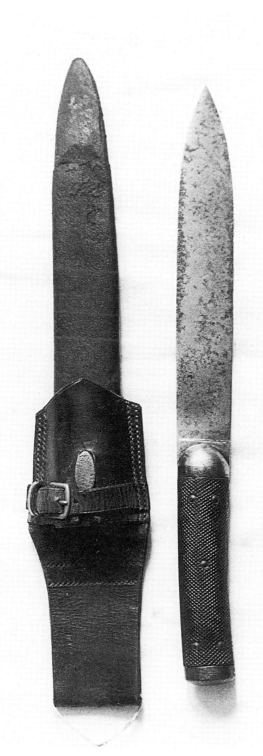

Plate 1

Plate 2 *Plate 3*

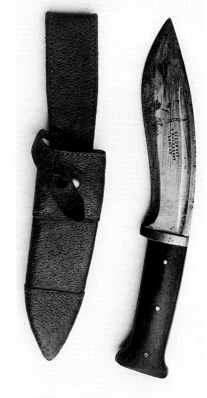

4 Very similar to (3), this knife has a 7.75-inch blade without fullers and is stamped

HOLTZAPFFEL & CO

LONDON

6

The hilt has hardwood grips and the white metal pommel is engraved H.C.P 60 RIFLES. The 60th Rifles, one of the forerunners of the King's Own Royal Rifle Corps, grew from the 60th Regiment of Foot. It carried the designation 60th Rifles in various forms between 1824 and 1881. The knife almost certainly dates from the latter part of this period.

5 Another knife in the kukri style, manufactured or marketed by Hill & Son. This 14.5-inch blade is etched GRAHAM GAUNTLETT and is stamped with the same Hill & Son mark shown in (3). The one-piece wood grip is secured to the tang by three small rivets and is fitted with a leather wrist thong. The leather sheath is of high quality. Overall length 20 inches.

6 This interesting hunting-style knife was carried by a member of the Coldstream Guards during the 1870s/80s. Made by Thornhill the knife has a clipped-point blade with round wood grip which is chequered overall. A German silver ferrule and pommel cap are fitted, the latter engraved with the name A or H (script form of engraving makes this initial difficult to decipher) G. FORTESCUE along with the Coldstream Guards badge. The black leather sheath is fitted with both belt loop and hanging ring, the locket being engraved with the Fortescue name. Blade length 7 inches; overall length 12.25 inches.

Research indicates that an Hon. Arthur Grenville Fortescue served with the Coldstream Guards. He

was the fourth son of the 3rd Earl Fortescue, and was born on 24 December 1858 and died on 30 October 1895. He was a Second Lieutenant in November 1878 and a Lieutenant in July 1881, (he did not appear in the 1886 Army List) and served with the 2nd Battalion in the Egyptian war in 1882, present at the engagement at Tel-el- and the Battle of Tel-el-Kebir.

Plate 4   *Plate 5*

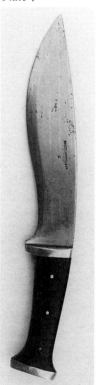
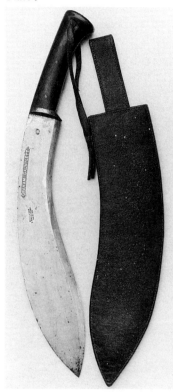

Plate 6

7 Like the previous knife the military provenance of this large large Bowie knife is established by the details provided by an engraved pommel. The knife was made or retailed in Edinburgh, though the actual maker/retailer cannot be established due to the name and some of the address being partially erased. The spear-point blade is some 9.5 inches in length. The crossguard and pommel are of white metal and the grip of stag. Overall length is 14.5 inches.

The pommel, although badly bruised, reveals enough of its original engraving to trace the owner and outline a potential history of the knife. The piece is named after a ? H. YOUNG with the regimental dedication appearing as the O HIGHLANDERS. Only a few Scottish regiments carried the latter designation and research indicates that none carried any numerical series that would have included a zero. The missing word must therefore be a Highland regiment whose name has a letter 'O' in it, which narrows the field down to the Gordons or Camerons. Enquiries with the United Services Museum in Edinburgh have identified a W. Young serving with the Cameron Highlanders in 1897 as the Quartermaster of the 1st Battalion, having the honorary rank of Lieutenant.

8 & 9 Patented in April 1902 by Major Charles Blair Baldock of the Merwara Battalion of the Indian Staff Corps at Ajmere, India, the Baldock Knife Spear weapon was described in the patent specification as providing an improved spear or knife for hunting, pig sticking, military or

Plate 7

Plate 8

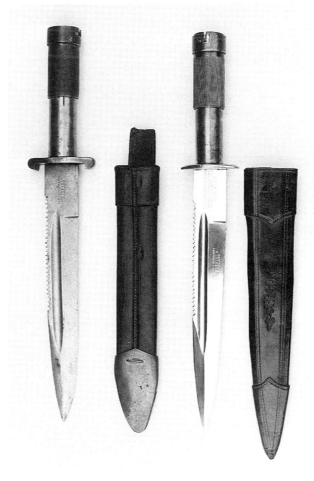

other purposes. The illustration shows two variations of this combination weapon; both have the same blade and hilt, but there are differences in the crossguard. The construction is all-metal and the tubular grip contains a sliding collar which could be compressed onto a wooden shaft to turn the knife into a spear. The left-hand example is marked on the ricasso

JAMES DIXON & SONS

SHEFFIELD

ENGLAND

The version on the right carries this mark on the blade with the ricasso marked

BALDOCK KNIFE SPEAR

MADE EXPRESSLY FOR

WALTER LOCKE & CO LTD

PATENTED

Note the two sheath variations and the fact that the left-hand specimen conforms more in style to the original design

drawing (9). Blade length 9 inches; overall length 13.75 inches.

---

10 Developed in the 1880s from a design by Major Henry John Childe Shakespear, the Shakespear Knife and variations of it were produced by Wilkinson up until at least 1910. Given Shakespear's background of hunter, soldier of fortune and Indian Army Major, it is highly likely that this knife was used by others in the military. The example illustrated has a 5.75-inch double-edged blade, steel crosspiece and plain wood hilt in which the top is chequered. On some examples the hilt is chequered overall. The sheath is leather covering a wood body and it carries a frog stud and spring clip which retains the knife in its sheath. Most examples of these knives carry an etched panel on the blade which reads

SHAKESPEAR KNIFE

WILKINSON PALL MALL

Overall length 9.5 inches.

Plate 9

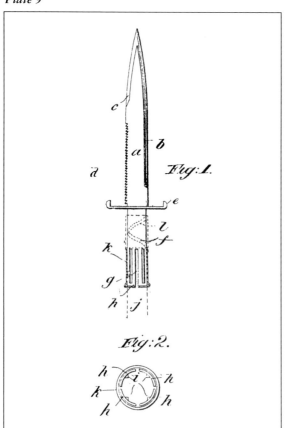

Plate 10

FIRST WORLD WAR

As mentioned earlier there appears to be no evidence to suggest that the British ever officially issued a trench or fighting knife during the First World War. Some unit and regimental level issue is known but most troops provided their own knives. These tended to be broken or modified bayonets or knives produced by those companies that recognised there was a market for a good fighting knife.

---

11 A typical example of a trench knife made from a converted 1879 Pattern Artillery Sword Bayonet. The blade on this weapon has been shortened to 7 inches and ground to a Bowie tip. Overall length 12.5 inches.

---

12 Another converted bayonet used as a trench knife during World War One. The piece is made from a Pattern 1888 Lee Metford Bayonet whose blade had been shortened to approximately 7.5 inches, with a highly effective knuckle bow added to the hilt. The present location of this knife is unknown and the illustration is taken from a copy of an old photograph obtained from its one-time owner.

Plate 11

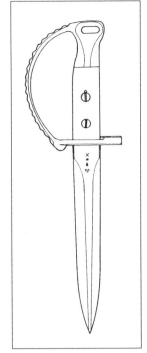

Plate 12

Plate 13

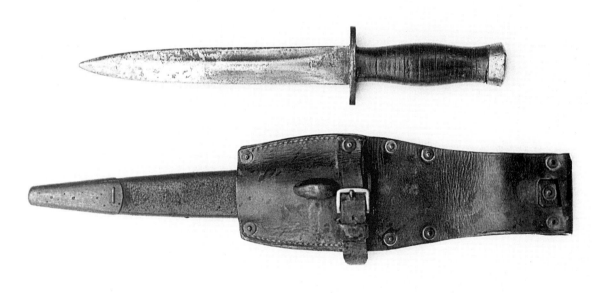

13 Almost certainly dating from the First World War period this conversion of a 1903 bayonet to a fighting knife has been very well carried out. The blade has been shortened to 7.125 inches and the original hilt replaced by one comprising leather washers, brass pommel and crossguard. The original sheath has been shortened to suit the conversion. Overall length 11.875 inches.

14 Converted from either a 1888 or 1903 Pattern bayonet this knife, like (13) has been very well made. The blade retains most of its original length but the hilt has been replaced with a short steel crossguard and shaped wooden grip with steel ferrule.

15 This 1888 bayonet conversion has almost certainly been professionally executed, and another specimen with a slightly differently shaped crossguard has been observed. The original blade complete with marks has been retained, with a large unusually shaped crossguard being added along with a completely new pommel of the correct 1888 design, though this lacks a bayonet slot, and new wood grips fixed with screw bolts. All metal work is blued. The original sheath complete with webbing frog accompanies this extremely fine and unique piece of First World War weaponry. Blade length 12 inches; overall length 16.875 inches.

16, 16A & 16B The famed and fearsome Welsh sword as

Plate 14

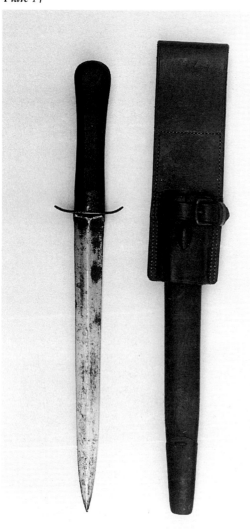

Plate 15

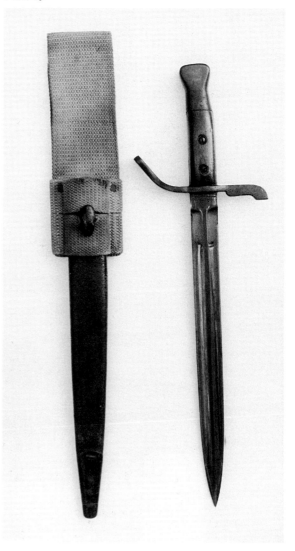

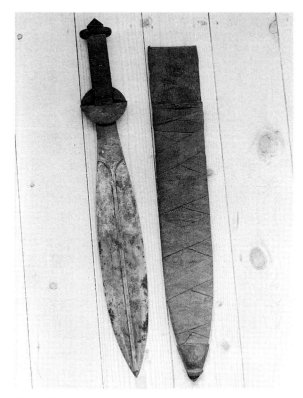

used by the Royal Welch Fusiliers during World War One. Privately provided by Lord Howard de Walden to his battalion it was based on the design for the ancient Welsh Cledd, and was designed and patented by Felix Joubert in 1917, the patent accepted on 23 August 1917. Joubert's patent drawing is shown in (16A). The blade and hilt are forged from one piece and a circular fold-back hand guard is fitted via a slot in the hilt. The hilts were cord-bound. The ricasso of some examples bears the motto DROS URDDAS CYMRU and the small mark of a J overstamping a O, but other examples are unmarked. The sheaths were either bound with webbing as in (16) or the leather left exposed as in (16B). Some sheaths have been noted, marked with the name Joubert along with the Royal Coat of Arms. Blade length 17.5 inches; overall length 23.5 inches.

A very unusual variation of the Welsh sword has been noted in the Welch Regiment Museum, Cardiff Castle. The piece has a crossguard of much larger than normal diameter which has one edge turned up to provide a degree of protection to the knuckles.

---

17 While originally manufactured as a dress weapon, the manufacturing date of 1916 of this Other Ranks Piper's Dirk makes combat use a possibility. The dirk illustrated is the Mk III which was introduced by List of Changes entry 16582 dated 21 July 1913. The dirk has a plain 11.75-inch single-

Plate 16

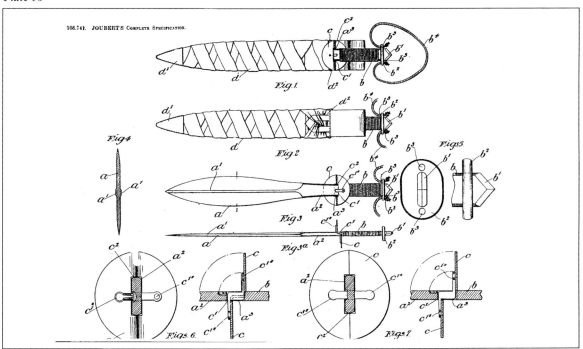

Plate 16A

edged blade, with a 5.25-inch sharpened back edge. The grip is of an early form of plastic called Dermatine, cast to form the Celtic interlacing pattern so typical of Scottish dirks, and is decorated with small bright headed pins. The hilt is topped with a pommel cap bearing a raised king's crown. It is interesting to note that a copy of Specification No. SA364A, approved 10 November 1913, held in my files which covers the manufacture and inspection of the Mk III states that the hilt should be manufactured from well-seasoned ebony. The use of Dermatine must therefore have been approved in the 1914–15 period.

The blade bears the Enfield inspection mark of a crowned

35

E

along with the acceptance date of 4'16 (April 1916). The other side of the blade also bears the Enfield inspection mark

along with a ↑ an the x mark indicating a bend test. The sheath is of black leather with four mounts bearing the thistle emblem. The reverse of the locket bears a bar which secures the belt loop. Overall length 17.375 inches.

---

18 Experimental trench knife. This heavy brass-hilted knife is reputed to be one of a batch of twenty pieces submitted by W. W. Greener to the War Department for trials as a trench knife during World War One. Apparently most of this batch were double-edged, with one of the edges being saw-backed, but five were like the example illustrated. Documentation is supposed to exist supporting these claims, but to date I have been unable to locate a copy of this. I am personally somewhat suspicious of the claims made for these knives, several of which appeared at auction a number of years ago. These knives are so obviously divers' knives, having been identified as such by the diving equipment manufacturers C.

Plate 16B

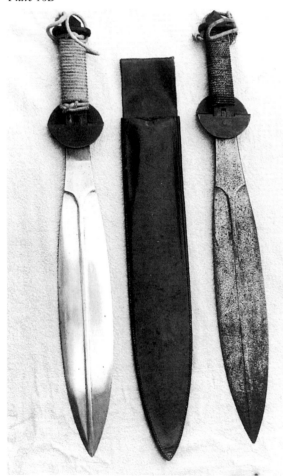

Plate 17

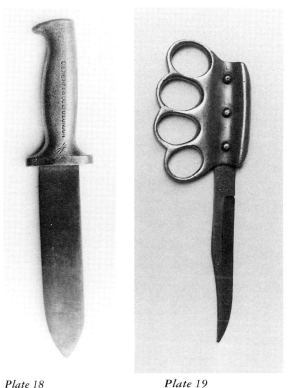

E. Heinke and Co. Ltd, whose name actually appears on the hilt. Besides bearing the Heinke name the hilt is also marked 19 and W.W.G. ENGLAND.

The mustering-out mark of two broad arrows tip to tip is also stamped on the hilt but this mark does not appear to be correct. Why Greener would have submitted Heinke-made divers' knives for trials as a trench knife is a mystery to me. Blade length 6.375 inches; overall length 11 inches.

19 Knuckle knives of this style were popular private purchase items during World War One and it is likely that such pieces also saw service during World War Two. All examples follow the same basic pattern, the only variation being in the hilt material and finish. This one is a brass-hilted version marked on the blade

CHAS	AND	SHEFFIELD
CLEMENTS		MADE

Clements are a long-established firm of cutlery retailers based in London. From information provided by them it would appear that the knife was made for them by George Ibberson. Blade length 5.375 inches; overall length 8.75 inches.

20 A fine example of this style of knuckle knife by George Ibberson, having nickel-plated knuckles.

Plate 18

Plate 19

Plate 20

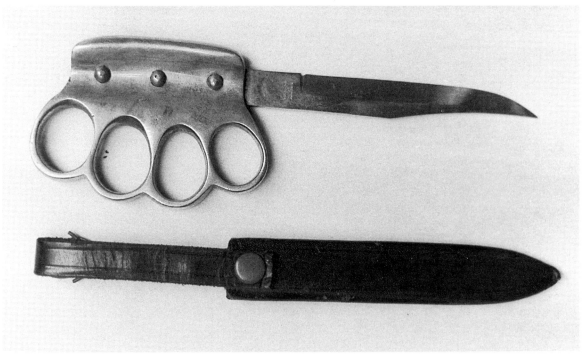

21 This piece in the collection of the Imperial War Museum also has a nickel-plated hilt, the palm piece of which is engraved 2ND LIEUT. FERGUSON THE BUFFS.

---

22 An example with alloy hilt, and the name SUTHERLAND & RHODEN SHEFFIELD etched on the blade.

---

23 & 23A Of the same type as (22), this knife is interesting in that the alloy knuckles are marked

REG NO. 654912

SHEFFIELD MADE

The sheath is also a little unusual as the body follows the general shape of the blade. A copy of the original Registration of Design drawing is shown in (23A). Unfortunately no information on who registered it has been located.

Plate 21

Plate 23

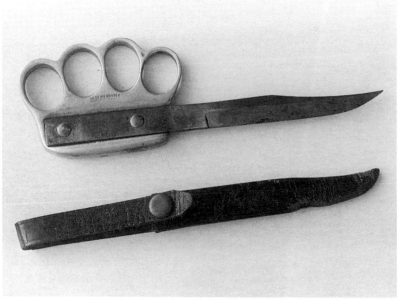

Plate 22

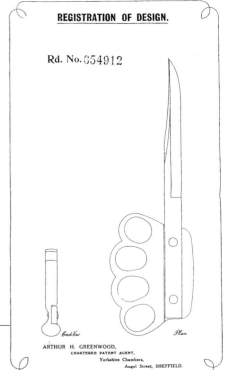

Plate 23A

REGISTRATION OF DESIGN.

Rd. No. 654912

ARTHUR H. GREENWOOD,
CHARTERED PATENT AGENT,
Yorkshire Chambers,
Angel Street, SHEFFIELD.

24 With the same style hilt as those knives shown left, this knife is fitted with an unusual double-edged blade with a waisted ricasso. The knife was made by E. Blyde & Co. Blade length 5 inches; overall length 8.5 inches.

25 The brass knuckles of this example are similar to that found on the World War Two BC41. The blade is marked LOWE SHEFFIELD. Blade length 5.375 inches; overall length 8 inches. (It is possible that this knife does not date from the

World War One period and is in fact much later, the name Lowe being associated with a joint venture which operated in the 1970s; see Appendix Four for information on Lowe.)

26 Another version with pyramid knuckle, which in this case retains the full width of the brass rather than being tapered in as on the previous example. The knife is unmarked.

Plate 24

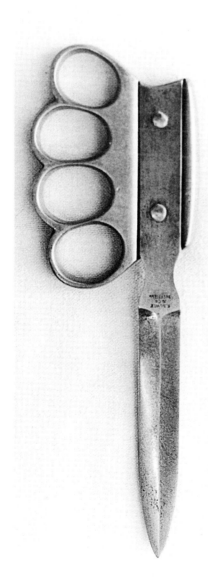

Plate 25

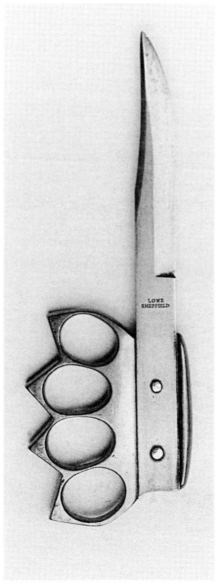

Plate 26

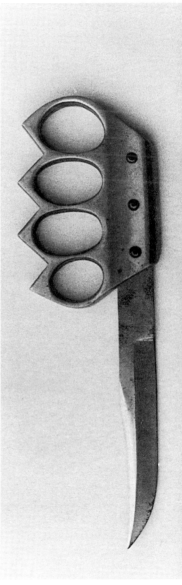

27 An unusual knife with only the centre two knuckles having pyramid projections. The knuckles are of brass and the blade is marked with the name JOHN WATTS. The sheath has a buckle hilt retainer rather than the normal press-stud. Blade length 5.5 inches; overall length 8.825 inches.

28 Similar to (290) in Frederick Stephens' *Fighting Knives*, this piece, unlike (290), has a ricasso and projections on the knuckles. The double-edged blade is 4.625 inches in length, the crossguard and brass knuckles have a plated finish. The scales are of stag secured by five nickel pins. The knife is of very high quality and bears the name CLEMENTS on the ricasso. Overall length 8.875 inches.

29 Another popular style of World War One knuckle knife with a slim Bowie blade of 4.75 inches in length, alloy knuckles and grips of chequered ebony. This particular example was made by Hibbert and Sons. Examples made by George Ibberson have also been noted. Overall length 8.875 inches.

30 With the same type of hilt as (29) this knife appeared in auction some years ago. The catalogue described the piece as having a 6.75-inch double-edged blade made by Beardshaw.[4] Overall length was not given, but this was probably in the region of 11 inches.

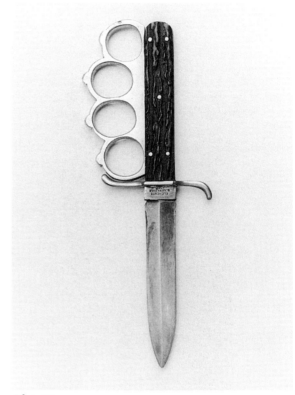

Plate 27

Plate 28

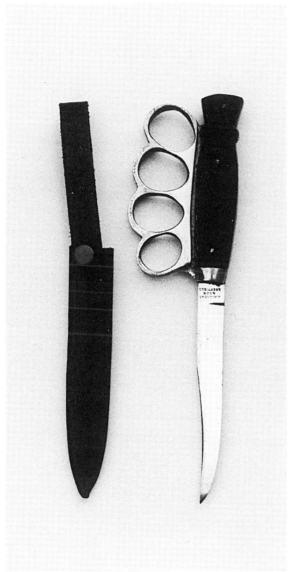

Plate 29

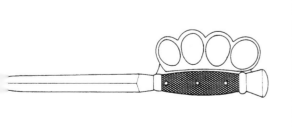

Plate 30

Plate 31

31 Made by William Rodgers, this piece utilises the same blade and grip material found on sheath knives of the period. The knife has a 5.5-inch Bowie blade, the hilt has a brass bolster and the grips are of a hard black ebonite-type material with a gouged bone finish. The knuckles are of alloy. Overall length 9.625 inches.

ROBBINS OF DUDLEY

Despite extensive enquiries I have been able to obtain very little information on Robbins other than that which has already been published by Frederick Stephens and Gordon Hughes.[5] Robbins was apparently a company which specialised in various forms of metalwork and operated in Dudley, Worcestershire from 1876 until about 1928, the last date at which their name appeared in local directories. It would appear that during World War One Robbins commenced the manufacture of a variety of knives for private sale to troops heading for the trenches. They used some unique designs, and examples of many of these are now rare. Unfortunately the increasing rarity of these knives has resulted in some very good fakes appearing on the market. (For further comment on this, see Appendix One on Fakes and Reproductions.)

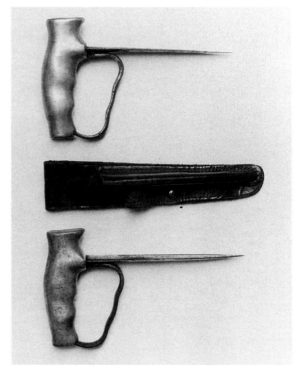

Plate 32/33

Plate 34

32 & 33 Probably the commonest pattern of Robbins' work encountered by the collectors, this push dagger is known to have been copied by other manufacturers. One example bearing the name SPENCER on the blade has been noted, and pieces by Underwood have been observed. In the illustration the top specimen (32) is unmarked, the lower example (33) being marked on the base of the hilt with the usual ROBBINS DUDLEY mark. Both knives comprise cast alloy hilts with a steel knuckle bow. The double-edged blade has double fullers on both sides. The brown leather sheath has the typical Robbins feature of a securing strap which wraps over the knuckle guard. The marked piece has a 5-inch blade, and the unmarked version a 4.75-inch blade.

34 An extremely rare variant of the standard push dagger is shown at the bottom of this illustration (photographed with a standard version for comparison). Only two examples of this knife have been observed and the piece is perfectly genuine and not one of the Robbins' fakes. The knife has the usual push dagger hilt but is fitted with a blade 6.25 inches in length. The blade length would indicate that it came from the same stock as that used to produce (37).

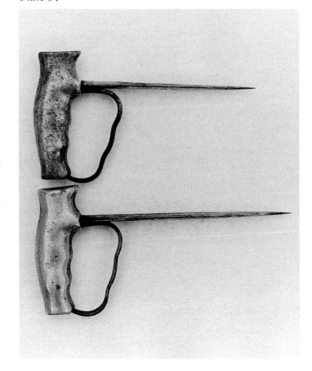

35 A further Robbins push dagger with double finger stalls and palm piece. The maker's name is stamped on the palm piece and the double-edged blade is 3.625 inches in length. Overall length is 6.5 inches. Fakes of this knife have been

noted; these have the Robbins name stamped near the junction of blade and hilt.

36 & 36A This Robbins dagger is in the collection of the Imperial War Museum and to date is the only example of this particular pattern seen or heard of, though fakes have recently been observed. The alloy 'ram's head' grip is designed for grasping between the middle three fingers. The blade is double-edged and similar to that used on (32). Blade length 4 inches; overall length 5.5 inches.

Plate 35

Plate 36A

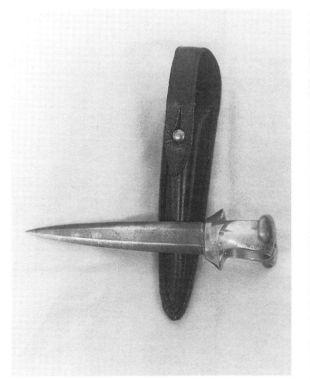

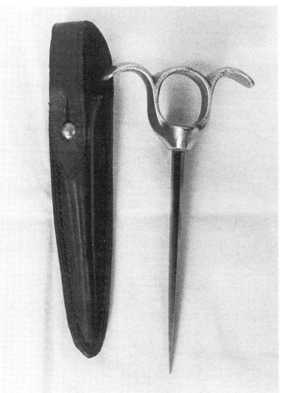

Plate 36

37 After (32) this is probably the next commonest style of Robbins' work encountered by the collector. It utilises the same hilt and blade form but these are mounted in a traditional knife manner. The maker's name is stamped into the pommel. Blade length 5.875 inches; overall length 9.625 inches.

38 Another variant with the hilt cast into two double finger stalls rather than a full knuckle bow. The plain double-edged blade is 5.625 inches in length and overall length is 9.75 inches. Physically larger specimens of this knife have been noted.

39 A rare variant with a kris-style blade. The hilt has a full bow with the maker's name stamped into the grip. The scabbard, while of the correct pattern, is of a different type of leather to that which is normally encountered on Robbins' scabbards, and is probably a replacement. Examples of this knife with the knuckle bow made from steel rather than alloy have been noted. Blade length 6.875 inches; overall length 11.25 inches.

40 With a blade almost like a miniature sabre this knife has a 8.875-inch double-edged curved blade and a hilt with a

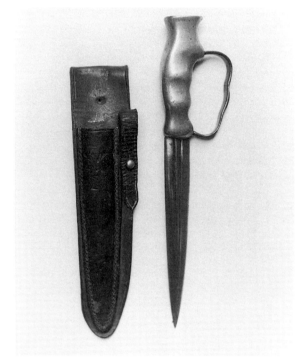

Plate 37

Plate 38

Plate 39

Plate 40

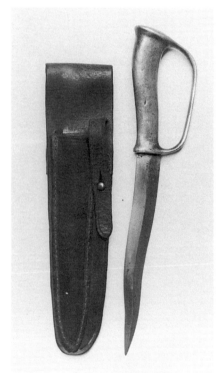

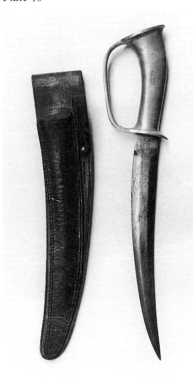

full knuckle bow. The maker's mark is stamped into the grip and the overall length of the knife is 13.475 inches.

41 The rare Robbins short-sword, copies of which have appeared. Some copies are of the correct dimensions while others have been noted with blades of about 8 inches. As usual the hilt is of cast alloy with integral pommel and crossguard. The double-edged blade is 12 inches in length and overall length is 16.5 inches. The Robbins name is marked into the side of the hilt. The sheath is of simple construction: a folded leather body with belt loop on the back and a wrap-around hilt retaining strap.

42 The very rare 'mushroom' pommel Robbins with steel disc/bowl style crossguard. Unfortunately no specimen was available for study and the illustration may be incorrect with regard to the blade. The original illustration showed this

knife in its sheath, but described the blade as an 8-inch hollow ground.[6] The hilt is stamped with the usual mark and the knife is accompanied by a sheath similar in style to that which accompanies (41). A few fakes of this type of knife have been noted – these have had the bowl guard made from alloy.

As indicated in (32) Robbins-type knives do exist which are either unmarked or bear names other than Robbins. The following pieces represent examples of such knives.

43 With the same blade as (41) this knife has a steel bowl/dish type guard and alloy hilt. The sheath is of the same type that accompanies (41). The knife is totally unmarked. Blade length 10 inches; overall length 14.375 inches.

Plate 41

Plate 42

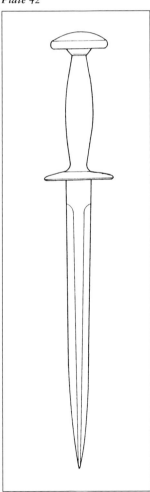

Plate 43

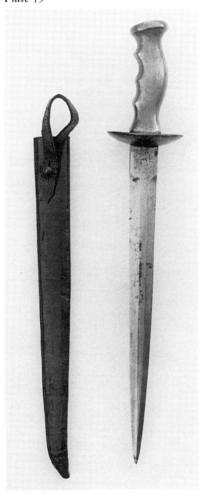

44 A push dagger in the Robbins style with several features which distinguish it from the Robbins-made versions. The hilt including the knuckle guard is cast in one piece, the blade has no fullers and the hilt retaining strap on the sheath has a press-stud rather than a pillar-stud. The knife is unmarked, but a similar example with SUTHERLAND & RHODEN lightly etched on the blade has been noted. Blade length 3.625 inches.

45 Another push dagger, except in this case the construction is all steel. The hilt of the knife is of hollow steel, the base of the hilt having a hole which exposes the innards of the hilt. This hole probably resulted from the casting process. The blade, unlike that of those used on Robbins knives, has no fullers. Both hilt and knuckle guard have been painted green and there are no marks to indicate the manufacturer. Blade length 5 inches.

46 This crude copy of a Robbins push dagger is thought to be authentic. One other similar example has been noted and this was in a scabbard of definite age, and was reputed to have been used by a member of the Welch Fusiliers during World War One. The hilt of this knife is made from one piece of brass with a guard which covers all four fingers. The finger guard is leather-covered, and the plain double-edged blade is brazed into place. Blade length 3.875 inches.

Plate 44

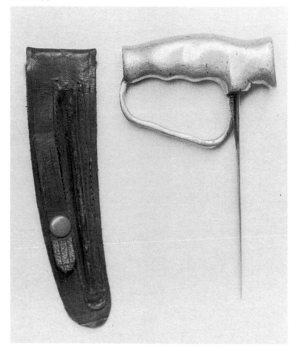

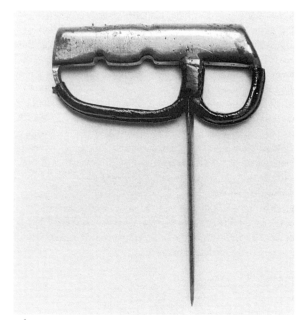

Plate 45

Plate 46

INTER-WAR YEARS

Between the wars only a few knives including pocket-knives (covered later in the book) were introduced into service. These knives were for survival and utility use, the authorities continuing to ignore the need for a combat knife.

47 Dating from the 1920s this knife was issued to the RAF Balloons and Kites Division for the purposes of cutting fouled lines and rigging. The knife is of simple construction, consisting of a 5.25-inch blade of single-edged spear-point form with ebony grips which are secured by three brass rivets. Overall length is 9.25 inches and the sheath is of black leather and of the pouch type. As will be seen the blade carries the name and trademark of S & J KITCHEN along with the Air Ministry stores code of 44/88. An example made by Hale Brothers has also been noted (see 48) along with one by Harrison Brothers & Howson.

48 A further knife from this period is the Release or Fireman's knife. As this knife is still in use today, and in order to keep the knives in some form of grouping, a full description of the 1920s version is included later in the book along with its modern counterpart.

Plate 47

Plate 48

SECOND WORLD WAR & POST-WAR

It was not until World War Two that the British authorities officially issued a fighting knife to its troops, the most famous example being the F-S or Commando knife. Once the need for combat and survival knives was recognised, a wide variety of different designs became available, in accordance with the nature of the warfare – jungle, airborne, clandestine or other forms.

HOME GUARD KNIVES

The shortage of weapons during the early part of the war resulted in the Home Guard using a great deal of initiative in arming themselves, and knives were no exception. Some special units, such as the Auxiliary Units, did receive Commando knives but most were private purchase or home-made.

49 & 50 Illustration (Plate 49) (IWM M7455) shows a display of Home Guard items which appeared some years ago at the Imperial War Museum, and according to them the knife on the left of the photograph came from a former member of the Chiswick Home Guard. This knife is shown in greater detail in (50), though the eagle-eyed reader will no doubt spot that this piece is now held with the sheath previously displayed on the left. The knife is well made, the blade having been crafted from an old round file forged and ground to form a 7.75-inch stiletto blade. A steel crossguard and Commando knife-style pommel are fitted, with the grip bound with thin cord. Overall length is 12.5 inches. The leather sheath is very well made and has CHISWICK scratched on the front.

51 This knife was originally described by Gordon Hughes as being of World War One origin,[7] but having examined this knife and the Imperial War Museum example a number of years ago I consider that this knife has Home Guard origins. The knife, with a 7.5-inch double-edged blade, was probably manufactured from an old file. The grip is made up of leather washers which are secured by a steel ball pommel. Overall length 12 inches.

52 In the collection of the Pattern Room this knife not only illustrates another form of Home Guard knife, but information obtained when researching it helped identify (50) and (51). The knife was made by a Mr Molyneux of Dorking in about 1940, and Mr Molyneux's son provided me

Plate 49

Plate 50

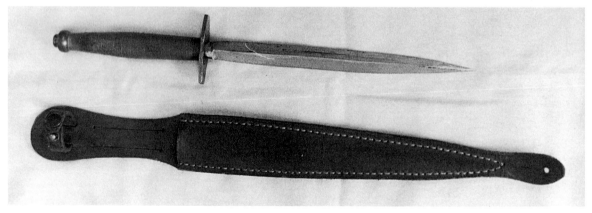

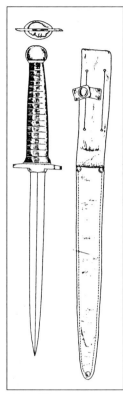

Plate 51

with the following information in response to my enquiries:

When World War Two seemed inevitable and the Local Defence Volunteers {the forerunners of the Home Guard} were resorting to pitchforks etc. as weapons my father decided that fighting knives would be useful as invasion by paratroops seemed certain. So he proceeded to make a few knives for himself and friends.

These knives were individually made and fairly conventional in design. The blades were mostly forged from old files, had a crossguard and the hilt was usually leather washers with the tang through the middle (very similar to the construction used on (50) and (51).

Following unarmed combat courses he decided on the combination knife/knuckleduster. The local military showed interest in it, as did the local Home Guard, but it never progressed beyond that stage. It was examined by other officials but was returned to him and he carried it throughout the war.

Plate 52

The knife has a cast alloy hilt with double finger stalls, somewhat reminiscent of Robbins' work, cast onto a 5.25-inch double-edged blade. Overall length 9.75 inches.

53 A rather nice Home Guard knife of Commando style. Made from an old file the blade is 6.5 inches in length with a short brass crossguard and a hilt taken from an old chisel. Overall length 11.625 inches. The sheath is wood fitted with a leather belt loop.

Plate 53

54 This curious piece in the collection of the Imperial War Museum is supposed to be of Home Guard origin. The knife comprises a length of gas pipe fitted with a 'T' piece which unscrews to reveal a 5.5-inch blade made from a file. Once unscrewed the piece which formed the 'sheath' then screws back into the other end of the 'T' piece to form the hilt. The weapon is well made and painted olive green Overall length 9.75 inches.

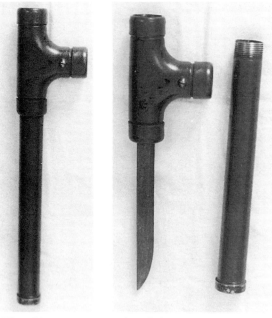

Plate 54   **Plate 54A**

55 While not confirmed, this knife is of likely Home Guard origin. The blade has been taken from a socket bayonet fitted with a brass crossguard, leather washer hilt and brass pommel cap.

56 Members of the 60 County of London Home Guard (London Transport) during a training exercise in 1942. Note the private purchase knife in wear.

MIDDLE EAST COMMANDO KNIVES

57 This knuckle knife is generally associated with the Middle East Commando and its design formed the basis of their cap badge. Three Commando Units were formed between July and November 1940 by GHQ Middle East Land Forces: 50 and 52 Commando were combined with Layforce early in 1941, and 51 Commando was disbanded along with Layforce in August 1941. Some ex-members of ME Commando did, however, go to China to form Mission 204.

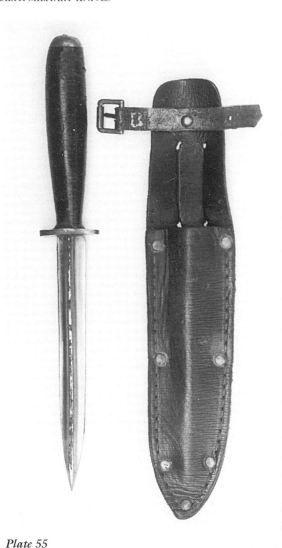

Plate 55

Plate 56

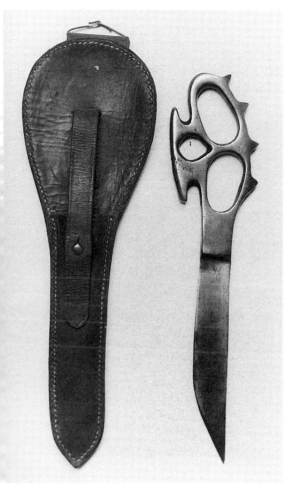

Until recently very little was known about this knife, but Charles Messenger's *The Commandos 1940–1946* threw an interesting light on its background. Apparently the idea for this knife came from a knife held in the Cairo Police Museum, and for some curious reason it was known as the 'fanny'. The book referred to also contains a photo showing the 'fanny' being carried during a raid in February 1941.

These knives are very well made and are usually accompanied by a sturdy leather sheath. The 'death's head' knuckleduster hilt is of cast brass, to which there has been brazed a single-edged Bowie-style blade. Examples using other blade forms have, however, been noted. This photograph shows a typical example of the knife: it has a 6-inch blade and is 11.75 inches overall.

---

58 The reverse of the sheath which accompanies the knife in (57), showing the name and serial number of its owner:

7944685

CPL BURDETT. J.

---

59 Middle East Commando knives are occasionally found with a four-figure serial number stamped into the grip, and more rarely carry a small official acceptance mark, as shown in this illustration.

---

60 This example in the collection of the IWM is marked

SGT

N HALL

L879670

Plate 57

Plate 58

Plate 59

Plate 60

61 A version with a double-edged blade as noted by Hughes,[8] but unfortunately dimensions for this variation are not available.

62 & 62A Two examples of the Middle East Commando type with blades taken from old bayonets have been noted. The first (62), is in the collection of the National Army Museum and was presented by Lt-Col S. Rose who served as second-in-command with 50 Commando; (62A) shows a further example with the blade made from a different portion of a 1907 blade.

63 I apologise for the poor quality of this illustration but it is a photo of a photocopy. It is, however, worthy of inclusion as it shows two Middle East Commando-style knives with very pronounced cog wheel projections to the knuckles. The knife on the left has a double-edged blade. The illustration on the right is from a World War Two German magazine and, as will be noted, the blade, besides being riveted in place, has a slight clip point. As an interesting aside to this photo, while the German text makes disparaging comments about the criminals of Whitechapel, an Australian collector recently provided me with a cutting from a World War Two Australian newspaper where this same photograph is shown with the text reading: 'This is the last picture-gram from Sydney to Melbourne. The service, which has been in operation for nearly 14 years, closed at midnight for the duration. Taken at a northern camp yesterday, the picture

Plate 61   **Plate 62A**

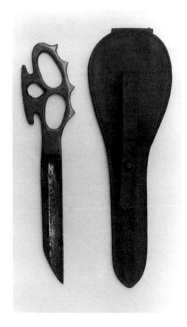

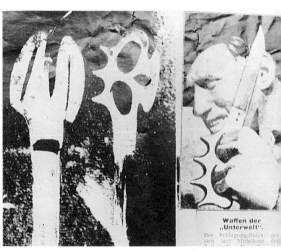

Plate 62

Plate 63

was transmitted a few hours before midnight. It shows Pte. Harry Langbein with a special dagger knuckleduster combination issued to outpost fighters of the A.I.F.'

64 An unusual, possibly bazaar-made or possibly spurious (though it does not exhibit the features normally found on fakes) version of the Middle East Commando knife. The blade is of different form to that usually encountered, as is the 'death's head' hilt. The knife is unmarked and no sheath is available for study. Blade length 6 inches; overall length 12 inches.

Plate 64

BC41 KNUCKLE KNIVES

The famed BC41 knuckle knife was reputedly issued to Commandos prior to the general introduction of the F-S Knife, and was undoubtedly modelled on some of the World War One knuckle knives. The knife is found in two variations, one with a cast-steel hilt, the other with a brass hilt, the brass version the rarer of the two types. The knives never bear any indication of the maker, just BC41 stamped into the tang and moulded into the grip.

65 A typical example of the BC41 along with its sheath. Blade length 5.375 inches; overall length 8.75 inches.

Plate 65

66 This BC41 has had the pyramid projections on the knuckles removed giving the knife the appearance of a World War One knuckle knife.

67 A brass-hilted version which, other than the hilt material, shows no detectable differences from the steel version.

68 Private Gilbody of the 2nd Parachute Brigade photographed during 1943 wearing a BC41. Note the broken finger stall, a fault which I have noted on several examples. One theory is that these were deliberately broken in this manner so as to enable a soldier to grip the knife and a firearm at the same time, the broken finger stall keeping the trigger finger free.

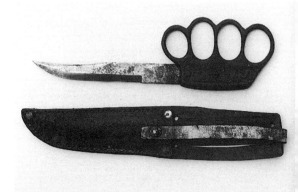

Plate 66

Plate 67

Plate 68

Plate 69

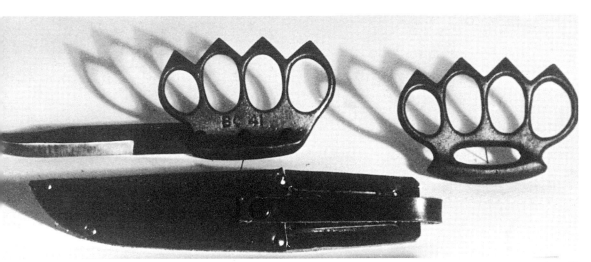

Plate 70

Plate 71

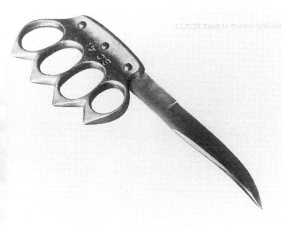

69, 70, 71 & 71A A set of rare BC41 knuckles which are included because they are closely related to the BC41 knife. Nothing is known about the history of these, but it is assumed they were made for Commando use. There has been some speculation about the authenticity of these knuckles, and while crude copies have been observed, generally made of brass and marked BC42, they are undoubtedly genuine. Photograph (70), reproduced courtesy of the Pattern Room, was located by Pattern Room staff in the files of a military establishment. It is from a series of photographs showing various knives (others are shown elsewhere in the book) including two others of the BC41; see (71) and (71A). These contemporaneous photos would certainly indicate that the BC41 knuckles are original.

RAF SERVICING COMMANDO KNIFE

This knife, first illustrated by Hughes,[9] was unattributed by him to any particular unit, but photographic evidence and information received from a relative who served with the RAF Servicing Commando indicate that these knives were an issue item to its members. Formed in 1942, the work of the Servicing Commando was primarily to service aircraft on front-line airfields. There were fourteen separate units and they saw service in North Africa, Sicily, Italy, France and the Far East.

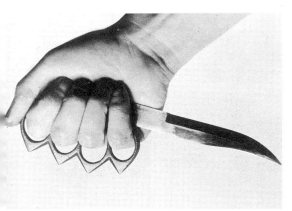

Plate 71A

72 This knife, which is of good quality, has a sturdy 6-inch Bowie blade, short alloy crossguard, grip made of leather and alloy washers and a staghorn pommel. Examples with a bone pommel have been noted, along with one example having a full staghorn grip, though this may be a replacement. The blade is marked on the ricasso as follows:

← 1943

W & SB

SHEFFIELD

W & SB is the mark of W. & S. Butcher. The grip is stamped with the official inspection mark of

↑

8

A plain natural finish leather sheath accompanies the knife. An example with a nickel finish guard and leather and brass washers making up the hilt has also been noted. Overall length is 10.5 inches.

73 Almost identical to (72), this piece may well have been bought in from commercial stock for issue rather than being

the result of a government contract. The blade does not bear the broad arrow or date and is marked

WADE & BUTCHER

SHEFFIELD

ENGLAND

The hilt does, however, bear the inspection mark of

↑

4

74 A member of the RAF Servicing Commando photographed in action in Normandy while servicing an aircraft at a front-line airfield. His knife is clearly shown in wear. (IWM CL261)

SMATCHET

In many respects the Smatchet is one of the most mysterious British issue knives of the period. Its

Plate 72   *Plate 73*

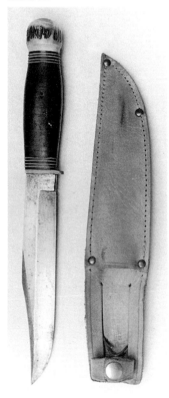

Plate 74

development appears to have been around the same time as the F-S Knife, i.e. 1940–41, with W. E. Fairbairn's book *All in Fighting* dated 1942 featuring it, and obviously posed photos of Commandos show it in wear with the first Pattern F-S Knife. Maurice Chauvet's *D-Day 1er B.F.M. Commando* lists the Smatchet among the equipment issued to Commandos for D-Day, yet despite examining many photos of Commandos in action I have yet to find one showing the Smatchet in actual wear during combat. This tends to make me wonder if it ever actually saw widespread combat use.

Another curious aspect is that the manufacturer of the British Smatchet has not as far as I am aware been identified. While some pieces bear broad arrow/number inspection marks, no specimen giving any indication of the maker has

ever been observed. Even enquiries with the few knife makers left in business have failed to produce any information.

75 This example is totally unmarked and has its grips rubber-covered, a feature which is removed on many examples. The large-leaf shape blade is 11 inches in length, the oval crossguard is of white metal, the grips under the rubber are wood and the large pommel is of alloy. The sheath is of black leather stitched over a wooden former. A belt loop is riveted to the back. Overall length 16.125 inches.

76 This example has its pommel stamped with a

↑

12

inspection mark. The grips are of wood secured by four rivets (occasionally five rivets are found) and they exhibit no signs of ever having been rubber-covered. The sheath is of webbing marked on the back with a ↑ along with M.E. & CO.1942. M.E. & Co. is the mark of the Mills Equipment Company.

Plate 75

Plate 76

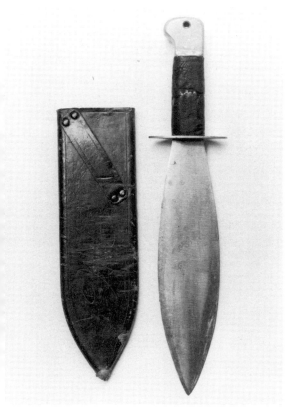

77 An example of the rare brass pommel Smatchet with its pommel stamped

$$\uparrow$$
$$13$$

These brass pommel Smatchets have a steel crossguard rather than white metal. It is interesting to note that several mint specimens of this rare knife, still with their blades grease-covered, turned up in Australia during 1992. Could these have been in store for some fifty-odd years?

---

78 This well-armed Commando not only has a rifle, bayonet and F-S Knife but a Smatchet as well. (IWM H17458)

BRITISH GRAVITY KNIFE

Known about by most serious collectors for several years these knives were fully documented for the first time by Frederick Stephens.[10] The knife, with certain refinements, was a direct copy of the German Gravity Knife, and was manufactured by George Ibberson and reputedly Joseph Rodgers, though no example of this particular model made by Rodgers has ever been heard of. Production figures of some 150,000 knives are quoted by Stephens, but despite this apparent high level of production this knife is extremely rare. If this level of manufacture is correct, what happened to all the knives is not known for certain. Stephens speculates that they may still be in store, but one story says they were never actually issued on a mass basis and those that were in store at the end of the war were broken up. Two versions exist: marked and unmarked. Unmarked specimens have been identified as being used by the SOE and OSS, the marked specimens for issue to Commandos and Paratroops.

---

79 This photograph shows a fine example of the Ibberson-made and blade marked version. As will be noted the only major difference between the British- and German-made versions is that the grips are of chequered Bexoid, an early form of plastic, rather than wood. The blade is marked with the name and violin trademark of George Ibberson, along

Plate 77

Plate 78

Plate 79

Plate 80

with the C.O.S.D./2194. These knives also bear another less obvious mark: in the marlin spike recess there is stamped on the body of the knife a small serial number, which in this case is 39. Blade length 4 inches; overall length fully open is 10.125 inches.

80 This is a totally unmarked example.

81 Besides the gravity knives shown left the British also designed several prototypes, only one of which ever seems to have reached a production stage. Five of these designs were rescued from the factory of Joseph Rodgers and Sons some years ago, and were illustrated by Hughes in his *Primer Part 1*.[11] The illustrations are reproduced by kind permission of Gordon Hughes and David Hayden Wright. The top two examples were found in an unfinished state and have hinged marlin spikes. The middle example has a gravity marlin spike and brass body. The lower two also have gravity-operated spikes but bodies of chequered alloy.

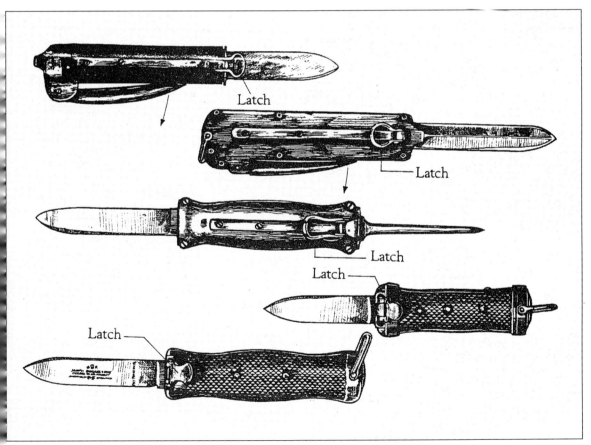

Plate 81

82 This is an actual example of the knife shown at the bottom of (81). The piece is in mint condition and is of very high quality. These knives are extremely rare. Only a few specimens are known about, and this particular example was found at an arms fair in the USA by an English collector who was on holiday. It is not known if these knives ever went into full production or were indeed ever issued to the military.

Plate 82A   *Plate 82B*

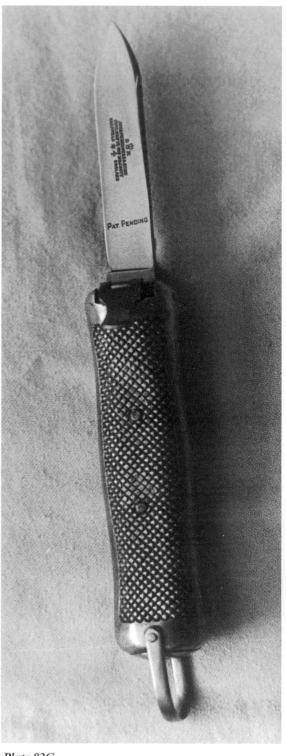

SPECIAL OPERATIONS EXECUTIVE AND OTHER CLANDESTINE KNIVES

During World War Two the area of operation covered by SOE included Scandinavia, Continental Europe, Italy, the Balkans, Greece

Plate 82C

and the Far East, and this led them to undertake a variety of clandestine duties such as sabotage, escape and evasion, assassination etc. To assist in these duties several varieties of knife were adopted, with many of these designs also being used by both the OSS and the Commandos. While the official issue versions were all unmarked, commercial versions were also marketed by cutlers and military outfitters for private purchase. All original SOE weapons are now scarce and this has led to many fakes appearing on the market.

83 A small thrusting dagger with double-edged blade, and hilt with a small indentation for resting the thumb.

84 This small flat knife is of very high quality and bears the name JOSEPH RODGERS AND SONS on the side of the hilt.

85 While not fully identified as having SOE origins the design of this knife makes such usage extremely likely. The blade is of very high quality and is made of thick stock very similar to that found on some early F-S knives. The grip is made of celluloid or similar material. The sheath, while possessing a belt loop, appears as if it was really designed for storage of the knife rather than actual wear.

Plate 85

Plate 83 *Plate 84*

43

86 A bright finish version of the SOE/OSS 'Nail'. The blade is triangular in form and is cut with fullers on each face. The hilt is oval in shape. These weapons also come in a brown finish and they were designed to be carried on the forearm or lower leg.

87 Utilising the same hilt as (86), this example has a narrow double-edged blade.

88 With a blade like that found on (87) the hilt of this knife is grooved for improved grip and has a very pronounced pommel.

89 The Lapel Dagger was designed to be concealed behind the lapel of a jacket or other areas of clothing. Very much a last-resort weapon, it was gripped between finger and thumb and used in a slashing mode at a captor's face. The leather sheath was designed to be stitched in place, and other varieties of both knife and sheath have been noted.

90 This illustration is taken from an SOE catalogue issued during 1944, and shows the official SOE version of the Thumb Knife along with its catalogue number and description.

91 This long and unusual spike blade has its pommel portion formed into a grapple. The weapon is simply formed from round section steel rod, with the lower half cut with three fullers and the top split to form the two arms of a grapple. The spike is blued overall. Similar weapons were typically cord-bound, and this example is pierced with a hole which would have acted as a securing point for such binding.

Plate 86

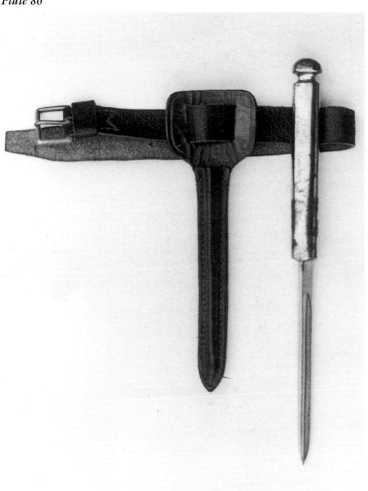

Plate 87

Plate 88

Plate 91

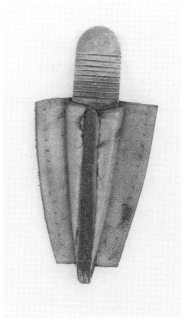

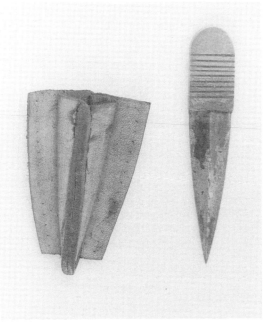

Plate 89

Plate 89A

KNIVES, THUMB

Catalogue No. JS 188.

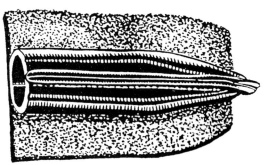

DESCRIPTION.   A very small, dagger-shaped knife, sharpened for the full length of the blade along one edge, and for three-quarters of the length along the other; the remaining quarter is flattened to give a grip for the thumb. The hilt is only one inch long, and the Knife can easily be concealed in the hand.

The Knife is provided with a leather sheath, with flaps which can be sewn to the clothing.

DIMENSIONS. In sheath 4″ x 2″. Knife 3¼″ x ¾″.   **WEIGHT.** ¾ oz.

PACKING AND SPECIAL NOTES. As required.

Plate 90

92 As far as I am aware no example of this knife has ever been recorded in any collection. The photo was copied from an unattributed book on escape and evasion equipment published in very limited numbers during World War Two. The book was reprinted in the USA during the late 1980s.[12] This book describes the knife as a 'Special Instantaneous Opening Knife', which presumably means that it is a flick or switchblade knife. If this is the case it is curious that the blade has a nail nick for manual opening. The grips appear to have a recessed dimple pattern like that found on (330).

93 to 96 Documented for the first time over a decade ago by Pierre Lorain the SOE Tyre Slasher Knife was only recently illustrated in H. Keith Melton's *OSS Special Weapons and Equipment*. Although it is possible that such knives did see service with the OSS, it was manufactured in England primarily for use by the SOE. The official SOE issue knives, as one would expect, are unmarked, but by a pure coincidence at least one manufacturer has been identified. In writing to John Watts Ltd about (271), without prompting, this type of knife was mentioned in their reply.

Plate 92

Plate 95

Plate 93   *Plate 94*

Two versions of this knife exist, one with a moulded bolster and the other with a white metal bolster not unlike that found on the Electrician's Pocket-knife. Whether Watts manufactured both styles is not known. The knife comprises a clip- pointed blade which locks into place and grips of chequered Bakelite or Bexoid. The grips on the version with the metal bolster are flatter than those on the other model. At the staple end of the knife there is a small folding hook-shaped blade which was designed for slashing the walls of tyres.

(93) shows the moulded bolster version, and (94) an example of the metal bolster version. (95) illustrates the two examples in comparison. Note the differences in the main blade and tyre slasher blade shapes. (96) represents a commercial/private purchase version of the tyre slasher. Although well worn this knife carries the marks of Joseph Rodgers and Sons on the blade. Note that the tyre slasher blade has been reshaped. This is the only commercially marked example of a tyre slasher knife so far noted.

97 Copy of the letter received from John Watts Ltd, which makes mention of these knives.

Plate 97

Plate 96

 WATTS ESTABLISHED 1765

John Watts (Sheffield & London) Ltd.

LAMBERT WORKS · SHEFFIELD S3 7AB · PHONE 0742-24301 (3 LINES)
Grams: Manhattan, Sheffield 3 · Telex: Chamcom Sheffld 547676 for John Watts

Our Ref: RB/CP.

Your Ref:

Mr. R.E. Flook,   23rd April, 1980.

Dear Sir,

        Thank you for your letter of the 15th April, I regret the original appears to have gone astray.

        The knife in question was manufactured by us during the war for the use of the Special Armed Services and also, we believe, for the French Resistance. The knife would therefore be made sometime during the war years. The scabbard was an ordinary leather one.

        During the same period we also manufactured knives for Commando Units and also Clasp Knives (a larger version of the old fashioned Boy Scouts Knife) fitted with a blade which locked in the open position, which was of similar shape to the blade in your sketch and also a similar knife with a sharp hook like blade which again was used by the French Resistance for the purpose of slashing the tyres of German vehicles.

        I am afraid that due to the passage of time and changing circumstances we are no longer manufacturing knives of a similar nature, being now mainly engineering and Machine Knife manufacturers.

        We trust the aforegoing will be of assistance to you.

                        Yours faithfully,
                  JOHN WATTS (SHEFFIELD & LONDON) LTD.,

                        R. Bishop
                        Chairman and Managing Director.

Grinding Wheel Dressers — Floor and Concrete Planing and Scouring Cutters — Machine Knives (Food and Industrial) — Shear Blades
Cutlery and Scissors — General Machining and Press Work
Directors: R. Bishop, Chairman & Managing Director · F. J. W. Mellowes · M. R. G. Bishop, Secretary · D. Beardshaw
Regd. Office as above. Regd. in the United Kingdom. Regd. No. 243860

98 The very desirable and much-sought-after Escape Knife was issued to members of the SOE, OSS, RAF, and possibly the Commandos, during World War Two. The actual design of this knife predates the war, though the Victorian examples do not have the saw blades.

Despite its early origins there are claims that it was developed during the war. Foot and Langley state in their book on MI9 that the knife was devised by Major Clayton Hutton, who was actually responsible for many other escape aids. While it is possible that Clayton Hutton did think of adding the saw blades, the idea for the remainder of the knife was certainly not original. Another erroneous claim by Foot and Langley is that the can opener is a lock breaker. It is a most interesting idea, but not a very practical one.

99 Illustrated for comparison, an example of the Victorian period 'Escape Knife'. Note the lack of saw blades. This piece was made by Joseph Rodgers and it carries the design registration number on the white metal scales. A number of

Plate 98

Plate 99

Plate 100

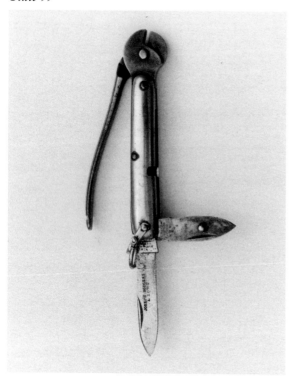

variations of this type of knife were 'rescued' from the Rodgers factory in the 1960s, and these are illustrated in M. H. Cole's book *US Military Knives*.

RDB Hunting Knife

100 From published information it would appear that before the introduction of the Fairbairn-Sykes Commando Knife the Commandos were issued with the Wilkinson pre-war hunting knife known as the RBD. Some time late in 1940 approximately 1,500 of these knives were ordered from Wilkinson at a cost of thirteen shillings and six pence each.[13]

The RBD, first made in 1869, was available in three models each with a different blade length, the shortest being 7 inches, the longest 10 inches. The three models were designated 1, 2 and 3, and all had staghorn grips. Besides bearing the Wilkinson Pall Mall address the blades were also marked in an etched scroll RDB HUNTING KNIFE NO. 1, 2 or 3. Exactly which model was supplied to the Commandos is unknown, and as far as I am aware no knife with recorded Commando use has yet been identified. From an historical perspective it can be argued that the RBD represents the original Commando knife.

The illustration shows an RBD model No.1 with a 6-inch blade, as opposed to the 7-inch length which published information indicates it should be. The sheath has its frog stamped with the initials M.J.H.

Fairbairn-Sykes Commando Knife

The Fairbairn-Sykes (F-S) Fighting or Commando knife holds for a variety of reasons a particular fascination for knife collectors. It is also a knife surrounded by stories and myths concerning its history, variations, meaning of marks etc. As with many knives, obtaining hard facts about the F-S is very difficult and made even more so by certain items of incorrect information published in several books. Approaches to the original makers

Wilkinson Sword achieve very little. The data sheet issued by them several years ago in response to enquiries is very inaccurate in many respects, and has helped fuel many of the fallacies surrounding the F-S.

The original concept and development of the Commando knife was well documented by Robert Wilkinson-Latham in his article in the magazine *Antique Arms and Militaria*.[14] From this article and other pieces of information it would appear that the development of the Commando knife was along the following lines:

1940: F-S with 3-inch wavy crossguard and knurled hilt – the original design.

1940–1: as above but with 2-inch wavy crossguard.

1941–2: straight crossguard and knurled hilt.

1942 to date: straight crossguard with ringed alloy hilt.

Of course there are other variations that do not fall into these three basic categories, but where these fall in the chronological history of the Commando knife is not known for certain. Wilkinson-Latham states that the Beaded and Ribbed was introduced in 1942, and I would personally date the all-steel version to around 1944.

Marks

Knives bearing the F-S Fighting knife and Wilkinson trademark logos are relatively common, but other World War Two vintage knives are rarely found with a maker's mark. Knives carrying the mark of J. Clarke and Sons and dated 1942 are known but are rare. Knife (128) is almost certainly World War Two, and (136) by George Wostenholm and Sons is possibly of World War Two origin. It is, however, generally the case that firms other than Wilkinson rarely marked their names on Commando knives during the war.

The marks usually found – ↑ and number, or more rarely letter code – are government inspectors' marks. Speculation did exist among collectors, and such speculation has been printed as fact in some books, that these marks were maker's codes. However, a letter from the MoD (Army) Quality Assurance Directorate states that such marks were those of the examiners of the Inspectorate of Stores (see 101). The letter indicates that the statement by Robert Buerlein in his *Allied Military Fighting Knives* that the

Plate 101

**QUALITY ASSURANCE DIRECTORATE
(STORES & CLOTHING)**
Didcot Oxon OX11 7HG

Telegrams Inspection Didcot   Telephone Didcot 815191 ext   540

Mr R E Flook

Please reply to The Director
Your reference

Our reference

Date 7 October 1981

Dear Mr Flook,

FIGHTING AND SURVIVAL KNIVES

Thank you for your letter of 28 September concerning the marking of knives.

You are correct in assuming that the marking of broad arrow and number were our examiners' stamps (in the days when we were known as the Inspectorate of Stores). Unfortunately the numbers you quote - 7, 56 etc are from a series that was discontinued about 1955/6 and all our records of that series have been destroyed.

The replacement series of examiners' stamps commenced at number 300 but most of these are now discontinued as we have changed our role from direct inspection by our own examiners to one of monitoring the manufacturers' quality control/inspection systems.

The number "474" which you quote later on in your letter is still current and is held by one of our few remaining examiners at Sheffield.

It is not possible to link examination stamps with manufacturers as our examiners could have visited each of several factories over a period of a few months.

Our contract records for purchases of knives go back to 1974 and suppliers of fighting and survival knives since then have been

> Joseph Rodgers & Sons Ltd
> (Rodgers Wolstenholm Group)
> 55 Moore Street
> Sheffield
>
> F E & J R Hopkinson Ltd
> 87 London Road
> Sheffield
>
> John Clark Ltd
> Mowbray Street
> Sheffield
>
> Geo. Ibberson
> Trafalgar Street
> Sheffield

I am sorry I cannot be of more help in your investigation.

Yours sincerely,

C ARMSTRONG
Director

number relates to a particular firm is untrue. An individual inspector to whom a mark was unique could visit several factories, so all the mark will prove is that the knife had passed inspection. While the ↑ and number stamps were still used up until quite recently, those found on Commando knives were from a series discontinued around 1955–56 and all historical records appertaining to them have been destroyed.

Although this information is very useful, amazingly no light was shed on the ↑ letter codes. Though such marks must obviously be those of inspectors they must come from a different series, possibly dating from pre-World War Two, or even from inspectors of a Commonwealth country. Both theories are credible, with some evidence to support both. I have, for instance, a World War One British machete marked ↑ over J, and a Canadian World War Two billhook marked ↑P on the sheath.

What, then, of the B2 mark found on both second and third Pattern Commando knives? It is the commonest mark found, yet it fits neither of the inspection mark series previously mentioned. Also, unlike number or letter marks, I do not know of it ever being noted on any other type of knife. The mark is almost certainly of British origin, but may well have been for an inspector based outside of the normal manufacturing centre of Sheffield, or even for an inspector attached to another government department.

Some World War Two vintage F-S knives can be found stamped ENGLAND on the crossguard, a mark was added to knives sold to the USA after the end of the war. From information provided by an American collector it appears that in 1947 a southern Californian firm purchased some 167,000 surplus Commando knives from the British government. The crossguards were stamped to reflect the country of origin and the knives sold on for two dollars ninety-five cents each. Another mark commonly found on Third Pattern knives is a small 1, 2, 3 or 4 on the hilt just under the

pommel. These figures are part of the hilt moulding and are thought to be a reference to the mould that was used to cast the hilt.

In the post-war era Commando knives which are issue weapons tend to be not only marked with maker's name but also with various stores codes. There are a few exceptions to this rule, but such instances are rare.

Variations

Of the standard patterns of Commando knife three styles are commonly quoted in books and auction catalogues: the First, Second and Third. These refer to the wavy crossguard, knurled grip and ringed grip respectively. However, besides these three basic categories many others exist. Some of these variations are well known — the Beaded and Ribbed, for example — others are not so well known and are not easy to categorise, such as (146) and (161).

Issue

As with all aspects of the Commando knife, stories concerning its issue abound. I have heard tales that particular sheath types were only issued to Paratroops, that type 137 was OSS issue, Beaded and Ribbed types were not issue but private purchase etc. Like a lot of information connected with these knives such stories are generally untrue. Once in production the issue of F-S knives was made to a variety of units i.e. Commandos, SAS, Paratroops, SOE and the Auxiliary Units. It was also available as private purchase. Although individual units may have had knives specifically commissioned for them, there was certainly no grand plan on the part of the authorities for certain units to be identified with a specific knife variation. The post-war story is somewhat different: (167) was held only by the RAF Stores Department, and (174) and (176) have been held by the Army since 1963 for issue to, and I quote a MoD (Army) letter, 'certain Special Forces'.

Illustrations

While the following illustrations show a selection of F-S or Commando knives, accompanied by additional information where available, I certainly do not claim that this section illustrates all the variations produced, nor does it answer all the questions. I know of variations that were unavailable for study and expect that many readers will know of examples not shown or mentioned. I do, however, hope that you will find this section useful in expanding your knowledge of this famous knife.

First Pattern

102 This illustration is a composite of illustrations (21) and (29) from Hughes's first *Primer Part 1*. It depicts what is thought to be the correct form of the extremely rare First Pattern with three-inch crossguard. The illustration in the *Primer* is believed to be incorrect in that the blade depicted is not of the true square shank type, despite being described as such in the text.

Apparently produced in very limited numbers this model had only a short service life. According to Robert Wilkinson-Latham in *The F-S Commando Knife* the large crossguard had a tendency to snag on clothing and was consequently shortened to two inches. No actual specimen was available for study, but except for the crossguard the piece was identical to the version with the two-inch crossguard, with the same blade and ricasso etching. The finish i.e. nickel and dimensions were also the same.

103 The F-S Fighting Knife First Pattern, second type. A production figure of 500 is often quoted for this pattern but this is almost certainly incorrect. Leroy Thompson in *Commando Dagger* gives a figure of 1,250, but I believe it could be much higher, especially when one considers the number of specimens that have appeared over the years. Also Wilkinson-Latham gives details of some First Pattern orders amounting to some 800 knives, though it is not clear whether these were a mixture of 3- and 2-inch crossguards, or all 2-inch versions.

The knife has a tapering double-edged blade with square shank ricasso which is etched THE F-S FIGHTING KNIFE on one side and, along with their trademark of crossed swords, WILKINSON SWORD CO. LTD. LONDON on the other. The 'S' crossguard is two inches in length and the hilt of coke bottle or skittle shape has a chequered

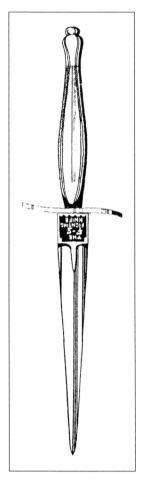

Plate 102   *Plate 103*

portion to improve the grip. A small pommel nut secures the hilt to the tang. The finish is nickel-plated overall. The dimensions of these knives vary because the blades were hand drawn and ground so no two knives will be exactly the same. Blade length 6.75 inches; overall length 11.75 inches.

104 to 106 Only four examples of this extremely rare variant of the First Pattern F-S have been noted at time of writing. As will be seen from the illustrations the ricasso of the knife bears the additional etching of an E. The significance of this is unknown, but it is possible that knives with this mark were commissioned by a particular commanding officer or unit. Illustrations 105 and 106 show comparisons in the length of ricasso and the etchings used on a standard First Pattern and that with the E etching. Note the longer and slimmer ricasso on the E version and the differences in the Wilkinson Sword mark.

Plate 104

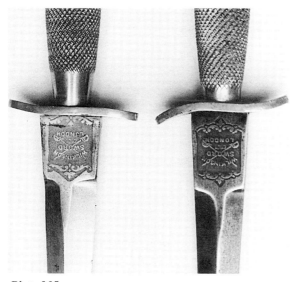

Plate 105

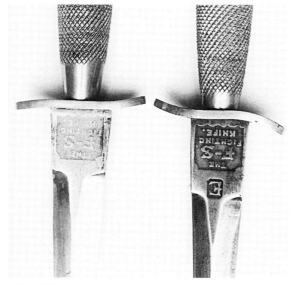

Plate 106

Plate 107

Plate 108

107 & 108 The hilt of a First Pattern with the numbers 30946 and 349 stamped in the pommel area. Hughes records three other examples besides this one, which along with the 30946 mark are marked 44, 47 and 449 respectively.[15] Two others have also been noted, one marked 358, the other 148. The exact meaning of these marks is unknown, but Hughes suggests that they are serial numbers and I would have no reason not to concur with this, although it is my view that the 30946 is a stores number rather than a unit number.

109 This First Pattern is very unusual in that the ricasso bears no Wilkinson or F-S etchings. It is not obvious why this should have occurred as the knife is almost certainly a Wilkinson product.

110 A further example of a First Pattern with no ricasso etching. However, this example is doubly unusual in that the crossguard has been removed.

111 While almost certainly of post-war origin, this First Pattern style knife is not only unusual but illustrates the difficulties that can be encountered during research. The knife has a highly polished blade with square shank ricasso of slightly different form to that usually encountered, an 'S' crossguard of unplated brass and an unplated brass hilt. The ricasso bears the Wilkinson and F-S logos. Three other similar examples have been noted, two like the piece illustrated, the other with an Ivorine hilt. When enquiries were made at Wilkinson about these knives they claimed that they did not make them, and that someone else had used their etching plates. Undoubtedly a very strange statement.

Plate 109   *Plate 110*   *Plate 111*

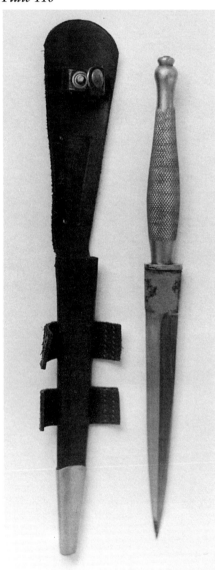
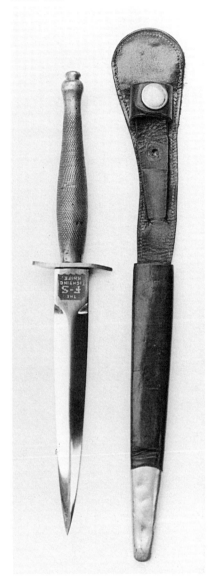

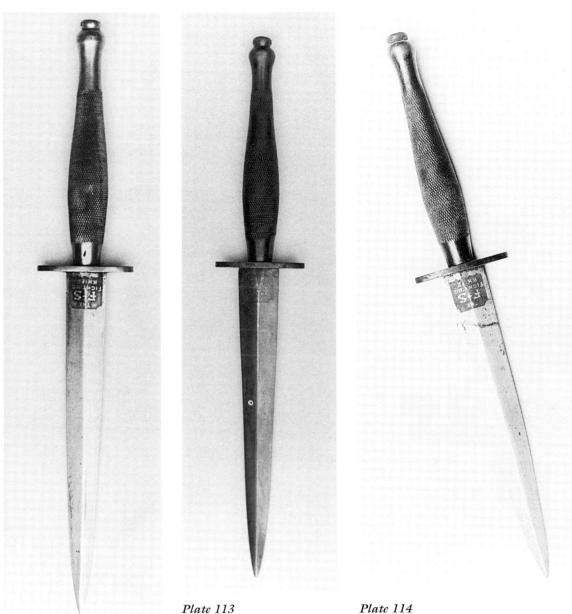

Plate 113

Plate 114

Plate 112

Second Pattern

In 1941 the design of the Commando Knife was changed to the style we know today as the Second Pattern. The square shank ricasso was dispensed with and the crossguard was straightened. Makers other than Wilkinson also commenced manufacture of the Commando knife.

112 Wilkinson-made Second Pattern which retains the same finish and etchings found on the First Pattern. Blade length 6.75 inches; overall length 11.75 inches.

113 While retaining the F-S/Wilkinson logos, this piece is blued overall. Blade length 6.75 inches; overall length 11.75 inches.

114 This version has a blued hilt and crossguard but a bright polished blade.

115 & 116 Only a few examples of this Wilkinson-made Second Pattern with the 'button' style pommel have been observed. As will be seen from (116) the pommel of this knife is much flatter than that usually encountered on this style of knife. Blade length 6.475 inches; overall length 11.25 inches.

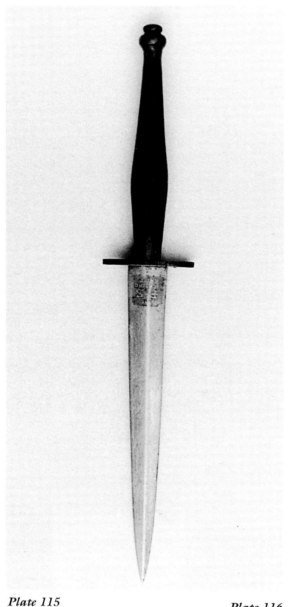

Plate 115

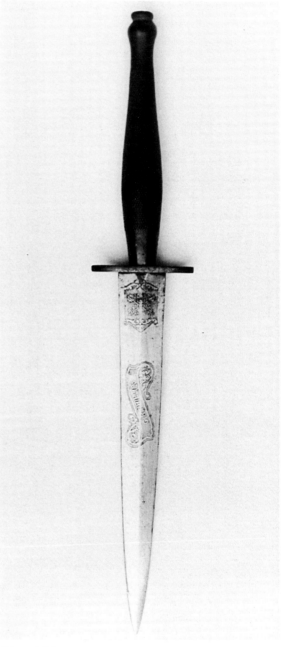

Plate 116

Plate 117

117 Second Patterns are occasionally found with an etched banner on the blade bearing the original owner's name or initials. These knives were privately purchased from Wilkinson during World War Two: this piece carries the name G. R. PHILLIPS. Blade length 7 inches; overall length 11.875 inches.

118 & 119 This knife uses a different banner etching to surround the initials M.L.S. These are the initials of M. L. Smith who was with the First Airborne Brigade.

120 Bright finish Second Pattern bearing on the blade an etched banner with the initials W.M.C.F.

Plate 118 *Plate 119*

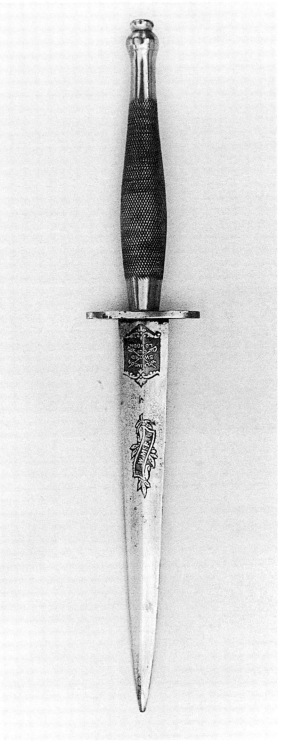

Plate 120

121 Marked D109209 E. THORNHILL, this knife is a little unusual in that it does not carry the F-S/Wilkinson logos. However, in view of the style of banner it is considered that this piece was at least etched by the company if not made by them.

122 Second Patterns are frequently found without the F-S/Wilkinson logo, instead remaining unmarked, or carrying broad arrow inspection marks or, more rarely, the name of the maker/retailer. These examples can be found with slight variations in the grip knurling, and the example shown which has fine knurling is marked

↑

60

on the base portion of the hilt. Similar nickel finish examples bearing the number 56 have also been noted. Blade length 6.875 inches; overall length 12 inches.

123 This Second Pattern, besides having its sheath modified, also bears a serial number on the edge of the crossguard. The numbers have been misplaced when stamped so could be either 547 or 745. Note the coarser knurling on the hilt.

124 Personalised by its owner this example has a name, number and unit stamped into the blade: i.e.

3053903 J.BATTEN
9 COMMANDO

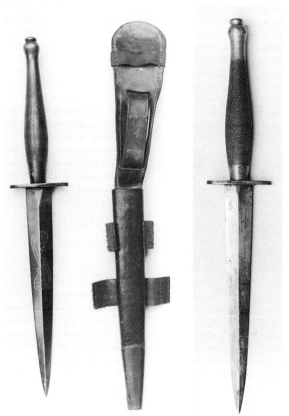

Plate 121   *Plate 122*

Plate 123

125 Blued finish Second Patterns are frequently found by collectors and, like the nickel finish versions, variations can be found to both knurling and other features. The knife illustrated is stamped ↑B2 on the crossguard. Other marks noted on this style of knife include ↑ over I, 9 and T, the latter in the following configuration:

$$\downarrow$$
$$T$$

Examples marked

$$L$$
$$\uparrow$$

have also been noted, but these are almost certainly a mis-stamped T marking.

126 This blued finish Second Pattern has a crossguard which has pointed ends rather than the rounded shape normally found and is stamped with ↑ over I (see 126A) whilst another similar example, with a crossguard 2.5 inches in length, is marked with the addition of a crown (see 126B). The I inspection mark would imply Indian issue (see comments on the ↑ I mark in Appendix Three) but not necessarily Indian manufacture. Blade length 6.875 inches; overall length 11.625 inches.

Plate 124 *Plate 125*

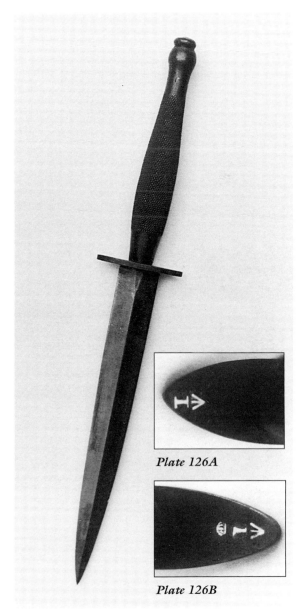

Plate 126A

Plate 126B

Plate 126

127 Besides Wilkinson very few manufacturers marked their names on World War Two Commando knives. This very fine piece is, however, marked on the underside of the crossguard:

1942

J.CLARKE & SONS

SHEFFIELD

In addition to this mark some examples also bear ↑ number inspection marks. These Clarke-made knives all tend to have knurling that gives the hilt the appearance of being dimpled.

---

128 This extremely fine example of a private purchase Commando knife was retailed by the Glasgow firm of J. & I. Marshall whose name is etched on the blade. Stephens[16] states that Marshall's was a firm of military tailors, but this

is incorrect. Marshall's is a long established firm of cutlery retailers with a history dating back to 1888. J. and I. Marshall ran the firm during the war and information obtained from the firm, which still exists, indicates that the knife was made for them by J. Clarke and Sons. Blade length 6.75 inches; overall length 11.5 inches.

---

129 This Second Pattern has a hilt finish which gives it the appearance of being covered in small beads. The knife is unmarked, giving no indication as to its origins. Blade length 6.75 inches; overall length 11.625 inches.

---

130 Similar to an example in the National Army Museum this knife has a slimmer hilt than that usually encountered on Second Patterns, and the grip portion is stippled rather than chequered with the extremities clearly defined by a

Plate 127   *Plate 128* 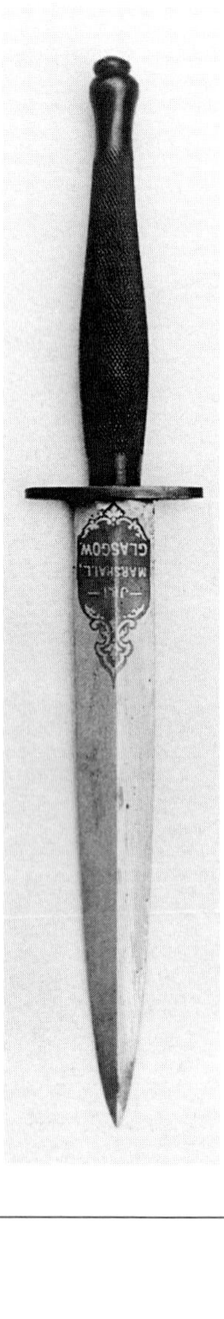   *Plate 129*    *Plate 130*

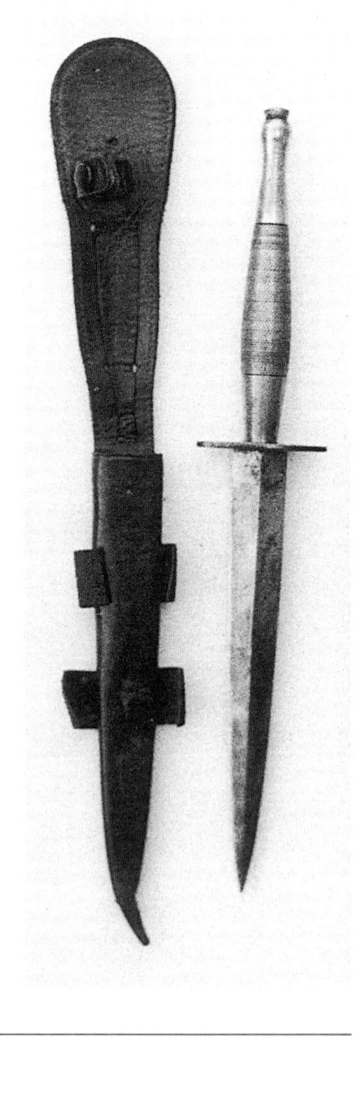

groove. Note the lack of a chape on the sheath. A similar example without the grooves on the hilt has also been noted. The sheath that accompanies this knife has an extended chape. Blade length 6.125 inches; overall length 11.0625 inches.

---

131 Three officers of the 1st Parachute Brigade in North Africa, 1942. The officer on the right, a Major Ashford, has a Second Pattern in wear on the left leg. This was a common method of carrying Commando knives, special tabs being provided on both the trousers and sheath for securing purposes. (IWM NA351)

Third Pattern

The Third Pattern introduced in 1942 marked yet a further change in the design and method of manufacture and gave us the design that has been retained to the present day. To ease manufacture and increase production the hilt was cast from alloy and the grip changed to a ringed design. The alloy was copper-plated to provide a base for

blueing. The blade remained as on the Second Pattern with regard to shape, but was in all but a few rare cases blued overall.

There appear to be very few design variations among wartime Third Patterns. Except for some bearing F-S/Wilkinson logos the only usual detectable manufacturing differences are the pommel nut shape and the number cast on the pommel portion of the hilt. As can be seen from (132) several types of pommel nut were used, ranging from the small button to a large dome. Regarding the small number cast on the pommel, as previously mentioned these are a reference to the mould used to cast the hilt. For some curious reason, however, Leroy Thompson identifies the 2 mark with knives manufactured by William Rodgers.[17] How he arrives at this conclusion is unclear, but it could be attributed to certain comments by Stephens.[18] In my view these marks give no clue as to the knife manufacturer.

Plate 131

Like other varieties of Commando knife many different inspector's marks can be found on Third Patterns. The following have been noted on World War Two examples: ↑ in conjunction with 15, B2, 2 (probably a mis-stamped B2), 21, 3, I, V, 7, 12, and 42. Post-war knives can be found bearing a variety of different stores marks.

---

133 Whether the changes which resulted in the Third Pattern were suggested by Wilkinson is not known. They did, however, make such knives etched with their trademark and the F-S logo. This photograph shows such a piece and like most Third Patterns it is blued overall. Blade length 6.25 inches; overall length 11 inches.

---

134 This Wilkinson Third Pattern is unusual in that it has a bright finish blade. Blade length 6.25 inches; overall length 11 inches.

Plate 132

| *Plate 133* | *Plate 134* | *Plate 135* | *Plate 136* |

135 A mint example of a Third Pattern marked on the crossguard

↑

21

Blade length 6.875 inches; overall length 11.625 inches.

---

136 This piece bears no marks indicating official issue and may even date from the early post-war years. It has, however, been well used and is unusual in that it bears the maker's name on the blade:

IXL

GEO. WOSTENHOLM & SON

SHEFFIELD ENGLAND

Adrian Van Dyk lists one of these knives in his sales catalogue, but for some unexplained reason concludes that the markings are fake.[19] This might be the case with his listed example, but the IXL marks on this knife are totally authentic. Blade length 6.375 inches; overall length 11. 0625 inches.

Other Variations

137 and 138 This style of Second Pattern (137) has several unusual features: the hilt is very chunky and bulbous, and the grip portion has very deep and coarse knurling; also the correct pattern sheath for these knives has a larger than usual chape and the tabs have no pre-stamped stitch marks. Both marked and unmarked versions of this knife exist, the example illustrated being marked broad arrow 2 on the base

Plate 137

Plate 138

of the hilt. 138 shows an almost mint example of this Second Pattern variant with a commercial-style sheath. Nothing definite is known about 137 or 138. I have heard one claim that they are OSS but have seen no evidence to support this. Some very limited photographic evidence does exist which may link these knives with Royal Marine and Royal Navy issue. In the book *SBS, The Invisible Raiders* by James Ladd one is illustrated along with other equipment used by RM swimmer canoeists in 1944. Also, in Charles Messenger's book *The Commandos* a Lt-Cdr of 30 Assault Unit is shown wearing one of these knives.

Beaded and Ribbed

According to both Stephens[20] and Thompson[21] the Beaded and Ribbed Commando knife was a commercial variant produced for private sale. This information is not totally correct. While many Commando knives were privately purchased the Beaded and Ribbed was officially issued as both (139) and (140) and bear arrow/number acceptance stamps.

---

139 This example is blued overall and is marked with a ↑ on the hilt. The hilt has nine rows of beads, and note the rather flat top to the pommel. Blade length 7 inches; overall length 11.875 inches.

---

140 The hilt of this knife has a rounded pommel rather than the flat top found on the previous specimen. This knife appears to have been originally blued overall but most of this

Plate 139	*Plate 140*	*Plate 141*	*Plate 142*

finish has been worn off. The hilt is marked

↑

4

Blade length 6.5 inches; overall length 11.5 inches.

---

141 The usual pattern of Beaded and Ribbed encountered

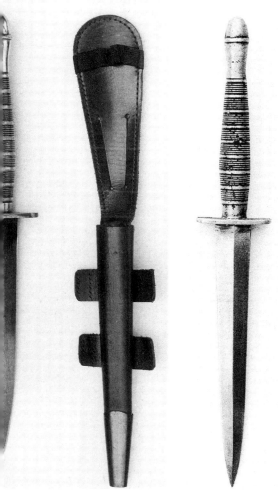

Plate 143

by the collector has nine rows of beaded rings. Examples with six, seven, and eight rows have been noted, the piece illustrated having six rows. The hilt and crossguard appear to have originally been blued with a bright finish blade. The knife carries no acceptance mark. Blade length 6.875 inches; overall length 11.9375 inches.

---

142 This example has a nickel-plated hilt, blued crossguard and bright polished blade. The sheath is of the normal pattern except for the hilt retainer which is a snap fastener normally associated with the First Pattern. This fastener is not an addition after removal of the elastic strap but an original fitting. The chape is nickel-plated. Blade length 6.75 inches; overall length 11.9375 inches.

Ribbed and Roped

---

143 A variation of the Beaded and Ribbed is the Ribbed and Roped. In these knives the beaded rings have been replaced by rings having a 'roped' pattern. This particular example has a nickel-plated hilt and blued crossguard and blade. Note the acorn pommel.

---

144 An unusual version of the Ribbed and Roped. The hilt and crossguard are cast directly onto the tang, and in common with (145) and many of the wood-gripped Commando knives, has parallel sides to the crossguard. Very few of these knives have been observed and they are of relatively poor quality. Blade length 6.625 inches; overall length 11.5 inches.

---

145 The hilt of this knife is made from a very hard grey alloy. The blade appears to have originally been blued, but the hilt shows no signs of ever having any sort of applied finish. Like other Ribbed and Roped knives this piece carries no official marks. Blade length 6.625 inches; overall length 11.5 inches.

Plate 144

Plate 145

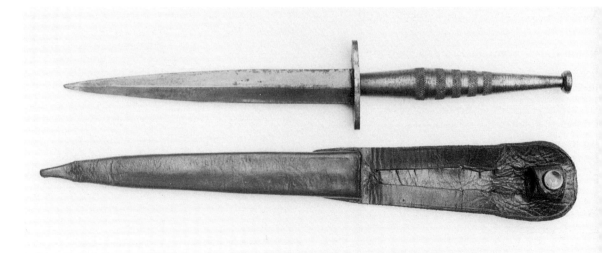

Plate 146

Plate 147

STEEL-HILTED COMMANDO KNIFE

146 to 148 Like many of the more unusual variants these all-steel versions are subject to much speculation regarding their origins. The commonest claim made for these knives is that they were made for dropping to the Resistance. I personally suspect that they actually represent an *ersatz* version made to meet the demands of D-Day. They could well have been dropped to the Resistance but they were also used by Allied troops. In the magazine *After the Battle* one of these knives is illustrated in a photo showing the contents of a Sherman tank salvaged off the D-Day beaches.[22] Examples are found with plated finish, and presentation inscriptions have been noted along with a spate of fakes. These knives have a standard type blade and crossguard, but the hilt is made from steel with five rings of knurling to provide a grip, and is very slim towards the pommel button.

(146) and (147) show two examples complete with sheaths of distinctive pattern. This type of sheath has been noted only with this style of knife, and that shown in (161). It would therefore appear safe to assume that it is the correct pattern for these knives. As will be observed the sheath has no chape and they appear never to have been provided with stitch tabs. The belt flap is not reinforced and the hilt retainer is of the press-stud type. Blade length is 6.375 inches; overall length 11.3125 inches.

(148) has been plated for presentation purposes and is represented by a form of sheath which could be a pattern also issued with this knife. The small rivets down the side of the sheath are not, however, original. Blade length is 6.5 inches; overall length 11.0625 inches.

WOOD-HILTED COMMANDO KNIFE

Wood-hilted Commando knives are reputed to have been used in the Far East in place of the metal-hilted versions. Some authors also state that they were made up after the war to use up surplus blades.[23] Whatever the truth of these claims, limited evidence does exist to indicate their use by the RAF during World War Two. At least one photograph exists showing a wood hilt in wear by a pilot and Wilkinson-Latham states that ex-World War Two pilots have identified such knives as issue items.[24]

One fact about these knives is clear, however, and that is they come with a large variety of hilt variations. The illustrations only show a sample of the many that may be encountered by the collector. Despite these hilt variations the one feature that is commonly found on these knives is the use of a parallel-sided crossguard.

Such knives almost certainly were not the subject of official inspection and this explains why they are never found bearing the ↑ mark. The example illustrated by Thompson with a ↑I mark on the crossguard is almost certainly a re-hilt.[25]

The dimensions of these wood-hilted knives vary between 11.25 inches and 11.625 inches overall and between 6.5 inches and 6.825 for blade length.

---

149 to 152 These knives follow in style the Third Pattern hilt, the hilts being painted black in examples (149) to (151), while the hilt of (152) retains a natural wood finish.

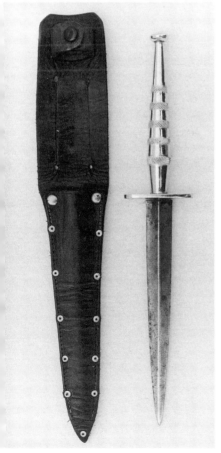

Plate 148

Plate 149

Plate 150

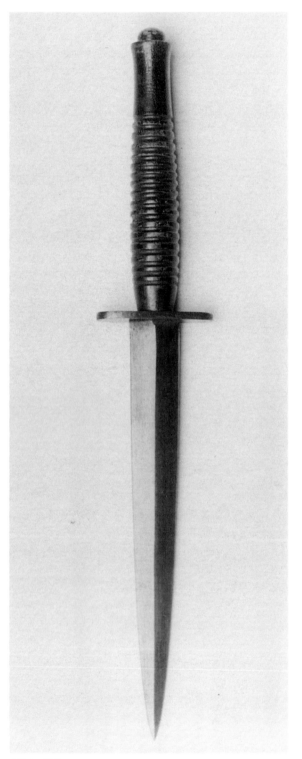

Plate 151

153 This knife is crudely put together but is not a one-off — a couple of other similar examples have been noted. The hilt is cut with very shallow grooves and is secured to the tang by means of a single pin through the hilt.

154 The hilt of this knife is cut with three groups of three bands. The crossguard is very thin and oval in shape, as normally found on Commando knives. Note the very small size of the pommel nut.

155 This style has a large oval-shaped hilt in which the pommel nut is recessed into the top of the grip.

156 With a hilt of the same style as (155), this knife has its blade marked with the name and trademark of John Blyde. One of the unusual features of this knife is the fact that the crossguard is made of alloy. A similar example has been recorded by Robert Buerlein.[26]

Plate 152   *Plate 153*

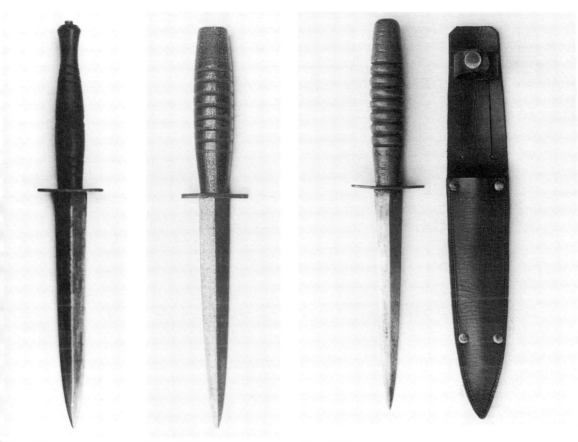

Plate 154   Plate 155   Plate 157

Plate 156

157 With round wooden grip cut with seven large ridges this piece is very similar to the knife shown in wear by the pilot in (158). In this example the crossguard is oval in shape and made of thin brass rather than steel.

158 RCAF pilot being debriefed at a front-line airfield in France shortly after D-Day. Note the knife in wear on the Mae West.

159 This knife has an unusual square section hilt made of ebony. This is not a one-off as other examples have been noted.

Plate 158

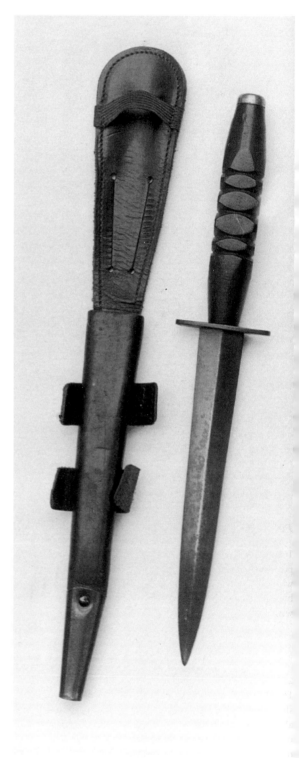

Plate 159

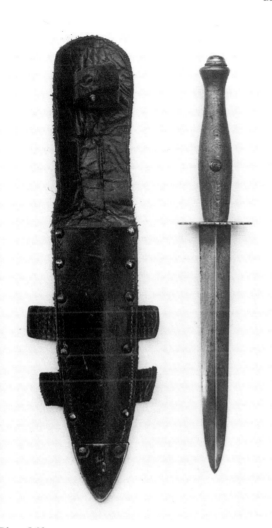

Plate 160

160 Although the accompanying sheath dates from the early post-war years the date of the knife is not certain. The grip, while of traditional shape, is unusually smooth and secured by a pin through the grip. The crossguard is of thin brass with a fancy edge.

MISCELLANEOUS TYPES

161 These Commando knives with alloy grips of octagonal shape are very scarce and have no recorded history, and although Buerlein states that the hilt is hand-worked this is not the case – the hilts have definitely been cast in this manner.[27] The sheath pattern that normally accompanies this type of knife is the same as that shown in (146) and (147).

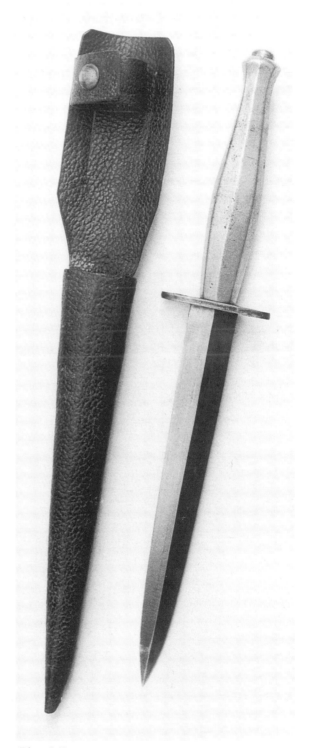

Plate 161

162 The true origin of these Commando knives, similar in style to the USMC Stiletto, is unknown, but a large number have turned up in this country and it is thought that they do originate from Britain. The hilt and crossguard are cast directly onto the tang, the hilt having rows of rings to provide a grip. The example illustrated has a coppered finish to the hilt and a blued blade, though examples with black paint finish to the hilt have been noted, along with those which only exhibit the alloy grey finish of the hilt material. Blade length 6.75 inches; overall length 11.625 inches.

163 These smooth alloy-hilted Commando knives have been attributed to use by the Free Polish Forces, but this is based on a single example which had a Polish badge attached to its sheath. It is unlikely that such knives were specifically

commissioned by such forces, and they are more likely to be private purchase variations. Genuine specimens of this knife are scarce, which has resulted in a number of spurious examples appearing.

164 With a hilt made of a synthetic, almost plastic-like material, this example is Third Pattern in style but the hilt is rather thick in diameter and does not taper in the usual manner towards the pommel.

165 This knife has in all probability been re-hilted but is interesting because of its accompanying sheath which is unlike anything previously noted. As will be observed the sheath is fitted with both locket and chape, the former being fitted with a bar which, it is assumed, accommodated a belt loop.

Plate 162

Plate 163

Plate 164

166 Of very late World War Two or early post-war origin the hilt of this knife is staghorn with a thin brass crossguard. The blade bears the violin trademark and name of George Ibberson along with the following:

SWAINE & ALDNEY LTD

185 PICCADILLY LONDON W1

Swaine & Aldney are a firm of high-class gentlemen's and military outfitters, so it is likely that this knife was an officer's private purchase. The leather sheath of substantial construction does not conform to the traditional pattern, but it is similar to other patterns observed with the Ibberson/Swaine & Aldney marking. Blade length 6.375 inches; overall length 10.125 inches.

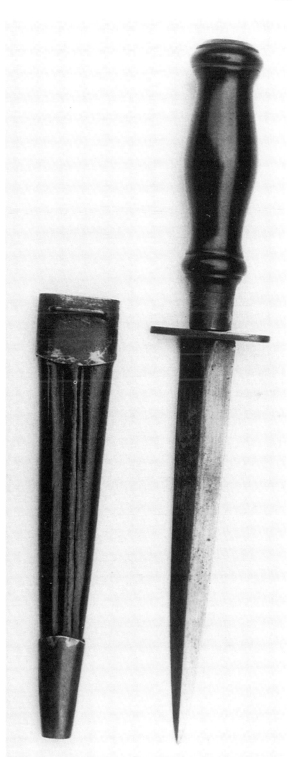

Plate 165

Plate 166

POST-WAR COMMANDO KNIVES

The history of Commando knives in the early post-war years is unknown, but it appears that with the disbandment of the Commandos the knife was no longer issued and large numbers were sold as surplus to the USA. Around the mid-1950s it came back into favour and has been held as a stores item ever since. However, despite the apparent commonality of equipment which NATO stores codification was supposed to bring about, the post-war knives have followed two distinctive trails.

167 & 168 This knife is currently held by RAF Stores for use in survival packs. Its official designation is 'Knife, Hunting G.P. with Sheath W.D. Pattern'. Under the NATO stores referencing system its number is 5110-99-4658827, but for RAF management purposes it is known as 1B/4658827. In service since at least 1966 it has been obtained from three suppliers: George Ibberson, John Clarke and Wilkinson Sword. The knives are not of particularly good quality and are in fact of the same commercial type that can be bought in many sports shops etc. The official issue examples are, however, marked on the crossguard with the maker's name, the year of manufacture and the stores number. The example illustrated in (167) is by George Ibberson and bears the pre-NATO codification stores number 1B/4432 on the crossguard; see also (168).

169 This photograph shows the crossguard of another example dated 1977 which bears the NATO number 4658827. This example does not give any clues as to the maker as the only other marks are SHEFFIELD ENGLAND. Blade length 6.875 inches; overall length 11.5 inches.

170 A reproduction of a letter from the RAF Stores Department giving the background to these knives.

Plate 168   *Plate 169*

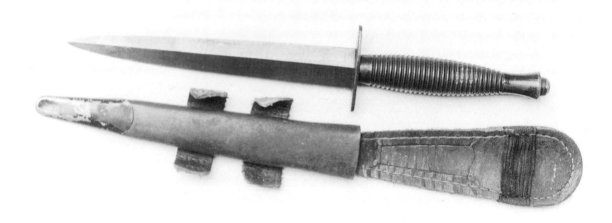

Plate 167

BP/3

Ministry of Defence
St George's Road Harrogate North Yorkshire HG2 9DB

Telephone Harrogate 68922 ext
Service Line Harrogate St George's

Mr Flook

Your reference
Our reference
D/DDSM1/35/6/47 SM 7a(RAF)
Date
28th July 1978

Dear Mr Flook

1. Thank you for your letter of the 24 July 1978. I have been able to identify from the detail given the knife you have acquired.

2. My records go back to 1966 when this equipment was known as 1B/4432 Knife Hunting G P complete with Sheath WD Pattern. Over the years we have provisioned these from 3 suppliers viz G Ibberson & Co Ltd, J C Clark & Son and Wilkinson Sword Co. Under NATO referencing philosophy this item was re-referenced as 5110-99-4658827. However, for RAF management purposes, it is known as 1B/4658827, with the same description.

3. Unfortunately due to destruction of old correspondence it is now difficult to give a valid reason for the introduction of this article into the RAF. Currently it has a general applicability covering such things as personal survival packs to bomb disposal, but I am not aware of it being used in the pursuit of animals human or otherwise. We buy many knives for the service, the function of which, in no way matches the description of the article.

4. I am sorry I cannot be more specific, but hope this information will be of some value to you in your study of the subject.

Yours sincerely

E. Snashall.

E R A SNASHALL

Plate 170

171 Capt. Robin Watts RAOC on attachment to the RM Logistic Regiment photographed during an exercise in 1975. Capt. Watts is carrying one of the commercial versions of (167).

172 to 176 The next post-war knife has a very involved and complicated history which has taken much research to unravel. In the Wilkinson Sword data sheet issued a number of years ago in response to enquiries about Commando knives there is a reference to a quantity of knives being supplied to the Admiralty in 1964 whose crossguards were stamped FR693. Even though Wilkinson supplied these knives in 1964 their origins go back to 1955. From information obtained from the Royal Naval Ordnance Museum this knife was first held as a Naval Armament Stores item, presumably for use by the Royal Marines, in 1955 Admiralty Fleet Order (AFO) P134/55 as FQ693 – Knife, Fighting and FQ271 – Sheath, Fighting Knife. Later it was held under series FR and then in the 1960s the stores numbers were changed to 247693 and 247271 respectively. The extracts from the AFO and stores catalogue reproduced in (172) and (173) illustrates the changes in stores designations.

   To date only one example of a knife bearing the FR693 designation has been observed and that is in the collection of the Pattern Room. The knife held there is shown in (174),

Plate 171

MISCELLANEOUS WEAPONS – CONTD.

STORE REFERENCE and remainder of nomenclature	Suitable for (see Key on page 1)	Drawing No.	V.R.A.F.E. or V.A.O.S. Cat. No.	Class	Remarks
FQ 134 HAMMER and striker – Assembly	o	Arm.1(E) 1413	–	– D	Identical with EV 056 HAMMER
FQ 641 HANDLE	g	NOD 3196/4/31	–	–	
FQ 654 HOOK, firing lever	a	NOD 1574	–	–	
		NOD 3597			
FQ 693 KNIFE, fighting	–	–	–	D	
FQ 160 LANYARD, firing – Assembly	a	NOD 1574	–	–	White Line 1½ lb. x 18in.
FQ 252 LANYARD, firing	a	NOD 1574	–	–	White line, 1½ lb. x 18in.
		NOD 3597			
FQ 278 LEVEL, spirit	g	–	–	–	Commercial pattern, approx. 2⅞ in. long.
FQ 291 LEVER, extractor	c,g,h	NOD 3196/3/27 SAID 1333C	BB.0491	–	Optional item
FQ 304 LEVER, extractor	d	DD(E) 3188/25	BB.6803	–	
FQ 317 LEVER, firing, rocket signal machine, mk. 4	a	NOD 1574	–	–	
FQ 005 LEVER, firing, rocket signal machine, mk. 4 – Assembly	a	NOD 1574	–	–	(25765)
FQ 330 LEVER, firing, rocket signal machine, mk. 5	a	NOD 3597	–	–	
FQ 018 LEVER, firing, rocket signal machine, mk. 5 – Assembly	a	NOD 3597	–	–	(B.9854)
FQ 343 LEVER, main spring	b,1	AID 1014B	–	–	
FQ 356 LEVER, main spring	c	Arm.1(E) 1412	–	–	
FQ 369 LIP, extractor	d	DD(E) 3188/21	BA.10023	–	
FQ 382 LOCKET, scabbard	j	–	6645	–	For Patt. 1900 Naval Sword (10419).58H5
FQ 395 LOOP, stock	d	DD(E) 3188/10	BA.10024	–	
FQ 121 LOCKET, SCABBARD	J	–	–	–	FOR PATT 1899 NAVAL SWORD N⁰ 20

A.F.O.P.134/55
(85650/3)14

4

Amendment No. 17

Plate 172

SECTION ER

SWORDS

KNIVES, FIGHTING

GUN, SHOT 12 BORE, DOUBLE BARRELLED

Inspection of the Stores in this section is carried out by the Director of Armament Supply

STORE REFERENCE and Remainder of Nomenclature	Interchangeability or Limitations in use	Drawing No.	V.A.O.S. Cat. No.	Class	Remarks
247 ER 666 CHAPE scabbard Pattern 1889 and 1900 Naval Sword	247 ER 022 and 247 ER 035 Scabbard	–	–	D	
247 ER 095 GUN, shot, 12 bore, double-barrelled – Assembly	–	–	–	C	
247 ER 693 KNIFE, fighting	OBSOLETE				
247 ER 382 LOCKET, scabbard, Patt. 1900, Naval Sword	ER 035 Scabbard	–	–	F	
247 ER 421 LOCKET, scabbard, Patt. 1889, Naval Sword	247 ER 022 Scabbard	–	–	F	
247 ER 009 SCABBARD, Mk. 2, 27 in. Naval Sword – Assembly	247 ER 102 Sword	–	–	D	
247 ER 022 SCABBARD, Patt. 1889, Naval Sword – Assembly	247 ER 115 Sword	–	–	D	
247 ER 035 SCABBARD, Patt. 1900, Naval Sword – Assembly	247 ER 128 Sword	–	–	D	
247 ER 048 SCABBARD, sword, Staff Sergeant, No. 4 Mk. 1 – Assembly	247 ER 141 Sword	–	B1/BB1284	D	For Royal Marines
247 ER 061 SCABBARD, sword, Regimental Sergeant Major, No. 4 Mk. 1 (Sam Browne)	247 ER 154 Sword	–	B1/BB1292	D	For Royal Marines
247 ER 271 SHEATH, fighting knife	247 ER 693 Knife OBSOLETE				
247 ER 558 SPRING, mouthpiece, sword scabbard	247 ER 022 Scabbard ER 035 Scabbard	–	–	D	
247 ER 102 SWORD, Naval 27 in., Mk. 2 – Assembly	247	–	–	D	
247 ER 115 SWORD, Naval Patt. 1889, 28 in. – Assembly	–	–	–	D	
247 ER 128 SWORD, Naval Patt. 1900, 28 in. – Assembly	–	–	–	D	
247 ER 141 SWORD, Staff sergeant, No. 1, Mk. 3 – Assembly	–	–	B1/BB1959	D	For Royal Marines
247 ER 154 SWORD, Regimental Sergeant Major, No. 4, Mk. 1 – Assembly	–	–	B1/BB1402	D	For Royal Marines 27 ¼ in.

Plate 173

(175) and (176) and, as will be noted, is complete with its issue box and labels. The box is marked

B1-1095-963-2037

KNIFE QTY 1

and the label attached to the knife and sheath is marked

KNIFE FIGHTING WITH SHEATH

PART NO. LDN 42260

FR693

FR271

The knife is by Wilkinson and is almost identical to the private purchase piece shown to the left of (180). Besides the Wilkinson crest on the blade the knife is marked FR693 on the underside of the crossguard, and the reverse of the sheath is stamped FR271.

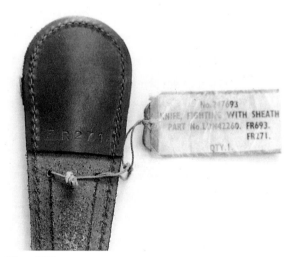

Plate 175

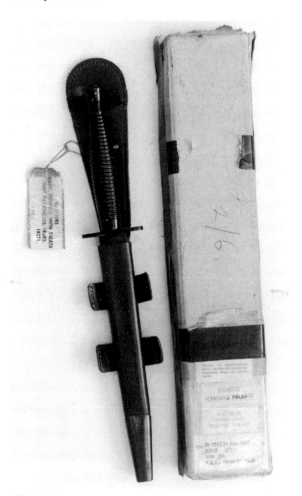

Plate 174

Plate 176

Plate 178

Plate 177

Plate 179

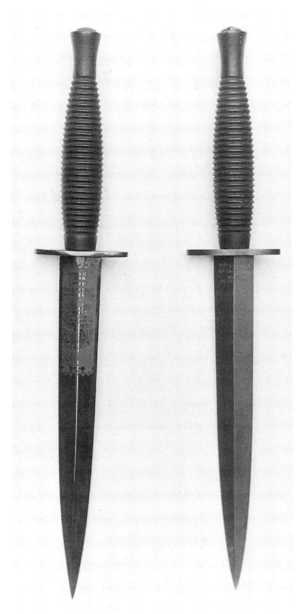

According to the RN Ordnance Museum these knives ceased to be held by the RN about 1965, but information received from the MoD (Army) Directorate of Supply Management indicated that knives with the B1-1095-99-963-2037 stores designation are still held by them.

---

177 The crossguard of a Commando knife of the same type as (167) with the crossguard bearing the above-mentioned stores number. It would thus appear that while the RAF have codified the knife under one description and number, the Army have it under another.

---

178 & 179 Another knife linked with this pattern is the so-called Falklands Commando Knife. These Wilkinson-made knives have a dull matt-black finish unlike that observed on any other Commando knife and bear a very basic trademark – see (179). According to Wilkinson-Latham, 200 of these knives were supplied to the MoD by Wilkinson in response to a telex order received during the Falklands War.[28] Enquiries made with Wilkinson confirm that this information is correct.

---

180 & 181 (180) shows one of these knives in comparison with a standard commercial finish product. Even though this knife bears no official marks it would appear that in Army Stores terms it is a B1-1095-963-2037 knife. In researching the RAF and FR693 knives, the Logistic Executive (Army) stated, and I quote: 'Additional purchases have been made

Plate 180

from Wilkinson Sword against specific projects, requirements for which could not be met from military stocks at that time.' So it would appear that at the outset of the Falklands War stocks of military issue Commando knives were low and that the 200 filled an urgent need.

F-S SHEATHS

Except for a few cases I decided to illustrate Commando knife sheaths separately. Over the passage of time knives have not necessarily stayed with the sheath they were issued with, and to attribute particular sheath types to knife

variations would in some cases be incorrect.

182 This sheath is the one always associated with the First Pattern, yet photographic evidence does exist which shows that it is also found with bright finish Second Patterns. Unlike later patterns of sheath the hilt retainer has a press-stud rather than the elastic strap. The belt flap is not stitched around its edge and is not fitted with a strengthening piece on the back. The press-stud and chape have a nickel finish. Like other F-S sheaths these are frequently found with the stitch tabs removed.

183 The standard sheath pattern of the type still in use today. Note the elastic hilt retainer. The chape of this example is nickel-plated.

DIRECTORATE OF SUPPLY MANAGEMENT (ARMY)
LOGISTIC EXECUTIVE (ARMY)
Portway Monxton Road Andover Hants SP11 8HT

Telephone: Andover Military
Direct Line (0264) 8 } Ext 2350
GTN Code 2077
Switchboard (0264) 82111

R E Flook Esq

Please reply to   S Man 1a(3)
Your reference

Our reference   D/DSM(A)152
(S Man 1a(3))
Date 20 th July 1982

Sir

KNIFE FIGHTING WITH SHEATH

I am directed to acknowledge receipt of your recent letter, which has been passed to this office, and which enquires into the background of the Knife Fighting with Sheath.

The subject item B1/1095-99-963-2037 is still in service with the Army Department but has always been for a specialised role. The item 1B/5110-99-465-8827 is in service with the Air Force Department and was purchased a long time ago as an integral part of survival packs. The similarity in design of the two items is coincidental.

The position is best explained by the fact that where a dependency is small, a limited one time buy would be effected either from items readily available from Trade or to a specialist specification, if necessary. The relevant Sponsor Branches retain management within each of the three Services where requirements are small, and individually biased; they do not lend themselves to a Single-Service Manager – hence the apparent anomaly.

The specific questions raised cannot be answered in other than broad terms for reasons of security. However, the two items in question are in service, the Air Force Department Knife as a Survival Pack item only, and the Army Department Knife since 1963 with certain special forces. Additional purchases have been made from Wilkinson Sword against specific projects, requirements for which could not be met from Military Stocks at the time.

I am, Sir,
Your obedient Servant

D St J EVE
Major
for Director

Plate 181

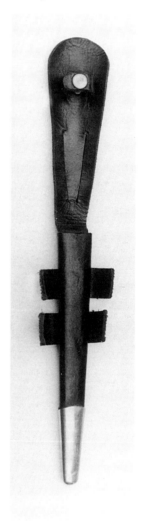

Plate 182   *Plate 183*

184 World War Two sheath with blued chape.

185 World War Two period sheath with square-ended chape. Commando sheaths are rarely marked, but this piece is stamped with a W on the rear of the body. This mark is sometimes found on bayonet scabbards and indicates that it has been waxed. It is a mark associated with Australian bayonet scabbards and thus may indicate that the sheath shown is of Australian manufacture.

186 Similar to (185), this piece has its chape secured by a rivet through the front rather than a staple at the rear. Possibly early post-war.

187 Relatively few of these back to front sheaths have been observed. What the exact reason is for the seam being down the front is unknown.

188 This sheath came with a Third Pattern marked ↑ over 7, but it is almost certainly a commercial post-war variety. The sheath originally had stitch tabs but these have been removed.

189 An intriguing all-metal Commando knife sheath of

Plate 184

Plate 185

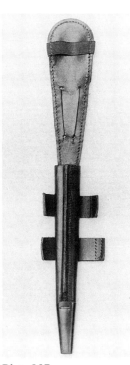

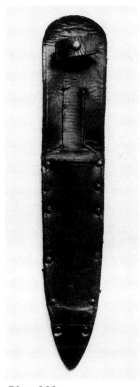

Plate 186

Plate 187

Plate 188

Plate 189

unknown origin. The body is formed from two pieces of tin plate soldered down the side. The belt flap is stepped back from the body to prevent the hilt and crossguard fouling. Holes in the belt flap were presumably made to take some form of leatherwork or other fastening. A small stitch tab at the tip of the sheath shows signs of age. The piece is painted dark green overall and the belt flap is marked

FPH

1943

This sheath came without a knife, but of all the specimens tried only those with relatively slim blades would fit. Only two examples of this sheath are known.

190 This sheath came with an unmarked Third Pattern. The sheath is without doubt factory-made and is the only example of such a design heard about. Made of light tan leather it has a small brass chape, but the belt flap lacks slots. The only means provided for attachment is the leather arm strap.

ROYAL NAVY DECK KNIVES

Besides clasp knives Royal Navy seamen also used fixed-blade knives when undertaking seaman-type duties such as working with ropes. While this practice has been going on for many years no knife, with the exception of one which could be World War Two vintage, has been identified which dates prior to the 1950s.

Plate 190

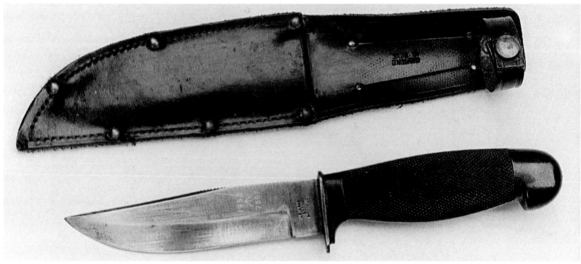

Plate 191

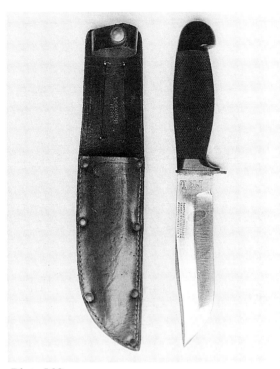

Plate 192

Plate 193

The 1950s knife (191), identical in form to (192), was supplied to the Royal Navy against Contract 6/HT/4232/50 and was designated 'Knife, Sheath, Pattern Number 0274/7587'. About 1970 this knife was replaced by that shown in (193). This knife has the same description but its Naval Stores number is 0274/437-5839. Also frequently used by the RN as a deck knife is 'Knife, Riggers 0274/910-5291'. How long this knife has been in service is not known but examples from the 1950s have been identified. Several manufacturers have been involved, each introducing slight changes in quality and style.

---

191 The deck knife used by the RN from the 1950s to 1970. The hilt is of black plastic with a short brass crossguard. The blade has a finely serrated back edge and is marked

1952

↑

7587

This mark is lightly etched in place. The ricasso is stamped with the maker's name of

J.CLARKE & SON

SHEFFIELD

The black leather sheath is stamped on the belt flap MADE IN ENGLAND. Blade length 4.25 inches; overall length 9 inches.

---

192 This piece is thought to be a World War Two version of (191). It bears no official marks, but this was not unusual on wartime RN knives. Except for the difference in the grind of the blade back edge the knife is identical to (191). The knife bears the name and trademark of G. Wostenholm on the blade. The tan leather sheath is marked on the belt flap MADE IN SHEFFIELD ENG. Another similar version by Taylor's Eye Witness has also been noted. Blade length 4.875 inches; overall length 9.25 inches.

---

193 Of rather flimsy construction this John Clarke-made knife is of a type which is still current issue. Besides bearing the maker's name on the blade it is also marked

1976

↑

457-5839

The grips are of wood secured by two brass rivets. The black leather sheath is of the pouch type. Blade length 4.125 inches; overall length 8.125 inches.

194 Officially known as 'Knife, Riggers', these knives come in a variety of qualities, some pieces having a substantial blade, others thin, whippy blades and crude grips. The piece illustrated is of sturdy manufacture and has its blade etched with the maker's name

F.E. & J.R. HOPKINSON LTD

SHEFFIELD ENGLAND

along with the stores mark of

910-5291

↑ 1980

The very basic sheath is the correct pattern for the knife, the strap across the front being for the carriage of a marlin spike. Blade length 5.75 inches; overall length 10.475 inches.

Other variations noted have been marked as follows: —

(1) Blade marked   910-5291

S&H 1977↑

The hilt is stamped ↑580

(2) Blade marked WM COOPER (HT) LTD

SHEFFIELD

The hilt is stamped 910-5291

(3) Blade marked as above with the hilt stamped H1528. This is a form of Naval Stores mark which dates from the early post-war years.

195 Another form of deck knife used by the RN is a special non-magnetic version for use on Mine Counter-Measures Vessels (MCMVs). The official designation of this knife is 'Knife, Seamen's NATO Stock Number 5110-12-155-9060'. The '12' in the number indicates the country of origin as

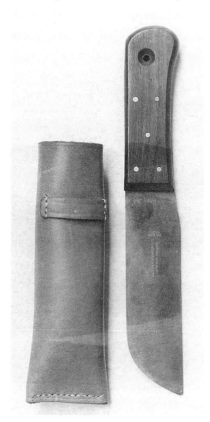

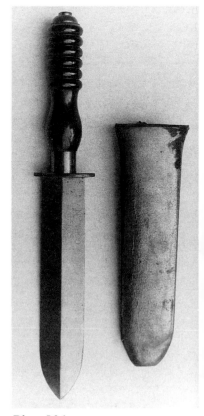

Plate 194   *Plate 195*   *Plate 196*

Germany and the notes on NATO Stores in Appendix Two will help explain the apparent anomaly of a German knife in a book on British and Commonwealth knives. The knife has a blade with a pronounced belly and hard chrome finish. The grips are of wood secured by three brass rivets, one of which is hollow, presumably to take a thong. The blade is marked with an electric pencil MCMV 4 over E30 and also carries a black and green stick-on label. The hilt is stamped NM on one side, and on the other it carries an unclear trademark which looks like LECIS along with NM116 5110 12 155 9060. The well-made brown leather sheath is stamped MADE IN GERMANY on the belt loop. Blade length 5.375 inches; overall length 9.5 inches.

DIVERS' KNIVES

As far as can be established RN divers have used six distinct styles of knife. Up until about 1962 the knife generally associated with standard (hardhat) diving was in use by all RN divers. From 1962 several other types of knife were issued, all with the common feature of having hard rubber handles. The importance which the Royal Navy places on the wearing of knives is reflected by the regulations contained in its diving manuals, which require all divers and attendants to wear knives.

196 & 196A The standard Divers' Knife is of a design that goes back many years, possibly even prior to World War

Plate 196A

One. It certainly saw service during World War Two and even though it is only officially issued to units complemented for standard diving it is preferred by many divers to the rubber-hilted versions. The knife has a broad double-edged blade 8.125 inches in length, a brass crossguard and ferrule, and grip of black plastic. In early versions the grip material was wood. The blade is marked

SIEBE

GORMAN

The official designation is 'Knife, Divers, Naval Stores Pattern 0887 431-7200'. The sheath is of brass and has an internal spring clip to hold the knife, and the sheath is secured to the belt by means of a strap. It is also sometimes carried in a diving boot, as shown in (197). The sheath is unmarked, but (196A) shows an original box of issue with labels indicating its official designation, stores and contract numbers. I have examined several of these knives with known RN origin but none bears any marks indicating official issue. Overall length 13.5 inches.

197 HM King George VI with Captain Fell inspecting 'human torpedo' crews in 1944. Note the knife visible in the bottom right corner being carried in the boot. (IWM A23302).

Plate 197

198 This piece is a non-magnetic version of (196). First issued in 1957 this knife was for clearance divers when working on magnetic mines. It was certainly still in service in 1983 but it is not known if it has been totally superseded by the type shown in (199), which has been in service since 1972. All examples noted to date have had a saw edge and, unlike (196), can be found bearing stores marks. This piece carries the pre-NATO codification marks of A.P. (Admiralty Pattern) 6260 on the blade and A.P. 6261 on the sheath. Both knife and sheath are additionally marked NON-MAGNETIC.

I have tried to obtain technical details of this knife, particularly the composition of the blade, without success. However, I did manage to establish that for stores costing purposes it was valued in 1983 at £72, which obviously reflects the high cost of the non-magnetic blade material. Under NATO Stores coding it is known as 'Knife, Divers, clearance, non-magnetic, 4220-99-431-7338', the sheath being 7339. Two versions of the knife are known to exist. In addition to the version shown another with the same blade form but with no stores markings and a sheath which is only marked NON-MAGNETIC has been noted. Blade length 7.75 inches; overall length 11.125 inches.

199 to 201B This non-magnetic knife is currently in service with the RN. Made by Life Support Engineering Ltd it was first manufactured in 1972 and seems to have had two blade forms, one single-edged the other double-edged. The blade and crossguard are made of copper beryllium and the hilt is hard black rubber. The sheath is of black plastic and is a standard commercial type bearing the emblem SOUS MARINE GUERNSEY. The knife shown in (199) bears no official marks but is stamped LIFE SUPPORT along the back edge. This design is shown in the drawings at (200) which are dated 1976. The current design for this knife is shown in the drawings at (201/201A), and an actual example is shown in the photograph at (201B). This indicates that these current knives bear the NATO stock number of 4220-99-758-6192 on the blade. Approximately 250 of these knives have been supplied to the RN. Blade length 6.875 inches; overall length 11.75 inches. Grateful acknowledgement is made to Life Support Engineering for much of the information and permission to reproduce the drawings.

Plate 198

Plate 199

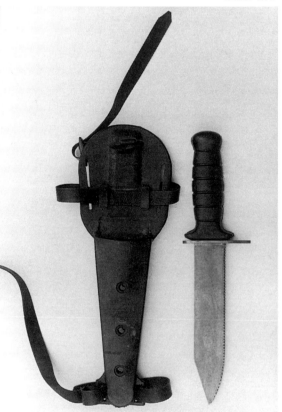

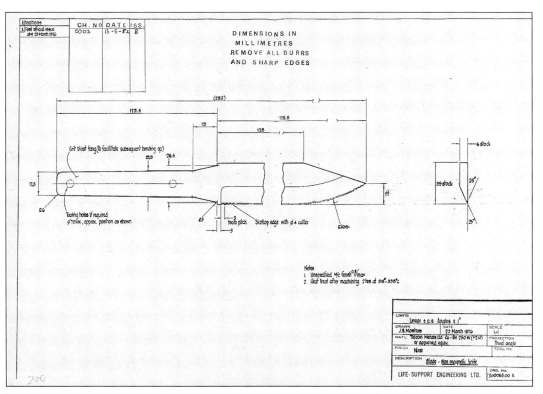

*Plate
200*

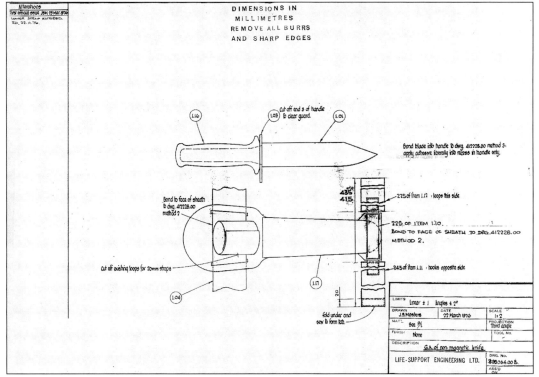

*Plate
200A*

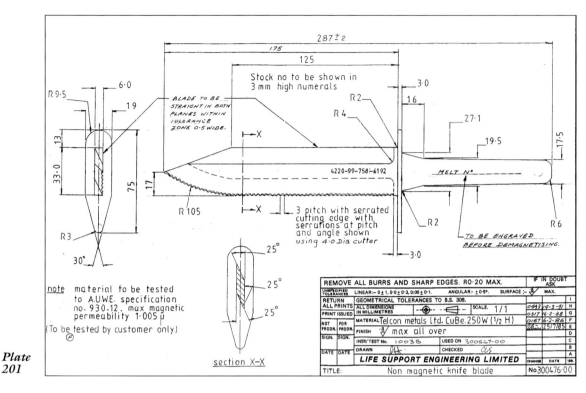

Plate 201

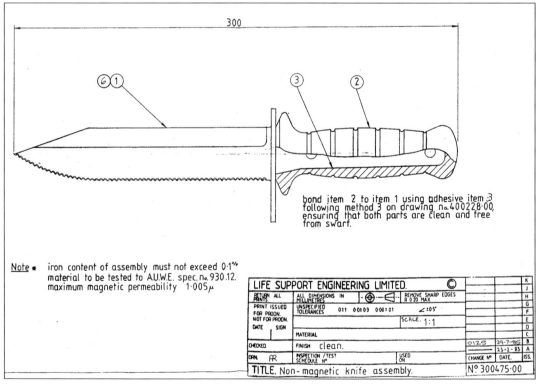

Plate 201A

Plate 201B

202 to 205 In about 1962 a new knife was introduced for divers, but despite being in service for about eight years it was never popular. Its short blade and lightweight construction made it generally unsuitable for underwater

Plate 202

TRADE MARK   TELEGRAMS EYE-WITNESS SHEFFIELD   TELEPHONE 24221/2

taylor's eye-witness limited
CUTLERY MANUFACTURERS

ESTABLISHED 1838   MILTON STREET . SHEFFIELD S3 7WJ . ENGLAND

YOUR REF.   OUR REF. GW/PAW

18th August, 1978.

Mr. R.E. Flook,

Dear Sir,

Thank you for your letter of the 11th August regarding the Diver's Knife.

Yes, this is a Knife which this company made during the last war - that is we made the blade for a customer who had the rubber handle moulded on.

Consequently, we did not supply the item direct to the Admiralty and your question on the dates taxes our memory too much. Those of our staff old enough to remember were not here during the war!

Answering your other questions:-

    a) Yes, this is a Diver's Knife.

    b) The purpose of the blade slot may have been to act as a shackle key, though one suggestion made today was that it served to reduce sideways water pressure.

    c) The hole in the handle received a button on the strap of the sheath.

Somewhere in London there used to be a firm called E.T. Skinner who were specialists in diving equipment and an approach to them might be more productive.

Yours faithfully,
Taylor's Eye-Witness Ltd.,

G. Wilson,
Director.

REGISTERED IN ENGLAND 55000   V.A.T. NO. 172 9799 07

TYPHOON INTERNATIONAL LIMITED

42-44 Arundel Terrace, Barnes, London SW13 9DS
Tel: 01.748 8341. Telex: 8953856 Tillon G. Cables: Typhoon London SW13

Your Ref: Our Ref: CVDL/B.MW   Date: 15 June 1982

Mr R E FLook

Dear Mr Flook

Thank you for your letter regarding the naval divers knives.

This was a knife developed by us for the Navy and as far as we can recollect, they were supplied for approximately six years up to 1970 or 1971.

It was not a successful knife. The blade was too short. and the whole thing was far too insubstantial for the average naval jack.

In fact. they used to buy their own knives and we have supplied our pic knife in quite large quantities to the Navy over the years which is one that we have as a standard item in our range of divers knives.

Yours sincerely
TYPHOON INTERNATIONAL LIMITED

C J van der Lande
Managing Director

Plate 203

work. It was, however, issued to ships and clearance divers, Royal Marine swimmer canoeists and members of the SAS Boat Troop.

The knife has a short Bowie-style blade with saw teeth on the back edge. Two blade variations exist, one with a slot in the blade, the other more traditional in style. The hilt is of hard black rubber and has a hole in both sides which mates with a stud on the hilt retaining strap. The knives bear the name TAYLOR'S EYE WITNESS on the blade and the stores number is moulded onto the hilt. The sheath is of hard black rubber and has its stores number moulded on the front.

The design and manufacturing history of these knives is somewhat curious. As already mentioned one version has a slot in the blade and it is my opinion that this was to allow it to be used as a shackle key. However, as will be noted from the letter at (202), the makers are not really sure of its function. Another odd aspect is that in this letter it is stated that Taylor's only made the blades. The letter is also incorrect in implying that the knife dates from World War 2. Subsequent research revealed that the knives were actually designed and assembled by Typhoon International Ltd (203).

Through the life of this knife a variety of stores numbers were used. Knife (204) is marked on the hilt A.P. 0433/1545 and on the sheath A.P.O. 0433/1546. Note the additional O in the AP marking. Knife (205) has the same hilt markings but the sheath is marked A.P. 0433/1546. An example with the sheath marked TYPHOON in place of the stores number has been noted, and knives bearing eleven-digit stores numbers of 0433-924-8626 and 0433-924-8625 respectively, and which represent a change to the NATO codifying system, have also been observed. It is also possible that knives with the stores prefix 0867 exist, as just prior to these knives being withdrawn from service the stores class group was changed to this new four-figure group. It is not, however, known if any were actually manufactured bearing this new number. Blade length 4.5 inches; overall length 9.125 inches.

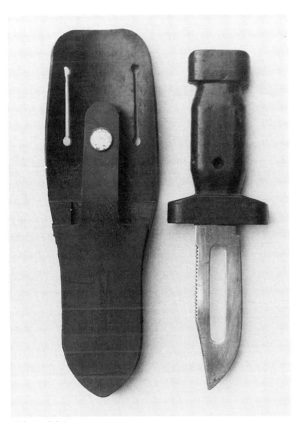

Plate 204

206 In 1970, as an interim measure between the phasing out of (204)/(205) and the introduction of the type shown in (208), the RN used this commercial divers' knife bought in from Typhoon International. This knife – as (207), a copy of the advertisement from a 1974 diving magazine, illustrates – was sold to the diving public as the Typhoon Pic Knife. The knife has a 7.25-inch Bowie-style blade with serrated cutting edge. The grip is of hard black rubber and the pommel of steel which, according to the maker, enables it to double as a hammer. The blade is etched with the maker's name and ruler marks. There are no marks indicating naval issue. The scabbard is of hard black plastic and carries the Typhoon trademark on the front. Overall length 12.5 inches.

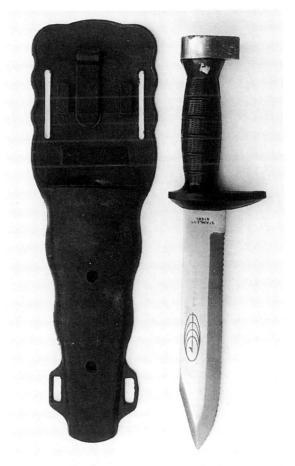

Plate 206

Plate 205

Plate 207

208 & 209 First introduced into service in the early 1970s and now the current issue divers' knife, this knife replaced the type shown in (204)/(205) and the Typhoon Pic Knife. It is manufactured by Hopkinson's, under both that and the John Nowill name. The example at (208) is etched as follows on the blade:

N.S. NO 4220-99-523-9744

JOHN NOWILL & SONS LTD

SHEFFIELD ENGLAND

The 'N.S.' number is the NATO stock number. This method of marking dates this example from the mid-1970s, as all examples seen since 1979 have had the stores number on the grip. The knife has a stainless steel double-edged blade with one edge serrated. The hilt is of hard black rubber and there is a heavy steel butt piece sunk into the pommel.

(209) is also by Nowill but it has the stores number moulded into the hilt. This knife is complete with sheath which bears its stores number on the front: N.S. NO 4220-99-523-9745. The leg straps are separately marked NSN 4220-99-523-9746. Blade length 7.75 inches; overall length 12.75 inches.

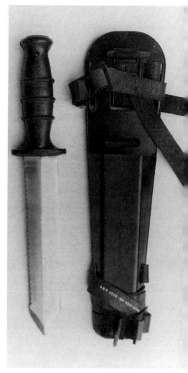

Plate 208   *Plate 209*

Plate 210   *Plate 211*   *Plate 212*

RELEASE OR FIREMAN'S KNIFE

In addition to requiring all divers to wear knives, RN manuals also state that SAR (search and rescue) divers should carry a 'fireman's knife' because of its superior qualities when cutting parachute shrouds.

---

210 Dating back to at least the 1920s, this type of knife is still in service today and is carried by fire and rescue teams and SAR divers for cutting free aircrew. It is also possible that it was carried by aircrew prior to the introduction of specific aircrew knives, but I have no evidence to support this.

The earliest dated specimen is from 1929, but the knife was obviously in service earlier than this as it is in a sheath dated 1927. This early knife is shown here and it has a couple of unusual sheath features. The knife, like its later counterparts, has a curved blade with a blunt rounded tip and is sharpened on the inner edge only. This feature was almost certainly adopted to prevent bodily damage when

trying to cut restraining straps. The hilt has wood grips held by three large brass rivets. The leather sheath has a belt loop on the back and is fitted with an internal spring clip which retains the knife; the spring clip on this version is in the bottom of the sheath, whereas on later versions it is in the throat of the sheath.

Both the blade and sheath markings are rather unusual. The blade is marked with a crown over AM for Air Ministry, and

M & Y

1929

The sheath is marked with the same marks but is dated 1927; the AM is, however, stamped over the arrow trademark of Maleham & Yeomans. It would appear that the AM marks on both knife and sheath have been added after manufacture, but they are not spurious. I would suggest that the knife was bought in for service use rather than manufactured against a specific contract with the marks added subsequently to indicate government ownership. Blade length 5.375 inches; overall length 11.125 inches.

211 to 213 (211) illustrates a version of this knife by J. Wilson and, as will be noted, both knife and sheath have extensive stores marks. The blade of this knife carries, in addition to the crowned AM and WILSON marks, the following:

STORES/4458/C42B

21E/254

A close-up of this mark is shown in (212). The sheath marks shown in close-up in (213) are in addition to the AM and WILSON marks:

1877/35MU/C42B

21F/254

The other knife shown on the right of (212) is by Rodgers and this bears totally different stores marks of B57966/40/C31A, and the mark on the sheath is B2856/39/C1.

The date of these two knives is not known for sure but it is thought they both are of the World War Two period. The Wilson example's blade length is 5.375 inches and its overall length 11.125 inches. The Rodgers example's blade length is 5 inches and its overall length 10.675 inches.

---

214 to 216 This illustrates a version of the release knife that is still current issue, with the original production drawings reproduced at (215) and (216). For some strange reason the drawings were converted from Ministry of Public Buildings and Works (MPBW) drawings. It is possible that this knife was phased out of military service at some stage while continuing with other government departments. When readopted by the military a suitable drawing was already available and was thus used for manufacturing purposes.

In general this modern example differs very little from its earlier counterparts. The most noticeable difference is that the grips are not so rounded and are secured by copper rather than brass rivets. The knife is marked on the blade 120-6199 along with the name and trademark of Joseph Rodgers. The sheath is marked on the front REAL HIDE, and on the reverse

120-6200

1977↑

Blade length 5.625 inches; overall length 11.125 inches.

A similar example with the blade marked as follows has also been noted:

JOSEPH RODGERS 1967

↑

RAF REF 21F/120-6198

Plate 213

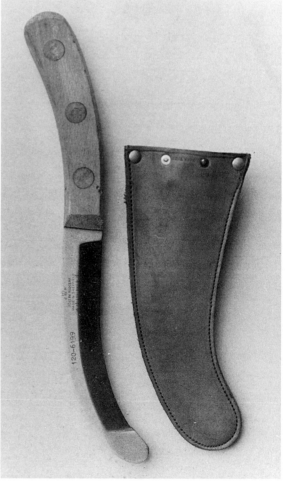

Plate 214

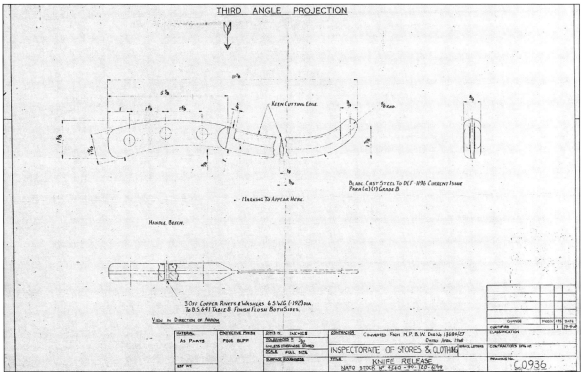

Plate 215

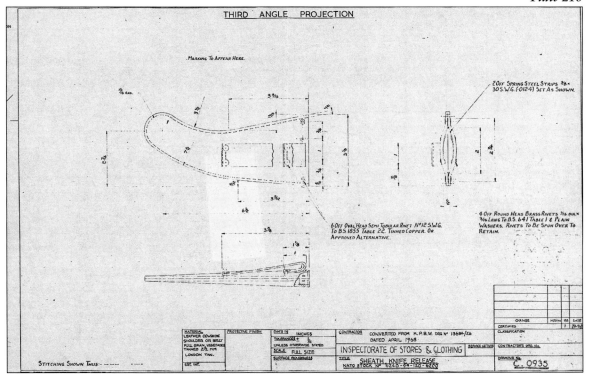

Plate 216

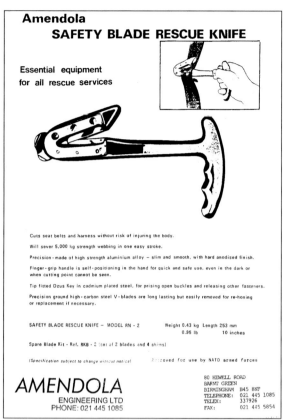

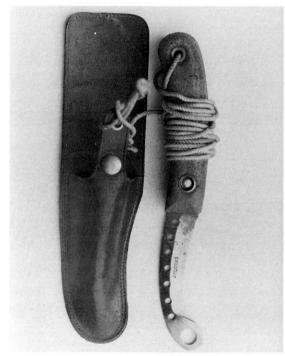

Plate 218

Plate 217

217 This rescue knife was introduced into at least naval service in 1990 under the authority of DCI RN 68/90 as 'Amendola Rescue Knife NATO Stock Number 4240-99-977-2081'. Other associated items were also listed in the DCI: 'Blade, Amendola Rescue Knife NATO Stock Number 4240-99-977-2082', and 'Sheath, Amendola Rescue Knife NATO Stock Number 4240-99-461-9020'. No actual example of this knife has been available for study, but the illustration shows the manufacturer's data sheet. It is believed that service examples are engraved with the year date and stores number.

DINGHY KNIVES

218 Incorrectly labelled by M.H. Cole as an American knife.[29] These knives are definitely British in origin as they bear RAF Stores codes and were packed in World War Two aircraft dinghies. Similar in style to the fireman's knife with a curved blunt-tipped blade, this knife has its blade holed along its length and is fitted with an orange cork grip. The

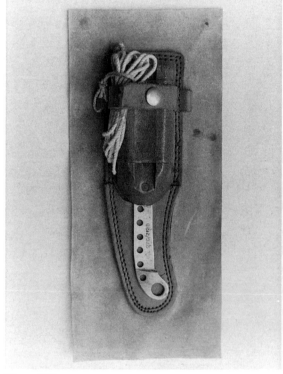

Plate 219

blade is marked 27c/2023. The leather sheath is backed by orange fabric, remnants of the patch that originally secured the sheath to the dinghy. The sheath is marked 27c/2024. To prevent loss of the knife it is attached to the sheath by a lanyard, and is retained in the sheath by a press-stud, the female portion of the stud being inset into the hilt. Neither knife nor sheath give any indications as to the maker. Blade length 4.375 inches; overall length 9.625 inches.

219 The exact date of this style of knife is unknown but similar pieces, such as (220), are known to have been carried attached to the Mae West of Fleet Air Arm pilots from late

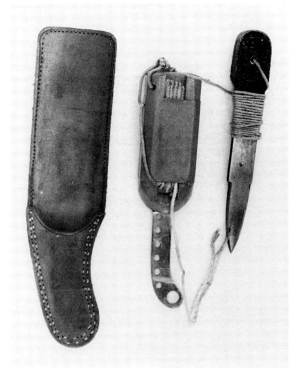

Plate 221

World War Two up until the 1950s. The blade is a smaller, less curved version of (218) and is marked ↑27c/2125. The grip is of orange-painted wood bound with a piece of tape. The tape is to retain the lanyard in a pre-packed stowage position, the lanyard being accommodated in a channel in the hilt. The sheath is of leather and is attached to a piece of yellow rubberised fabric which would have been stuck to the Mae West. Blade length 2.375 inches; overall length 5.75 inches.

220 The figure shown was photographed at the Fleet Air Arm Museum and shows the form of flying clothing used in the 1950s. Attached to the Mae West is a dinghy knife which, as will be seen from close examination of the photograph, is accompanied by another knife. From first glance it would appear that this type of dinghy knife is identical to (219), but it does in fact have a half-round groove in the back of the hilt. This groove accommodates the additional knife when the knives are in the sheath.

221 & 222 This smaller knife has a wooden hilt, painted black, to which is riveted a small double-edged spear-pointed stainless steel blade. The purpose of this knife was to puncture the dinghy if it accidentally inflated in the cockpit, or to sink it if the pilot was washed up on a hostile shore.

Plate 220

Both knives are unmarked, although the dimensions of the dinghy knife are the same as those for (219), and those for the small knife are blade length 1.75 inches, overall length 5.5625 inches.

___

223 Another version of the puncture knife, but in this case carried in its own right rather than as a companion to a dinghy knife. Of crude manufacture, the knife has a roughly shaped wooden hilt fitted with a small triangular-shaped alloy blade. The sheath is of thin leather stitched to a fabric patch, and has both an elastic and press-stud method of securing the knife.

224 This style of knife is currently packed in the Royal Navy's twenty-five-man liferafts and is listed in Naval Stores Catalogues as '0472/472039 Knife'. The knife has the same type of hilt as (219) but the blade has a can opener tip. This is apparently provided to allow the opening of cans of water packed in the liferaft. The blade is marked with the name and trademark of Joseph Rodgers along with STAINLESS AND PAT PEND.; the other side of the blade is marked E3/2228. This mark/number does not, however, tally with the official stores numbers given in the catalogues, and its meaning is unknown. Blade length 2.75 inches; overall length 6.25 inches.

___

225 Three different labels on the back of the type of sheath used with (219), (221) and (224). Curiously these three sheaths, although in two cases carrying the correct stores code for (224) type knives, came with the type shown in (219).

AIRCREW EMERGENCY KNIFE

Despite extensive research I have been unable to obtain any firm information on the dates of introduction of these two knives. However, from the few threads of information that are available it would appear that (226) was introduced in the 1960s, being replaced by (227) in the early 1970s. With the current model designated the

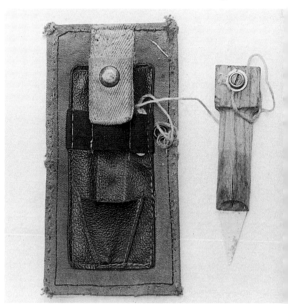

Plate 222

Plate 223

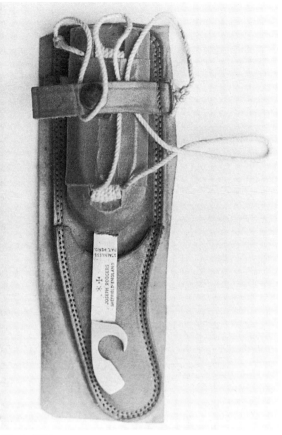

Plate 224

Mk 3, and assuming that (226) is the Mk 2, it is interesting to speculate what the Mk 1 looked like. These knives are worn attached to the right leg of the flying suit by means of an orange or green fabric patch. They are worn in the hilt-down position, and to prevent loss of the knife a lanyard attaches it to the sheath. The excess length of the lanyard is wound around a cleat which tucks into a pocket in the sheath.

It is interesting to note that besides use by aircrew of the three services these knives were carried by the SAS teams that entered the Iranian Embassy during the siege in 1980. Photographs of the raid clearly show these knives in wear, but whether it was the Mk 2 or Mk 3 knife is not known.

---

226 This knife has a 4-inch Bowie blade and is 8 inches; overall. The blade is of stainless steel and bears the name and violin trademark of George Ibberson, along with AM22C/1996. The name LT. HUDSON has been added in electric pencil. The grips are of black plastic with a form of simulated staghorn finish. The hilt contains a spring lock mechanism activated by two levers on either side of the hilt. This mechanism locks onto a stud on the sheath and so retains the knife. The sheath is marked 22C/2202.

Plate 225

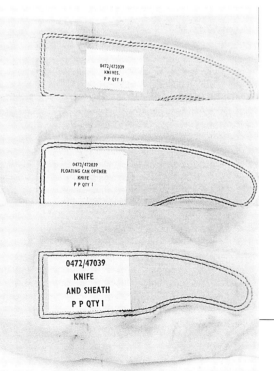

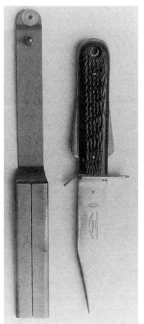

Plate 226   *Plate 227*

227 This knife is the Mk 3 version. Note the change in blade shape which was adopted to prevent bodily damage while trying to cut oneself free from harnesses etc. Despite this change in blade shape the dimensions of the knife remain the same, and the same type of sheath was used. This knife was made by Joseph Rodgers and carries the stores code 22c/2966↑ on the blade. Note the different type of hilt pattern compared to that on (226).

228 This photograph shows a comparison of the two blade styles.

229 This photograph shows a Mk 3 with its orange fabric sheath holder/patch.

230 This is the original packet for the metal sheath used with the Mk 2 version of the knife.

231 This Mk 3 is complete with its green fabric patch, lanyard and cleat. The blade is marked 22c/1278106↑. This change in stores number reflects the influence of NATO codification on British military stores.

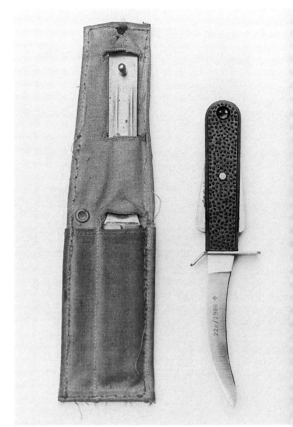

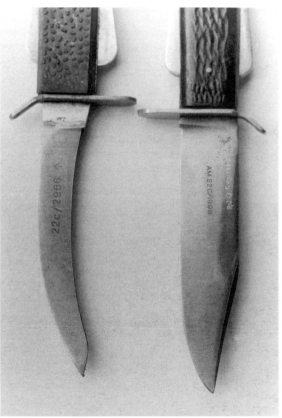

Plate 228

Plate 229

Plate 230

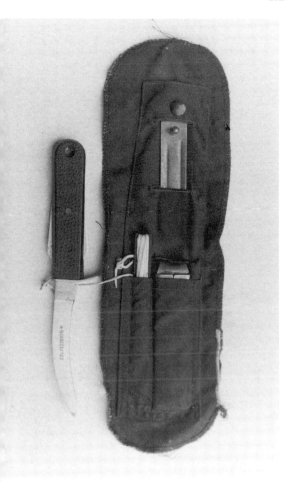

Plate 231

TYPE D SURVIVAL KNIFE

Introduced into service in the late 1950s or early 1960s this survival knife is still in service today, and is an issue item to all three services. Originally manufactured by Wilkinson Sword and presently by Hopkinson's, the knife has also been made by several other manufacturers. This fact is reflected in the varying degrees of quality and style which can be found in specimens examined. A variety of stores marks are also found on these knives which indicate the different marking systems adopted by the three services before the introduction of NATO codification. The stores codes used pre-NATO markings were:

1B – This was used by both the Army and RAF, and indicates an item in the 'Small Handtools' category.

27C – This is an RAF code indicating a survival item. It should be noted that the 22C used on the aircrew knife is believed to indicate aircrew equipment.

0274 – Royal Navy stores code indicating 'Tools, General'.

Later models bear the NATO Stores code which is common to all three services. The NATO Stores code is 5110-99-127-8214 and the official designation is 'Knife, Survival, Type D without sheath'. The sheath is designated 'Sheath, Knife, Survival, NATO Stock Number 5110-99-127-8215'. As the knife is designated the Type D, one wonders what Types A, B and C were like.

The Type D has a heavy single-edged blade between 7 and 7.25 inches in length. The crossguard of steel is oval in shape and the hilt has wooden grips which are secured by two screw bolts on early examples or three copper rivets on later versions. Blades may be found either bright, blued or Parkerised. All the known issue sheaths observed to date, apart from (240A), are of leather, but these are subject to variation in terms of quality and style. Overall length of the knife is between 12.375 and 12.5 inches.

232 The well-contoured lines of the original issue version made by Wilkinson, with bright finish blade. The knife bears the Wilkinson trademark on the blade along with REG DESIGN APP FOR, and on the other side 1B/4594↑.

233 & 234 This piece, complete with its original box of issue, was manufactured by Rodgers and has a blued blade. The blade bears the RAF Stores code of 27C/2360↑.

235 This knife is undated but its style represents the design changes which took place around the mid- to late 1970s. These changes brought about a reduction in quality, presumably to reduce cost. Unusually there is no maker's mark on this knife but the blade bears the Royal Naval Stores code of 0274/4594↑.

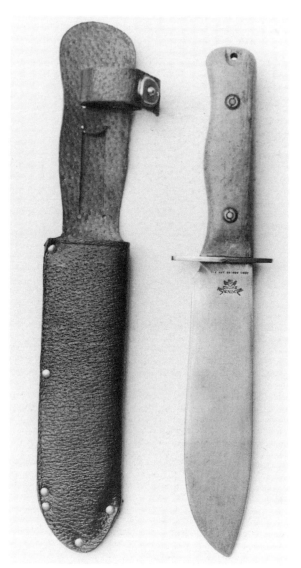

Plate 232

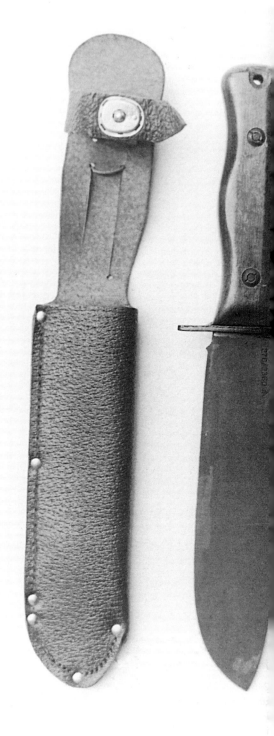

Plate 234

Plate 233

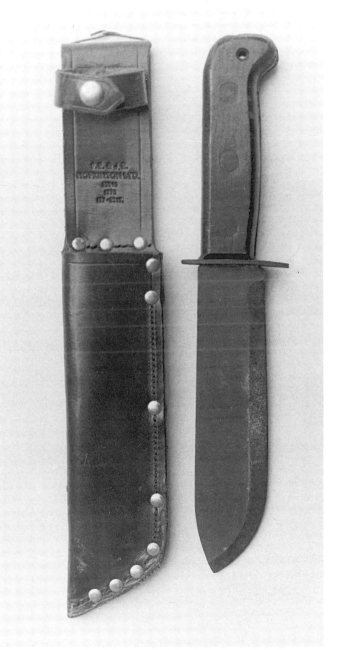

Plate 235

Plate 236

236 This piece from 1978 reflects a further design change, this time in the scabbard. This scabbard design did not last long as another type was introduced in 1979. The knife illustrated is marked 127/8214 on the blade and 474↑. The belt loop of the sheath is marked

F.E. & J.R.
HOPKINSON LTD
30910
1978
127-8215

237 This knife is marked on the blade

JR 1979

127/8214

The grips on this piece are rather square and uncomfortable in the hand. The blade has a Parkerised finish, and note the change in sheath design.

---

238 This 1982 version is the type still in use today. It has a blued blade and the grip is stamped 1278214 with the Hopkinson mark of an H within a diamond, along with ↑82. The sheath is of poor quality and is marked on the back with the Hopkinson mark and 1278215 ↑84. According to an article in the magazine *Soldier of Fortune*, one of these knives dated 1984 was described as the very latest issue 'Paratrooper Survival Fighting Knife'.[30] The 1984 date is reputed to indicate the year of introduction of this pattern, but the article is basically nonsense.

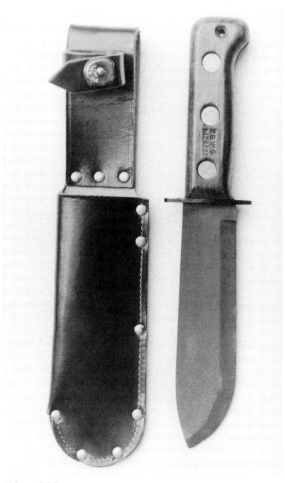

Plate 238

239 Hughes, in his *Primer Part 2*, shows a knife similar to this.[31] When I first saw the *Primer* illustration I assumed it was a private conversion, but after examining the knife shown in the photo I am not so sure. The Bowie point of this knife has been applied in a highly professional manner and was probably factory-done. The knife, manufactured by Wilkinson, is marked 27c/2630 and has a bright blade. It is accompanied by the early pattern sheath. If this knife does represent a distinct pattern it is curious that it bears the same stores number as (233). If any reader has any firm information on this variation of the Type D I would appreciate hearing from them.

---

240 & 240A The two nylon sheaths illustrated, one olive green the other camouflage and which are designed for the Type D survival knife, bear no official marks and may represent a commercial variant. If it is an official issue item it is obviously an improvement over the poor quality leather

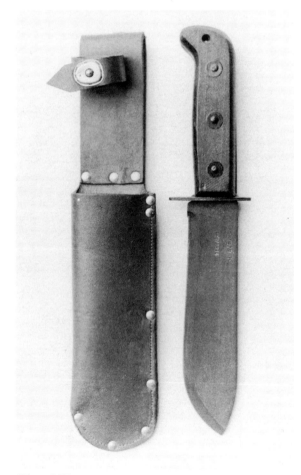

Plate 237

sheaths and does provide the useful facility of a pouch on the front for the storage of a sharpening stone or other survival items. (240A) which is a slip over cover for the Type D leather sheath is in the Disruptive Pattern Material (DPM) currently used by the British Army. Although it is not marked it is almost certainly official issue. Compare with the DPM sheath which is shown at (260A).

241 An early pattern Type D in wear during RAF survival training.

Plate 240　　　　　　　*Plate 240A*

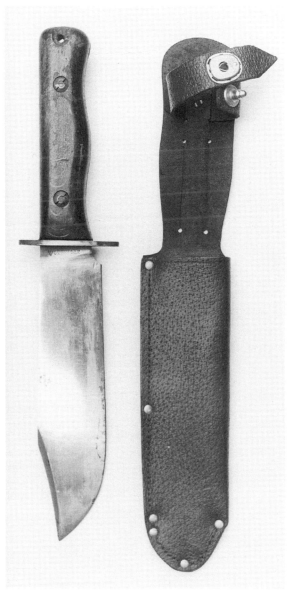

Plate 239

Plate 241

Plate 242

242 Late pattern Type D in wear by Royal Artillery officer after a parachute drop during an exercise in 1992.

BILLHOOKS AND MACHETES

The farmer's implement of a billhook or fascine knife does not obviously seem to have a military connection. Such implements were, however, issued by the military during both world wars and also probably between the wars. Post-war issue has also taken place. Billhooks would have been used for cutting brush etc. for firewood or when creating emplacements.

The machete is more obviously associated with jungle use, although some limited photographic evidence does exist to show that it was occasionally carried in the European theatre during World War Two. Up until the war the British had used only one style of machete and this pattern is still in use today. It has also been copied by both the Canadians and Australians. During World War Two several new patterns were introduced, some of which had specialist roles, but none of these remains in service today. The only two patterns issued are the traditional type and a

post-war design with a parang-type blade.

It is interesting to note that the official British nomenclature for the 'jungle knife' is 'matchet', whereas in the US it is 'machete'. This latter designation is as per the *Oxford English Dictionary*, and thus the one I have used.

243 This billhook was made in 1916 by A. & F. Parkes & Co. Ltd of Birmingham. The blade carries, in addition to their name and the date, the trademark of two feet and the word BIPED along with the small inspection mark ↑36. The blade is thicker towards the tip in order to add weight at that end of the blade. The grip is of round section with a metal ferrule. Blade length 10.5 inches; overall length 16 inches.

Plate 243

245 This billhook dates from 1949. Note the differently shaped hilt. The blade is marked

STANIFORTHS

SEVERQUICK

1949↑

Blade length 9.5 inches; overall length 15.75 inches.

Plate 244

244 Dating from 1940 this billhook was manufactured by Elwell and is marked on the blade

ELWELL

1940

along with a large broad arrow mark. The blade is some 10.25 inches in length, and the tang goes right through the wood hilt and is peened over at the top. The metal ferrule at the base of the hilt is also marked with the Elwell name. Overall length 15.75 inches.

Plate 245

246 A very early British machete which, while in a sheath dated 1917, is probably of pre-World War One origin. The blade with upswept point is very heavy and is marked with the trademark of a blacksmith at an anvil, along with the only partly decipherable name EDWARDS & ----------
SHEFFIELD, with LUCAS inside a scroll device. The grips are

Plate 246

of leather secured by five copper rivets, and the hilt is of much larger proportions than those found on later models. The leather sheath is marked on the back of the belt loop

JAS DAWSON & SONS LTD

1917

along with 125. Blade length 13.125 inches; overall length 19.375 inches.

247 The piece shown is a typical representative example of the standard pattern British machete. This example dates from 1944 and bears the maker's stamp JJB (J. J. Beal). It has the same style blade as (246) but is of lighter stock. The grips are black fibre secured by five copper rivets. As will be noted, the hilt is a different shape to that found on (246), being the style that is still used today. One unusual aspect of this example is the sheath construction. Unlike the usual pattern which is all-leather, this example is made from a rigid fibre material stuck to wooden side walls and fitted with a leather belt loop. The back of the belt loop is marked

↑

B.H.G. 1944

and has the inspection mark of

↑

10

Blade length 14.75 inches; overall length 19.875 inches.

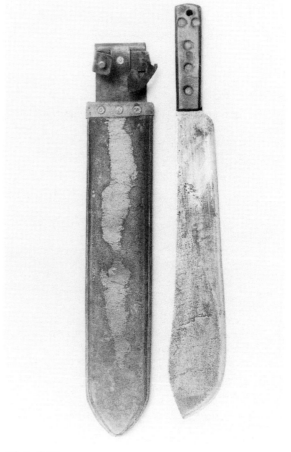

Plate 247

Plate 248

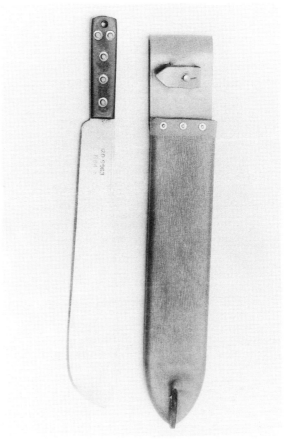

248 This photograph shows from top to bottom:
Early post-war blade markings of

↑KE8277   1952

This piece was made by Martindale and has red fibre grips. The sheath that accompanies the piece is marked on its belt loop P.I. 1952 over a broad arrow and KE3513. An inspector's mark of 077↑ is also stamped into the belt loop.

World War One piece by S. & J. Kitchen with wooden grips secured by five steel rivets.

World War One example dated 1918 bearing the name SAMUEL KITCHEN along with the XCD trademark. The blade is also marked with a

J
↑

---

249 A 1984 version of the standard British machete. The official designation in the stores catalogues is 'Matchet, Rigid Handle, NATO Stock Number 5110-99-120-9963'. Note the spelling of machete, and the fact that this piece has the same designation as (259) and (260). The piece is made by Martindale and bears their name and crocodile trademark on one side of the blade; on the other it is marked

120 9963

1984↑

The black composition hilt is marked with the inspector's

Plate 249

stamp of 466↑. The back of the sheath belt loop is marked

120-9964

BHE

1983

Blade length 15.125 inches; overall length 20.25 inches.

Paratrooper Machete

---

250 According to the manufacturers of this short machete it was made for paratroops operating in the Far East during World War Two. However, as can be seen from (251) it also found use with at least one RAF pilot operating in that theatre of war. The machete was manufactured by Ralph Martindale and it carries the company name and trademark on the blade, along with ↑1943. The blade is double-edged and 2.25 inches wide at its broadest point. The grips are of a chequered composition material secured by three copper rivets. The sheath was specifically designed for attachment to

Plate 250

Plate 250A

the legs by means of two straps, there being no provision for attachment to the belt. The back of the sheath is marked ↑ over B.H.G. 1943, along with two separate marks of 360 and 10. Blade length 9.75 inches; overall length 14.875 inches.

251 An RAF fighter pilot dressed in his Beadon flying suit complete with machete, screwdriver (?), and a Commando knife carried under his Mae West. (IWM CF203)

RAF Survival Machete

252 To those familiar with US military knives this piece will be recognised as the same style of folding machete used by the USAAF during World War Two, and the US origin is reflected in the official designation. According to the RAF Stores Department this machete was known as '1B/4465 Matchet, Folding US Type'. It was last procured in 1951 and ceased to be held as a stores item in 1970. No information was available on when it was first introduced into RAF service, but this is thought to be late in World War Two. As will be noticed, the only apparent difference between the British and American versions is that the British example is fitted with a lanyard ring. These knives are known to have been made by E. & C. S., George Butler, Joseph Westby, and Harrison Brothers and Howson. Unmarked examples are also known. Blade length 9.75 inches; overall length when open 15.75 inches.

253 This photograph shows the blade markings on the E. &

Plate 251

C. S. example; note the ↑ over 4 inspection mark on the crossguard.

I also have in my collection a US version manufactured by Camillus which bears the mark of a ↑ along with EH over a 9 within a mis-stamped circle or a C.

Pattern AF 0100

254 This design appears to have been influenced by the Americans, the large blade being similar to that found on several World War Two American issue machetes. Dating from 1945 this machete and sheath were introduced along with the 1944 Pattern Webbing. To match this webbing the sheath, besides having a belt loop, also has US-style belt hooks for attachment to the eyelets on the 44 Pattern Belt.

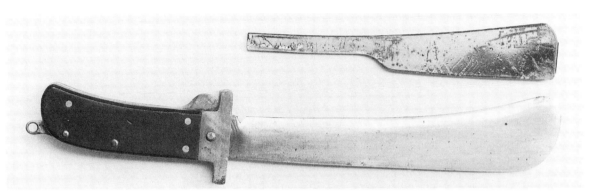

Plate 252

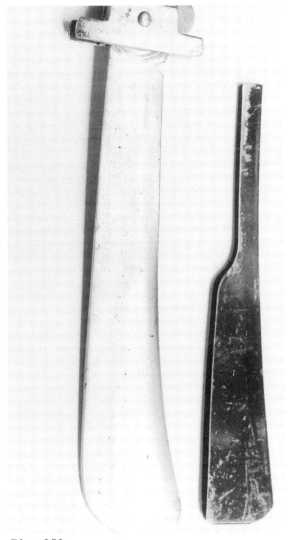

Plate 253

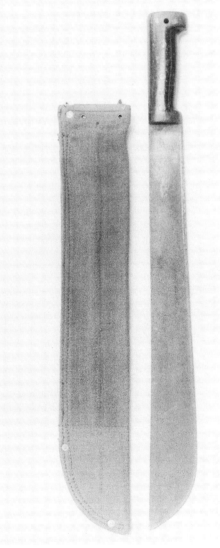

Plate 254

The machete has a 17.375-inch blade and hilt with black plastic grips. The blade carries the name and trademark of Martindale along with the date of 1945, the ↑ mark and the pattern of AF0100. The grip is stamped with the inspection mark of 80 over a ↑. The green webbing sheath has a strengthened throat, and is marked on the reverse M.E. Co. 1945 ↑ and A F 0101. Overall length 22.25 inches.

255 Made by Joseph Rodgers and Sons, this AF0100 has wood grips and, like the previous specimen, is dated 1945. The wood grips are also stamped with the inspection mark of broad arrow over 12. The sheath is marked on the reverse M.W.&S. Ltd 1945↑. Examples with black plastic grips by Thomas Turner, and ones with wooden grips by M.S. Ltd, have also been noted.

256 to 258 The photographs of these machete types are from the same series as those which contained the illustrations of the BC41 Knuckleduster and appear to be of trials or experimental items. (256) shows a large parang-type machete with a blade not unlike that found on the current issue parang, and a hilt similar to that found on some of the Indian-made machetes. The piece is marked on the blade with the name BRADES along with some figures which appear to be either 1938 (the year?) or 1638 (a pattern?) and MADE

Plate 256

Plate 255

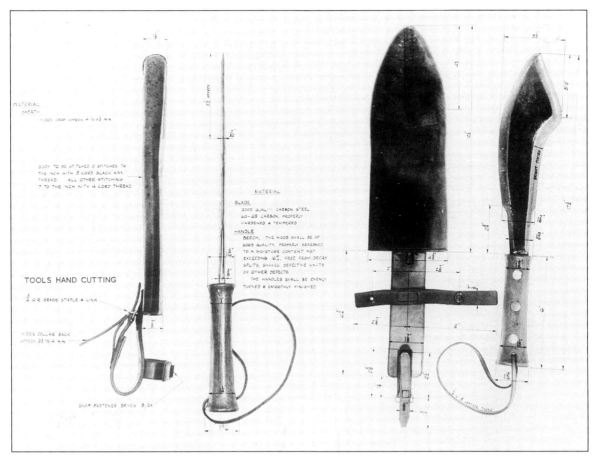

Plate 257

IN ENGLAND. The blade is also marked with a PAGODA trademark which is also found on a label attached to the hilt. No further information on this type of machete has been forthcoming, neither has any actual example been observed.

(257) and (258) show a rather strange piece which appears to have a description of 'Tools, Hand Cutting'. The illustration at (257) gives all relevant dimensions but also shows that the item was produced with a sheath. (258) has a different hilt but is generally the same shape and is marked on the blade with the maker's name, which appears to be PARKES. Again no other information is available on these pieces, and whether they ever saw actual military use is not known. To date no actual examples have been observed.

Golok

The exact date of the introduction of this machete is not known but it certainly saw service during the Borneo campaign which took place between 1962 and 1966. The machete is still in use today and is also used by the New Zealand forces, and has been stylistically copied by the Australians – see (381).

According to Martindale, one of the manufacturers of this type of machete, it is known as the Golok pattern, but in my opinion the blade is closer in shape to the true parang. The present official designation is the same as that for (249) and the NATO stock number is 5110-99-120-9242.

---

259 The example shown here is by Elwell and the blade is marked

ELWELL 1964

KE18731

along with a ↑. The hilt is stamped with the inspector's mark

277

↑

The green webbing sheath is fitted with both belt loop and US style belt hooks. Another manufacturer, Bullock Bros, has been noted for examples marked with the KE18731.

---

260 This photograph shows a version by Martindale manufactured in 1975 bearing the stores number 120-9242. The sheath which accompanies this piece is marked on the reverse

MECO 1972

1B/8465-99-120-9243

This mark is interesting in that it shows that despite the NATO Stores marking system the Army has retained the 1B code to indicate that this item is in the 'Handtools' category. The official description of the sheath is 'Sheath, Matchet, Webbing, hook attachment, mildew and water resistant, for 120-9242'. A further sheath for the Golok is shown in 260A

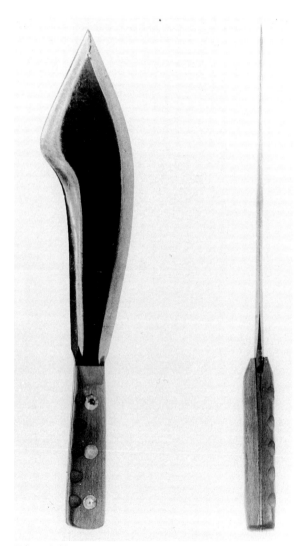

Plate 258

Plate 259

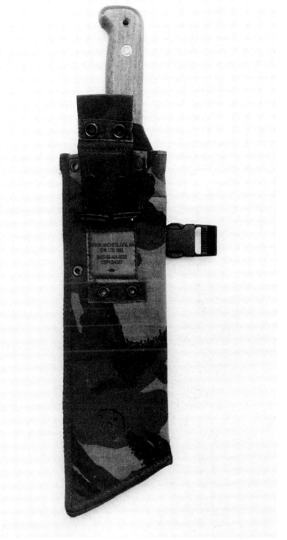

Plate 260   *Plate 260A*

Plate 260B

and 260B. This style of sheath, introduced in the early 1990s is made from DPM material and is described on the label affixed to the reverse of the sheath as:

SHEATH, MACHETE, DPM, IRR

O.W. LTD 1993

8465-99-495-9250

CSP 1B/4387

↑

Note the 'correct' spelling of machete. The O.W. LTD is assumed to be the maker but the meaning of the IRR is not known. Dimensions for the Golok are: blade length 13 inches; overall length 18.125 inches.

SNOW/ICE KNIFE

261 A snow/ice knife as used by British forces when operating in Arctic conditions to cut and fashion blocks of ice to make a shelter. The single-edged blade is 12 inches in length and is marked

DOUBLE SHEAR	I. WILSON
STEEL	EX. SYCAMORE ST
HAND FORGED	SHEFFIELD ENGLAND

The grips are made of a light composition material and

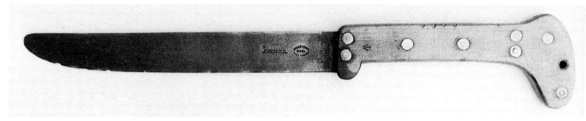

Plate 261

secured by eight steel rivets, and are stamped on one side with the ↑. The grips are very large in comparison with the blade length at 9 inches. Overall length is 21 inches.

---

262 A Royal Marine on exercise in Norway *circa* 1960 using one of these knives to construct an ice wall.

MAGAZINE KNIVES

Specifically designed with non-sparking blades for work in magazines and armament works, three versions of the magazine knife have been used by the British, two of which are illustrated. No actual specimen of a Mk I has been observed, but according to the details in the List of Changes 11913 the only difference between it and the Mk II is that, and I quote from 11913, 'It differs from the Mark I (not published in List of Changes) in

Plate 262

being of a strengthened pattern.' List of Changes 24402 dated 4 August 1921 also refers to the 'Knife, Magazine, Mark II'. This is sub-headed 'Separate drawing for Naval Service', and states: 'With reference to 11913: A separate drawing (N.O.D. 1545A) of the above-mentioned knife has been sealed to govern manufacture for Naval Service.'

---

263 The official designation of the knife is 'Knife, Magazine Mk II'. This type of knife was introduced into service in 1903 by List of Changes entry 11913 dated 20 June 1903. The knife has a plain wooden hilt of round section fitted with a brass ferrule. The blade is of phosphor bronze, marked

ECH

1966

III

Blade length 7.75 inches; overall length 11.25 inches. Another example has been noted which is marked with a broad arrow and

II

BF LTD

1944

---

264 Thought to be the current issue version of the magazine knife, this knife has its blade made of what appears to be some form of alloy with bronze finish. The grips are of wood secured by three aluminium rivets. The knife is totally unmarked and the date of its introduction into service is unknown. Blade length 7 inches; overall length 12.25 inches.

MISCELLANEOUS KNIVES

This section contains knives of British origin or

Plate 263   *Plate 264*

use which do not fall into any particular category.

265 Locally made knives found considerable use during World War Two and this piece is similar to others I have seen. Obtained from an ex-RAF pilot who purchased the knife in Egypt, the knife has its blade brazed to the crossguard in the same manner as the Middle East Commando Knife. The hilt, is of black plastic/Bakelite material, fitted with a brass ferrule and pommel. Blade length 6 inches; overall length 11 inches.

Plate 265

266 This knife appears to have been converted out of another knife, possibly the Italian Paratrooper Knife. The hilt comprises green horn, alloy washer and ebony pommel piece. The extensive blade markings read as follows:

LAW CIAKLES RICHARD BASIL

30 YEARS 86257 15 M N.B. ADDIS

ABEBA

22.6.41

While the name and place are obvious, exactly what the 30 YEARS and the 15 M.N.B. mean I have not been able to establish. It would seem likely that Richard Basil Law Ciakles had something to celebrate in Addis Ababa on the 22 June 1941. Blade length 7.25 inches; overall length 11.75 inches.

267 This private purchase knife has an authenticated World War Two history which is a rare occurrence. The knife is a skinning knife manufactured by the Sheffield firm of Christopher Johnson, and bears the designation WOODCRAFT KNIFE on the blade. The ricasso bears the Johnson trademark of CJ within a flag along with

JOHNSON

WESTERN

WORKS

SHEFFIELD

The knife has a short crossguard, wood grip and alloy pommel. Blade length is 3.875 inches and overall length 7.5 inches. This knife was carried by Sgt Bill Jones, Flight Engineer with 419 Squadron RCAF on bombing operations over Europe during 1944.

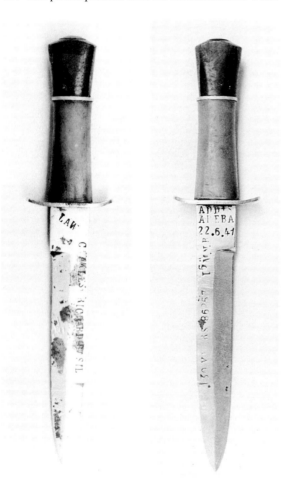

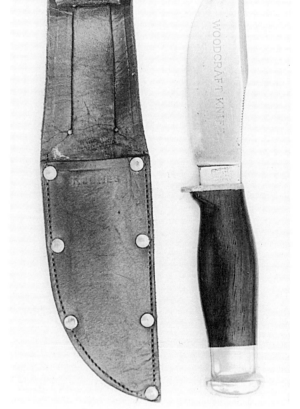

Plate 266   *Plate 266A*   *Plate 267*

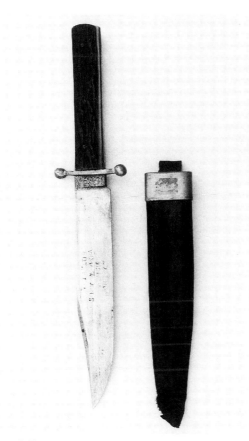

Plate 268

knife is similar to others heard of which have reported Chindit and Commando use. I have examined this knife and, as noted by Stephens, despite its basic design it is of very high quality. The knife is made from one piece of steel with cord binding to form a grip. No sheath or further information is available.

---

271 The date of this knife is not known for sure, but I would personally date it as World War One despite the original maker's claim that it was made during World War Two. The knife has brass knuckles with integral crossguard, ebony grips and a blade with very pronounced clip point. The blade is marked

JOHN WATTS

SHEFFIELD

ENGLAND

Blade length 6 inches; overall length 10.25 inches.

268 A Victorian or possibly Edwardian period Bowie knife which has seen World War Two usage. The knife has a 7.25-inch blade, white metal crossguard and staghorn grip. The blade is stamped

T TAYLOR

SQUK EL ARBA

TUNISIA

JAN 1943

The SQUK EL ARBA should more correctly be spelt Souk el Arba. This important airfield in Tunisia fell to the Allies on 16 November 1942.

---

269 This very professionally made weapon was carried by Major G. L. Dickinson of 6 Commando. It is constructed out of a Mk 1 No.4 Spike bayonet blade with a nickel-plated brass, not steel as stated by Stephens, hilt added.[32] Blade length 7.875 inches; overall length 11.875 inches.

---

270 First illustrated by Stephens in *Fighting Knives,* this

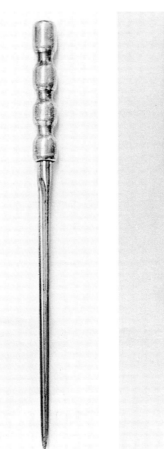

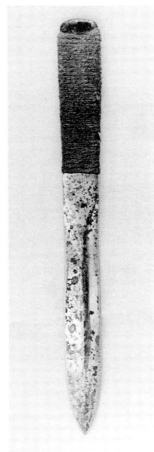

Plate 269   **Plate 270**

272 This very high quality knife was described by Hughes in his *Primer Part 1* and was dated as World War One.[33] Enquiries and correspondence with the Victoria and Albert Museum have indicated, however, that W. J. Waterer, the manufacturer, actually resided at Pughs Place between 1939 and 1958. The wood grip is nicely contoured and the steel crossguard is of 'S' form. The blade has a square shank style ricasso and this is etched

W.J. WATERER

55 YEARS

SWORDMAKER

& CUTLER

9 PUGHS PLACE

CARNBY ST

LONDON W1

ENGLAND

The leather sheath is of high quality with a large belt flap and hilt securing strap which snaps across the hilt rather than around it. Blade length 6.25 inches; overall length 10.5 inches.

---

273 As will be noted, this knife is very similar to the previous specimen but in this case it was made or retailed by Cogswell Harrison. The major detectable differences are that the hilt finish is somewhat rough and the maker's name is stamped rather than etched. Also for some curious reason the sheath has no hilt retaining strap. Whether or not both these knives date from World War Two is difficult to establish conclusively, but it is highly likely that both Waterer and Cogswell Harrison made these knives for private sale during this period. Blade length 6.375 inches; overall length 10.625 inches.

---

274 to 276 These three push daggers all date from World War Two and were manufactured for private sale rather than as issue items.

(274) was made by Cogswell Harrison. The grip is of alloy fitted with a 6-inch double-edged blade, the junction of the blade and hilt being fitted with a leather washer form of crossguard. The hilts of these knives are known to bear a serial number and the leather sheath is stamped with the name of the manufacturer. The main illustration is courtesy of Gordon Hughes, and is supplemented by a sketch which gives a more three-dimensional view.

Plate 272

Plate 271

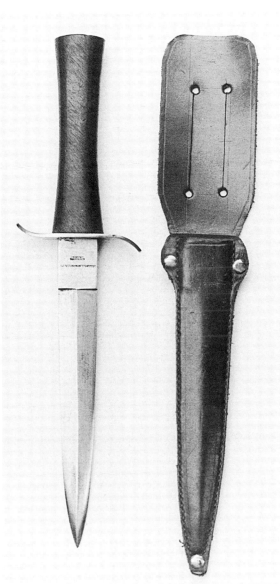

Plate 273

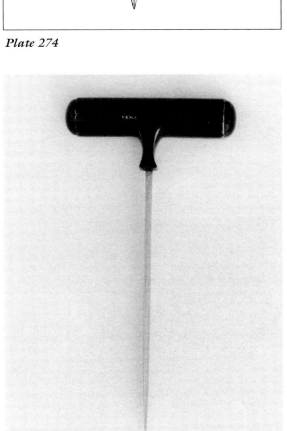

Plate 274

Plate 275

(275) is a specimen made by Lockwood Brothers and bears their trademark of C + X, and the name of the retailer, Ferraby and Hare of Hull. This knife differs slightly from the previous specimen in that the junction of hilt and blade has a properly cast section rather than the leather washer.

Plate 276

Plate 278

Plate 277

(276) is also by Lockwood Brothers, made *circa* 1942, according to Joseph Elliot and Sons Ltd who now own the Lockwood name. The grip is of alloy and the double-edged blade is 2.875 inches in length.

277 to 279 (277) shows a conversion of a 1903 bayonet to a fighting knife. The blade has been shortened to 6.75 inches and ground to a stiletto shape. The sheath has been shortened to suit this new blade length. Overall length 11.5 inches. Several other examples of 1903s shortened in such a way have been noted, and it was originally thought that such conversions dated from World War One. However,

Plate 279

Plate 280

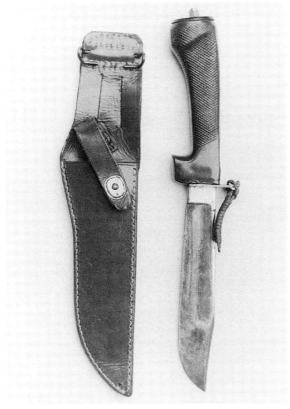

photographic evidence – see (Plate 278) (IWM E29064) and (Plate 279) (IWM E29057) – indicates that such knives were carried during World War Two. Both photographs show members of the SAS on operations in the Aegean carrying these 1903 conversions. The officer third from the right in (279), is Ian Lapraik of SAS fame. His knife is now in the Imperial War Museum, having been donated by Lapraik's widow. The fact that these conversions were carried in World War Two cannot be disputed, though when the actual conversion took place is unknown.

280 This No. 5 bayonet with knuckle guard was first mentioned by Anthony Carter in his book *The Bayonet*. The piece is in the collection of the Imperial War Museum and has been the subject of much speculation as to whether or not the knuckle guard is an official addition. Other examples have been noted, but these are considered to be of dubious origin; rumours of knuckle guards bearing official marks have been heard, but no actual example observed. The guard has been made from a length of steel rod bent in such a way that it secures between the bayonet slot and the crossguard hole.

281 Manufactured by Wilkinson this knife was commercially marketed as the RJH Jungle Knife during the late 1960s. According to Robert Wilkinson-Latham these knives were intended for the MoD but at the last minute they (the MoD) stuck to the old-style survival knife, presumably the Type D. Approximately 7,000 of these knives were made, a high proportion of which were sold to overseas countries. A

Plate 281

prototype Mk 2 was produced with a different type of hilt designed to contain survival aids. The RJH designation was made up from a composite of the designers initials: R – Robert Wilkinson-Latham; J – John Wilkinson-Latham; H – Howard Evans (armourer at Wilkinson).

The knife has a 7.875-inch Bowie blade with fullers, and is etched RJH JUNGLE KNIFE. There is a small brass crossguard and the hilt is of brown plastic and in the same shape as that found on the 1908 Pattern Cavalry Sword. The sheath of rather low quality has a wrap-over strap with a 'lift the dot' type snap. While Wilkinson state that the MoD showed no interest in these knives, I have heard stories of troops in the Far East being issued with them; the example illustrated indicates signs of military use. The sheath has been fitted with belt hooks and the reverse of the sheath is marked

972 WHITEHOUSE 2 PARA

SP COY

It is of course highly likely that the knife may only be a private purchase item, and I would appreciate any information on whether these knives were ever officially issued. Overall length 14.5 inches.

282/283 A rare example of a Wilkinson-made official issue kukri of which only 1,400 were manufactured in 1951. Of very high quality, the piece is made in the traditional style with the only unusual feature being a plated pommel cap. The blade is stamped 51 over WSC, which also appears on the two small knives, along with a ↑48D mark stamped in a most unusual configuration. The sheath is of black leather fitted with a lace-up frog. Blade length 12 inches; overall length 16.5 inches.

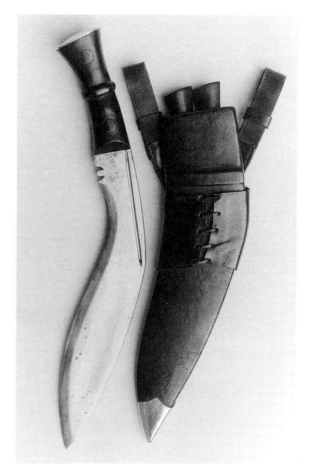

Plate 282

284 This push dagger of previously unrecorded style is post-war and was the former property of a member of the SAS who served between 1966 and 1985 and saw service in Oman and the Falklands. The blade is double-edged with a square shank; the knuckle guard, centre column and hilt bar are of alloy. One unusual feature of the knife is that the centre column is mortised into the hilt bar rather than being cast in one piece. The piece is unmarked and no sheath was available for study. Blade length 4.25 inches; overall length 5.75 inches.

POCKET, FOLDING, CLASP OR JACK KNIVES

The folding knife probably represents the earliest official issue of knives to British military and naval units. As will be seen from the letters from

Plate 283

the Royal Army Ordnance Corps and Royal Naval Museums – see (285) and (286) – records relating to the issue of such knives go back well into the 1800s. The variety of these knives used by the British is also quite amazing, ranging from the square-pointed versions of the 1800s through to the specialist knives of the SOE, RAF escape knives and the all-stainless versions issued today.

Prior to 1939 several variations of the military folding knife were issued but many of these are unmarked making a correct chronological listing difficult. However, from the information that is available the knives that follow have been placed into some form of date order.

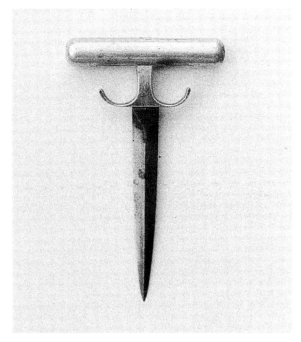

Plate 284

Plate 285

Curator:
Lt/Col W E SAUNDERS (Retd)
Telephone:
Brookwood 4511 Ext 650
Ref: CS/M/10

RAOC MUSEUM
RAOC TRAINING CENTRE
DEEPCUT
CAMBERLEY
SURREY
GU16 6RW

Mr. R.E. Flook, 18 February 1976

Dear Mr. Flook,

Thank you for your letter of 13th February reference clasp knives.

I am very sorry to inform you that this is not a technical museum and therefore the research sources are limited. However, I have been able to elicit the following.

Clasp knives were in use in the Army as early as 1865 and possibly before this by mounted troops.

Clothing Regulations of 1881 state "Each Pioneer of Cavalry will be furnished with a clasp knife as part of the equipment of a Pioneer".

By 1909 the use of the clasp knife had been extended to others and was issued to Mounted Infantry, Regimental Transport Drivers and other Dismounted soldiers engaged on, or under training for, Mounted Duties.

This regulation was not amended by Clothing Regulations of 1914 or 1936.

Cont'd

CS/M/10   February 1976

Even as late as 1943, these knives were not a general issue but were confined to men with Regiments and Corps connected with mounted duties.

Specialist soldiers would also be issued with this knife ie., Mountain and arctic areas. The marlin spike was of course used for "getting stones from horses hooves".

I am sorry I cannot help you with dates of issue or manufacturers but you can see that the period covered is nearly 100 years.

Yours sincerely,

Curator

-2-

SQUARE-POINT FOLDING KNIVES

Typically associated with naval use, square-point jack knives were produced in relatively high numbers but today are quite scarce. One article I have on the work of Thomas Turner quotes that 441,800 were supplied to the Admiralty over the last twenty years.[34] Unfortunately the article is undated and not of good enough quality to reproduce, but I would guess that it was written in the early 1900s. The illustration page of the article is reproduced at (287). The handwritten notes on this illustration highlight the various markings. Besides issue to the Navy, these knives

Plate 286

From: Captain R. H. Parsons, M.A., C.Eng, MIERE, Royal Navy (Rtd)

PRNM 591/3

Royal Naval Museum
HM Naval Base
Portsmouth
Hants. PO1 3LR

Portsmouth 22351 Ext. 23868/9

15th June, 1982.

Mr. R E Flook

Dear Sir,

In reply to your letter of 6th June, we have consulted the Seamanship Manuals back to 1883 and although knives are mentioned as part of a seamans kit issue, they are not generally illustrated. In the 1898 Manual for boys a knife is illustrated as part of a kit laid out for inspection, but on too small a scale to be of any help. However it could be a simple horn handled clasp type of knife.

I am sorry that after that insufficient detail we are unable to answer your query fully.

Yours faithfully,

Director.

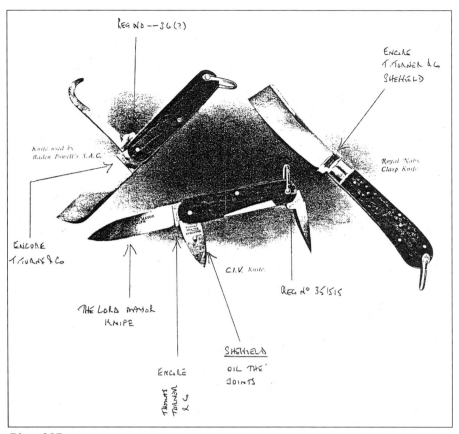

Plate 287

Plate 288

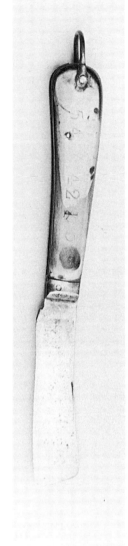

Plate 289

also appear to have been issued to the Army as examples with WD (War Department) marks are known.

---

288 This knife is by Thomas Turner and has the name of its one-time owner engraved on the blade – A.H.DENTON – along with what appears to be the name of a ship. This portion of the engraving is worn away and is not readable. The knife has an iron bolster, stag scales and copper staple. The blade length is 3.625 inches and overall length with blade open is 9 inches. The tang is marked

ENCORE

T. TURNER & CO

BEST STEEL

---

289 This knife is unusual in that it has smooth horn scales stamped with a serviceman's number. The tang is marked

J IRELAND

CONTRACTOR

It may be noted that neither (288) nor (289) bear any marks indicating official naval issue. This is not unusual as the marking of RN jack knives did not become common practice until World War Two and then the only mark was the year.

---

290 This was made by the Sheffield firm of Clarke Shirely and beside their name is marked w↑D2 indicating Army issue. I have a similar Clarke Shirely knife which carries the same WD mark but which has had its staple flattened and stamped 6495.

---

291 This example is very unusual in that it is dated. The tang is marked with the maker's name DEANE & CO, w↑D19, and the date 1878. Examples bearing the name of Parkin & Marshall have also been noted.

BOER WAR PERIOD FOLDING KNIVES

Dating from around the Boer War period these knives are frequently found with service numbers or inscriptions cut into the grips. All examples examined have been identical with no design varitions noted.

---

292 Made by Joseph Allen, this knife has a sheep's-foot blade 3.75 inches in length, steel bolster, horn scales, marlin spike and copper staple. The quality of the piece is high. Overall length 8.5 inches. Tang markings are

NON XLL

JOSEPH

ALLEN & SONS

SHEFFIELD

along with the acceptance mark of w↑D2. Other makers noted are Brookes and Crookes, Atkinson Brothers, Mappin Bros and H. G. Long. Both Brookes and Atkinson examples were marked with the w↑D mark with the suffix 18.

Plate 290

Plate 291

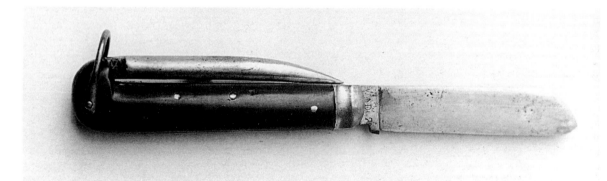

Plate 292

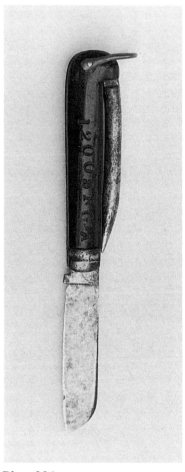

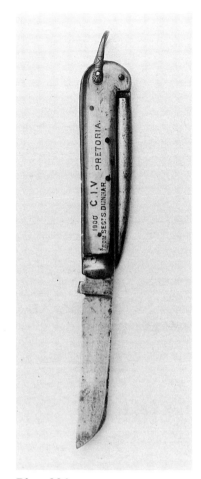

Plate 293   *Plate 294*   *Plate 296*

293 Made by Atkinson Brothers, this knife has one grip marked

A. WARREN G COY 6 ROYAL
WARK REGT SOUTH AFRICA

294 Made by H. G. Long, this knife has its grip marked 12005 RGA.

295 During the campaign in South Africa a pocket knife was made for the City Imperial Volunteers (CIV), a yeomanry regiment raised in London. The knife associated with this regiment was also known as the Lord Mayor's Knife and was also supplied to 15,000 other British and colonial troops serving in South Africa. If the Thomas Turner article on which this information is based is correct it would appear that this was one of the first British military clasp knives to be fitted with a can opener. The article states:

...and it is provided with a tin opener. This was the idea of a member of the present firm {i.e. Thomas Turner} who had been in South Africa, and in view of the fact that so much food was being sent to the troops in tins he was led to wonder what would happen when the soldiers received their tins and found that the tin openers which ought to accompany them had got mislaid or were at some more or less distant spot.

. . . The suggestion therefore that a strong tin opener should be added to the pocket knives sent out to the seat of war was adopted, and when the knives were ordered for the Duke of Cambridge's Own, the Duke described them as absolutely the best and most useful knife he had seen, while Major Mackinnon of the CIV described the tin opener in the pocket knife as 'invaluable' and quite as useful as the blade.

The advertisement/Thomas Turner illustration is taken from a 1900 magazine and shows the knife as available for the sum of four shillings and six pence. No other information is

Plate 295

available on the CIV knife, and despite the reported production of at least 15,000 knives I have been unable to locate an actual specimen for study.

The illustration at (287) also shows a knife used by Baden Powell's South African Constabulary. No specimen of this knife has been available for study either, but according to the article the knife has a 4-inch hilt with staghorn grips, with a 3.5-inch sheep's-foot blade, and a well-finished hook for removing stones from a horse's hoof. There is also a copper shackle with which it can be attached to a cord suspended round the possessor's neck.

---

296 Besides the official CIV knife, another knife with CIV connections has been available for study. This is the same pattern as (292) and was made by J. Tidmarsh; it has the grip engraved in a professional manner as follows:

1900 C.I.V.

FROM SEGT S. DUNBAR PRETORIA

ADMIRALTY PATTERN 301

In the early 1900s the square-pointed RN knife appears to have been replaced by a piece designated Admiralty Pattern 301. The Maleham and Yeomans document shown at (297), although dated 1915, quotes an earlier paper CP 7182 1910, so it would appear that Admiralty Pattern 301 was introduced at least as early as 1910. Further documents (298) show that the knife saw service in World War One, a contract for 64,000 being placed in 1915.

Two patterns of this knife are known, one which complies with the specification and another with chequered alloy scales. One of the latter has been noted dated 1932, and would appear to be a step towards the development of the pattern of RN jack

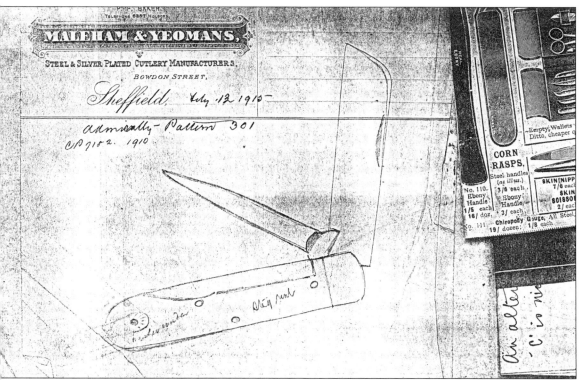

MALEHAM & YEOMANS,
STEEL & SILVER PLATED CUTLERY MANUFACTURERS,
BOWDON STREET.

Sheffield. Feby 12 1910

Admiralty Pattern 301
CP 7182. 1910

Plate 297   **Plate 298**

SCHEDULE.

Pattern No.	Description.	Quantities required and places of delivery. To be consigned to the Superintendent,			Total.	Net price per dozen including delivery.
		Royal Victoria Yard, Deptford.	Royal Clarence Yard, Gosport.	Royal William Yard, Plymouth.		
301	Knives, clasp, 4½ inches, stag, round end, iron bullet bolster forged solid. Best cast-steel hand-forged sheep-foot blade. Cast-steel marline spike, properly tempered, 3½ inches long; rivet through bolster, No. 12 L.S.W. Gauge. Copper shackle, No. 8 L.S.W. Gauge.	No. 29,000	No. 13,500	No. 21,500	No. 64,000	

knife used between 1940 and 1986. One stag-gripped example has been observed bearing the WD mark but no specimen bearing any form of identifiable naval acceptance mark has been studied.

---

299 This knife complies with the original specification by having stag scales. The knife was manufactured by Harrison Brothers and Howson and has a 3.5-inch sheep's-foot blade. Its overall length is 8.125 inches. An example made by Hunter has also been noted.

---

300 This example has chequered alloy scales and was manufactured by Joseph Allen and Sons. An Allen-made version with stag scales has been noted.

---

301 This knife dated 1932 is also by Joseph Allen and is identical to (300). Whether this was the first pattern of knife to be dated by the RN is not known, but it was certainly not common practice until World War Two.

---

302 This AP. 301-style knife obviously saw Army service,

the blade being stamped w↑D1; this WD mark overstamps the mark of Thomas Turner. The knife is unusual in that it has full stag scales, there being no bolster. The marlin spike is stamped RE13165 (RE for Royal Engineers?).

CLASP KNIFE, WITH MARLIN SPIKE AND TIN OPENER

If the documentation reproduced at (303) is correctly interpreted, this knife was officially designated Pattern 6353/1905, with the manufacturing specification updated in 1913. Manufactured for the Army, it was produced up until at least 1938 when it seems to have been phased out in favour of the smaller knives with chequered Bexoid scales. During its life the knife was the subject of some design and specification changes, but the general configuration remained the same right up until its demise.

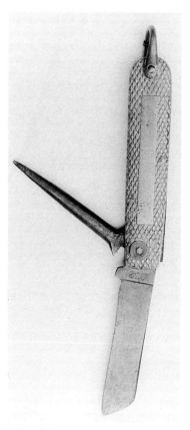

Plate 299   **Plate 300**   **Plate 301**   **Plate 302**

SPECIFICATION No. $\frac{\text{A.C.D.}}{685}$

N.B.—This supersedes Specification No. $\frac{\text{A.C.D.}}{429\text{A}}$

| KNIFE, Clasp, with Marline Spike and Tin Opener ... ... | Pattern No. $\frac{6353}{1905}$ |

$\frac{57}{24}$
$\frac{}{9389}$

Approved, 22nd July, 1913.

To govern manufacture and inspection.

1. *Patterns.*—The knives must correspond in every particular with the Standard Pattern, which may be seen in the Pattern Room, Royal Army Clothing Department, Grosvenor Road, London, S.W., as regards shape, make, workmanship, and quality of materials, and with this Specification as regards measurements.

2. *Material and Dimensions.*—The Blade and Tin Opener to be made of best cast steel, free from flaws, properly hardened and tempered, and to be as thin and as well ground as the Standard Pattern; the edge of the Blade to be whetted on an oilstone; to be $3\frac{1}{2}$ inches long from "kick" to point, to be $\frac{11}{16}$ inch wide; the Tin Opener to be $1\frac{5}{8}$ inches long and to be $\frac{11}{16}$ inches wide; the Bolster to be $\frac{1}{2}$ inch long, to be solid, and made from the best iron; the "Springs" to be made of best spring steel, properly hardened and tempered. The Marline Spike to be made of cast steel, properly hardened and tempered. Length of Marline Spike when shut to be within $\frac{1}{8}$ inch shorter than the Spring; and the point, when shut, to be fitted close on the Spring to prevent catching in the pocket.

3. The length of the Handle to be $4\frac{7}{8}$ inches; the Scales to be checkered black horn, $4\frac{3}{8}$ inches long, Bolster $\frac{1}{2}$ inch; to be riveted to plates with two iron rivets; the Shackle to be made of copper wire, No. 11 gauge, same size and shape as that of the Standard Pattern, and riveted with brass wire. The Blade, Tin Opener, and Marline Spike to be firmly riveted in, and to bear the maker's name on the Tangs.

H. A. ANLEY, *Colonel,*
for Director of Equipment and Ordnance Stores.

WAR OFFICE.

(B 9664) Wt. w. 1796– 843   230   7/13   H & S   G. 13,504.

Plate 303

304 This knife complies exactly with the specification and was manufactured by Wade & Butcher. The knife is dated 1938 and bears the inspection mark of ↑6 on the marlin spike.

---

305 Also dated 1938, this example has pressed leather scales but otherwise conforms with the specification. The knife was made by Joseph Rodgers & Sons and bears their 6 Norfolk Street address along with their star and cross trademark. The marlin spike is stamped with a ↑.

---

306 & 307 Neither of these knives carries any marks indicating military issue, but except for the scale material they conform with the specification. (306) carries the name of SCOTIA and J MCCLORY, and has scales of a hard black synthetic material with gouged bone type pattern, while (307) by Walker & Hall has pressed flat fibre scales.

---

308 The label attached to this example of a Pattern 6353 knife is most intriguing; it appears genuine but certain items of the text are somewhat odd. The knife was made by Joseph

Rodgers and has chequered Bakelite or Bexoid scales. The marlin spike is stamped w↑D8.

The label claims that the knife was one of 500 issued for 1937 troop trials and that the pattern was not adopted. It also states that the star and cross markings on the blade are experimental. Both these statements are of course incorrect: this pattern of knife was obviously issued and had been in service for many years prior to 1937. The star and cross marks are, of course, the well-known trademark of Joseph Rodgers. If the label is a fake then someone has gone to an awful lot of trouble to produce something that adds little to the financial value of the knife. If the label is genuine it is possible that the design was put up for readoption by the services in 1937, but that it failed the trials and was phased

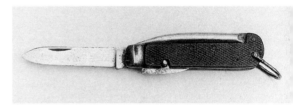

Plate 307

Plate 308

Plate 304   *Plate 305*   *Plate 306*   *Plate 308A*

Plate 308B

out in favour of the standard World War Two pattern. This, of course, does not answer the question of how someone got the interpretation of the Joseph Rodgers markings so completely wrong.

---

309 Despite being undated, Thomas Turner is known to have made this style of knife as early as 1914 – see (450) – and while the blade, marlin spike, can opener and shackle all comply with specification ACD 685, the white metal scales certainly do not. Whether white metal was approved by a specification amendment or was introduced by Turner on a commercial basis and then taken into service is not known. The blade bears the name THOMAS TURNER & CO. SHEFFIELD along with their ENCORE trademark. The scales are marked

ENCORE

T.TURNER & CO

along with W↑D.

---

310 The same type of knife as shown in (304) but bearing an interesting set of marks on the marlin spike. The spike is stamped from a proper die B 668 38. Another example has been noted marked D – 1445–45. The meaning of these marks is unknown, but could the last two digits of the number relate to the year?

Plate 310

VICTORIAN AND WORLD WAR ONE PRIVATE AND PRESENTATION POCKET KNIVES

During the Victorian and World War One periods private purchase and gift knives were frequently

Plate 309

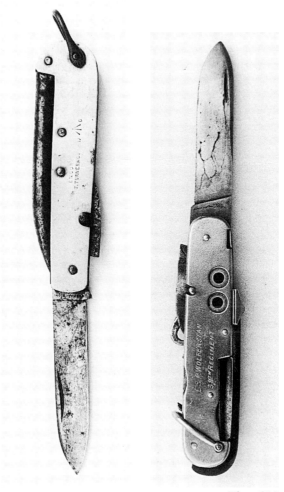

Plate 311

utilised. It is obviously difficult to identify such knives unless, like some examples, they bear an inscription or have been otherwise identified.

---

311 The personal knife of Captain E. S. P. Wolferstan, 38th Regiment (The Staffordshire Regiment). This type of knife, typically known as the Horseman's Knife, is marked on the can opener, cartridge extractor and button hook ARMY & NAVY C.S.L. ('C.S.L.' stands for Co-operative Society Ltd). The knife has white metal scales and is fitted with main blade, button hook, corkscrew, can opener, cartridge extractor, leather punch and a hook for removing stones from horses' hooves. These knives typically have two screw bolts fitted to the hilt, for repairing the reins; they are, however, missing in this example.

Plate 311A

As will be noted, the scales of the knife have been engraved with Capt. Wolferstan's name and regiment. Capt. Egerton S. Pipe-Wolferstan's record is: Second Lieutenant January 1881, Lieutenant July 1881, Captain April 1889, Major November 1900. The last entry in the Army List is in 1902. From at least 1899 to 1902 he served with the militia. During his line service the 38th were based in Malta, Egypt and Gibraltar.

312 This photograph shows two versions of the knives that were believed to be packed in some of the gift boxes given to troops during World War One. The knives have gouged bone scales with 3.35-inch blades and are 3.375 inches; overall. They are fitted with copper shackles and the typical period spear-point can opener. The top example is by E. Blyde & Co., and the lower by G. Butler.

Plate 313

Plate 314   **Plate 315**

Plate 312

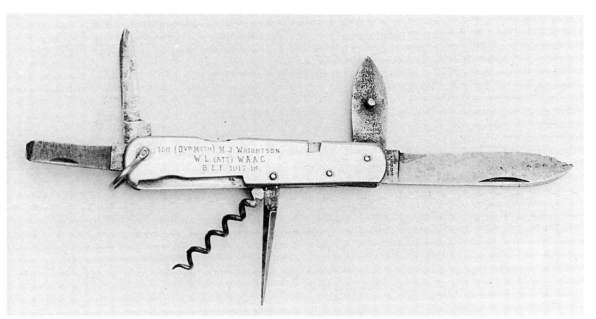

Plate 316

313 This knife is a mystery piece which, despite being of similar form to (312), may well be later than World War One or, indeed, an official issue version. The knife is by Joseph Allen and has chequered Bakelite scales. Blade length is 3.125 inches.

---

314. This rather interesting pocket knife manufactured by Thomas Turner was typical of the rather low-quality products rushed out at the outbreak of World War One, marketed to inspire patriotic feelings. The knife has main and pen blades along with spear-point can opener. The alloy scales are marked 1914

DURALIMIN

WAR KNIFE

Due to the low quality the survival rate of these knives is poor and examples are difficult to locate.

---

315 A fine gentleman's knife with its shield inscribed to Colonel Lawrence of the 17th Lancers. Lawrence was Colonel-in-Chief of the 21st Lancers and Honorary Colonel of the 17th Lancers. In 1915 he was a Major-General on the British staff in Europe. The knife has chequered ebony scales, nickel shackle and a metal bolster. The main blade is marked PAGET KNIFE and the ricasso bears the name GILLES UXBRIDGE. As Uxbridge is not particularly known as a cutlery centre I suspect Gilles is probably the name of a retailer. The knife also has can opener, corkscrew, punch, button hook and small pen blade.

316. A rather nice presentation knife commemorating service with the British Expeditionary Force (BEF) between 1917 and 1918. The knife is marked on both main blade and can opener ROUTLEDGE, BIRMINGHAM. The knife also has punch, corkscrew, small pen blade and file blade. The scales are of white metal, one of which is engraved

450 (DVR MECH) M.J. WRIGHTSON

WL (ATT) W.A.A.C.

B.E.F. 1917–18

WORLD WAR TWO AND POST-WAR ARMY JACK/CLASP KNIVES

Of all the patterns of pocket knife issued to British troops over the years those made during World War Two with the black plastic (Bexoid) scales represent the type most likely to be encountered by the collector and the style which was probably the most prolific in terms of production numbers. The actual date of introduction of this type of knife is not known, the earliest date observed on any specimen being 1939, but Brian Davis states that they date from 1933.[35] On what basis this date was arrived at is not known, but as Pattern 6353 was still being made into the late 1930s it is my view that they were not made as early as 1933. These knives saw service up until at least 1952, and through this 1930s to 1950s period the total production must have been staggering. At least one manufacturer claims to have produced at least one million of Type 317, and when one considers the number of manufacturers involved in making these knives the total production must have run into many millions.

The knives can be found in three basic forms: three-piece (main blade, can opener and marlin spike) with steel bolster, three-piece with moulded bolster and two-piece (main blade and can opener) with moulded bolster. Other design variations generally based on these three themes do exist, and some of these are today quite scarce. Dates for some of the more distinctive design features can be established from known specimens. The use of copper for the shackle material appears to have been phased out around 1940, and the bottle opener was first included on the can opener around 1945. The steel bolster does not appear to have been used after 1945.

The following list of manufacturers was drawn up from all variations, and while not every one made every variation, it certainly does indicate the effort put into the production of these knives. It should be noted that the list is probably not totally comprehensive.

DAWES & HALL	THOMAS TURNER
A. DOBSON	NEEDHAM
JOHN PETTY & SONS	TAYLOR (EYE WITNESS)
H. M. SLATER	WARRIS
E. BLYDE	F. GRAVES & SON
HARRISON BROTHERS & HOWSON	BAXTER
	J. STEAD
JOSEPH WESTBY	HERBERT ROBINSON
C. MYERS	HUMPHREYS
GEORGE ELLIOT	A. H. BISBY
JOHN MILNER	J. WATTS
H. ROWBOTHAM	J. ALLEN
WRAGG	I. WILSON
C. JOHNSON	R. GROOVES
G. BUTLER	J. RODGERS
G. WOSTENHOLM	W. SAYNOR
ALBERT OAKES	RICHARDS
G. IBBERSON	ABRAHAM BROOKSBANK
WADE & BUTCHER	J. H. THOMPSON
T. ELLIN	DCC (Davenport Cutlery Co.)
J. B. HOLLAND	J. B. & S
SSP (Sheffield Steel Products)	HALE BROTHERS
ROCKINGHAM PLATE & CUTLERY (R.P.&C)	HARRISON FISHER
	JOHN BROOKES
J. CLARKE & SON	W. MILLS & SON
J. NOWILL	
GEORGE GILL & SON	
TRAFALGAR (possibly a trade name)	

Plate 317

317 Made by Harrison Brothers and Howson, this three-piece example has a steel bolster and copper shackle but, like all early patterns, lacks the bottle opener on the can opener. It also bears the earliest recorded date for a World War Two pattern knife of 1939. The main blade has been ground but is 2.625 inches in length. Overall length is 6.25 inches.

318 This example by Joseph Rodgers is dated 1940 and is unusual in that it has pressed leather scales.

319 A late, 1945, version by Richards having the bottle opener attachment and steel shackle. The knife has the overall appearance of superior quality. Blade length 2.625 inches.

320 What exactly prompted the introduction of the moulded bolster is not known for sure, but it was probably due to ease of manufacture and/or a saving in steel. The example shown was made by George Ibberson in 1943. Blade length 2.75 inches; overall length 6.375 inches.

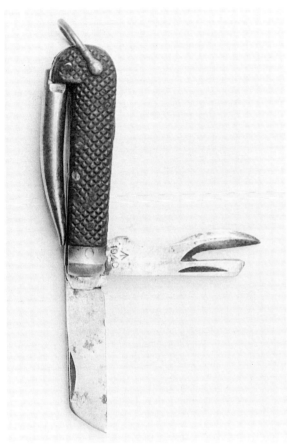

Plate 318

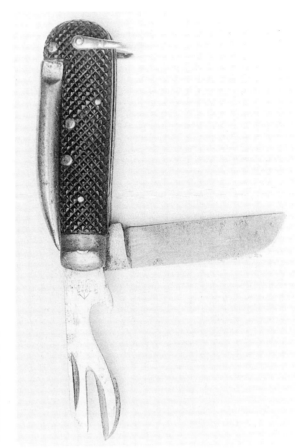

Plate 319

Plate 320

321 This 1944 knife by Wostenholm is unusual in that it carries a very early form of stores mark, the can opener being marked

CC

0532

The CC mark is a clothing code. According to information received from the MoD (Army) pocket knives are considered to be items of personal clothing and equipment, hence the clothing code mark. Three-piece moulded bolster examples can be found bearing the mark ABL, generally along with 1951 dates and another name such as LIBERT, COLIN WINAND or COLASSE. These knives are thought to be of Belgian origin, but one example I have is just marked ABL along with the code CC0530. It is not clear why the Belgians would have adopted a British clothing code for their knives.

322 Post-war, 1949 example by H. Rowbotham which has the bottle opener attachment. Blade length 2.625 inches; overall length 6.25 inches.

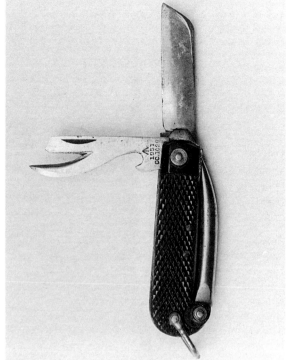

Plate 322

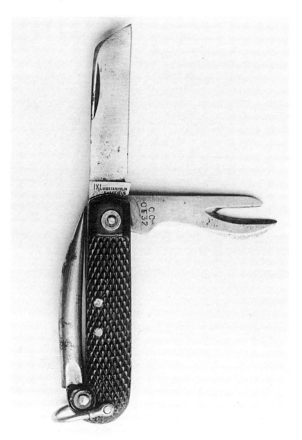

Plate 321

Plate 323

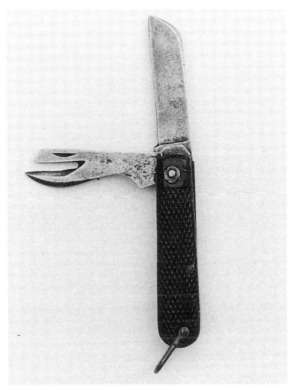

Plate 325

Plate 326

Plate 324

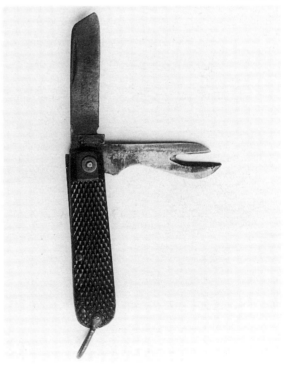

323 Also by Rowbotham, this 1951 knife carries, like (321), a CC mark, although in this case it is CC1029 which seems to indicate that a new numbering sequence was adopted post-war.

324 This 1943 three-piece knife has no bolster, the grips being chequered overall. The grips are flat and of very thin section. Considering the piece is by Ibberson the quality is rather poor. Blade length 2.5 inches; overall length 6.25 inches.

325 Manufactured in parallel with three-piece knives throughout World War Two, two-pieces appear to have fallen out of favour in the early post-war years as no example dated latter than 1946 has been observed. The example illustrated is by E. Blyde and Co. Ltd and it exhibits all the features of early manufacture – copper shackle and no bottle opener.

326 The mysteries of the CC numbering system are deepened by this version, which is marked CC1001. The knife was made in 1944 and carries the mark IXL WOSTENHOLM. Blade length 2.625 inches; overall length 6.25 inches.

327 1945 version by Taylor with bottle opener.

328 & 329 Very few of these knives with two blades and
steel bolster have been noted, but at least two manufacturers
produced them.

328 This example was made in 1940 by Harrison Fisher and
Co. Ltd.

329 This knife was also made in 1940, but by Taylor. Note
that it has flat scales. Whether the early 1940s were years for
trials of various scales is not known, but it is certainly the
period from which most variations date.

330 As will be noted, (330) has scales with a recessed
dimple pattern. This example was made by George Ibberson
in 1941. Another example by Rodgers, also dated 1941, has
been noted.

331 This knife has similar grips to (324) but of more
substantial thickness. It was made by J. Rodgers, is dated
1941, and like most knives from 1941 or later has a steel
shackle. I have two other examples of this type of knife, both
are dated 1940, and both have copper shackles. One is by
Albert Oakes, the other by Hale Brothers.

332 This unusual variant is fitted only with main blade and
marlin spike. Only two examples have been noted, both by
Watts; the one shown dates from 1944, the other is dated
1943. What prompted the manufacture of a knife without a
can opener is unknown, but it is an amazing omission when
one considers that such a feature had been fitted to Army
Knives since at least the Boer War. Blade length 2.625
inches; overall length 6.25 inches.

Plate 328

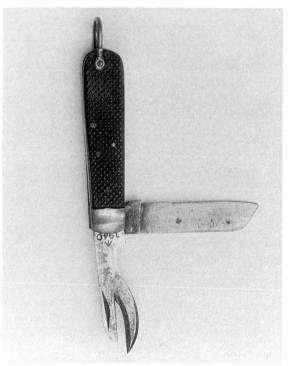

Plate 327

Plate 329

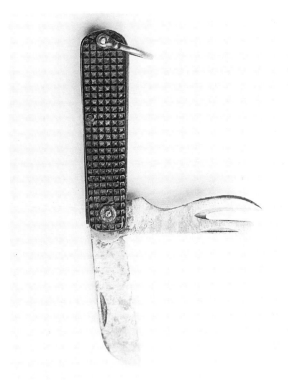

Plate 332

Plate 330

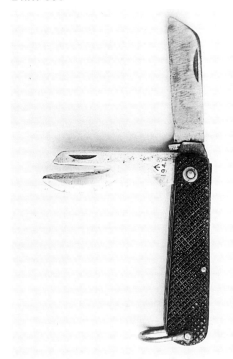

Plate 331

NAAFI OR SUDAN LINESMAN'S KNIFE

333 to 336 The exact origin and identification of this knife was unknown until a fellow collector gained access to a cutlers daybook for the firm Maleham and Yeoman. In this book a line illustration, reproduced as (333), shows this style of knife under the designation NAAFI (Navy, Army, Air Force Institute) and Sudan Linesman's Knife, with apparent orders in May and December 1943. The reference to the NAAFI would appear to indicate that this organisation purchased these knives for sale to servicemen. The reference to 'Sudan Linesman' possibly indicates that such knives were used by telephone linesmen in the Sudan.

These knives have typical-of-the-period Bexoid scales but are fitted with two pen blades, one large and one small, rather than the sheep's-foot type normally found on World War Two period knives. The example in photograph (334) (top) is by Baxter Ltd, and that in (335) (bottom) by Needham Brothers. Another specimen by H. M. Slater has also been noted. The dimensions of these two knives are not available, but those for the specimen by Slater are main blade 2.5 inches in length, secondary blade 2.25 inches in length, overall length 6 inches. It is interesting to note that on these knives the centre liner is not formed into a screwdriver tip as is normally found on official issue knives.

(336) is a previously unrecorded version of the NAAFI knife having a sheep's-foot main blade. The knife bears no

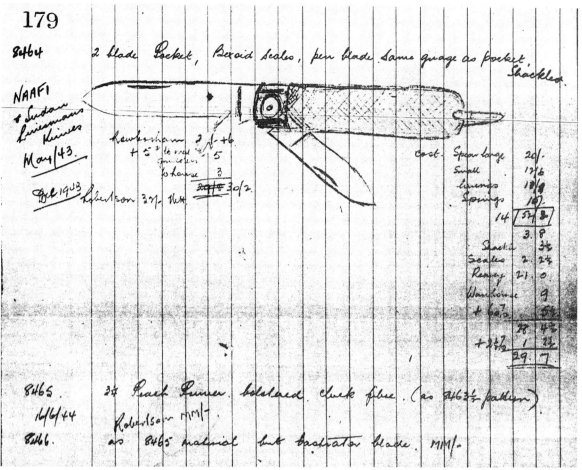

179

8464

2 blade Pocket, Beroid Scales, pen blade same guage as pocket.
Shackled.

NAAFI
+ Sudan
Frincemans
Knives

May/43.

Oct 1943

Rawkesham 2/- +6.
+ 5 + to rest   5
to house   3
29 + 30/2.

Robertson 3/-. Nett

cost. Spear large   20/.
Small   17/6
linings   18/8
Springs   10/

14   5/   8

3. 8
Shackle   3½
Scales   2. 2½
Reavey   21. 0
Warehouse   9
+ 60%   5½

78   4¾
+2½   1   11½
29. 7

Plate 333

8465.
16/6/44
8466.

3¼ Peach Pruner. bolstered. check fibre. (as 8463½ pattern).
Robertson MM/-.
as 8465 material but bashrator blade. MM/-.

Plate 334 top   335 bottom

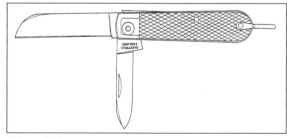

Plate 336

Plate 337

indication of the maker, the blade being marked SHEFFIELD ENGLAND. Main blade length 2.625 inches, secondary blade 2.25 inches; overall length 6.125 inches.

ALL-METAL KNIVES

All-metal knives underwent a brief period of manufacturing in 1939–40, then for some unknown reason they dropped out of favour until 1944. Other than the ARP knife – see (344) and (345) – made by DCC and George Gill in 1939, the predominant manufacturer of these knives in the 1939–40 period was George Ibberson. In these early years Ibberson made three different all-metal knives whose common feature was the STAYBRITE stamp on the scales.

---

337 This example utilises a canoe-shaped body fitted with main blade, can opener and marlin spike; the shackle is of copper. Besides the STAYBRITE mark on the scales, the can opener is marked with the Ibberson name, the violin trademark and the date 1940. Another example dated 1939 carries a W↑D mark on the marlin spike. Blade length 2.5 inches; overall length 6.125 inches.

---

338 & 339 Both these knives are dated 1940 but use totally different forms of body construction, despite having the same blades. (338) has a body formed out of one piece of metal which is folded over to give a rolled back; (339) has slab-

sided grips of a style used later in the war. The knives bear the Ibberson name and trademark on the can opener and STAYBRITE on the grip.

After a gap in the production of metal knives an all-stainless pattern appeared in 1944. Known in the cutlery trade as the Burma Knife it was apparently designed to replace the more traditional pattern for use under corrosive conditions. The body shape of these knives is similar to (339) except that they have a cut-out in the body which gives access to the blade finger nicks. The can opener has the bottle opener attachment which appeared on most patterns at

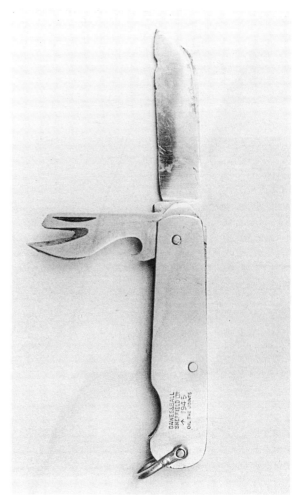

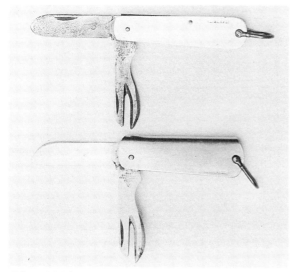

Plate 338 bottom   339 top

Plate 340

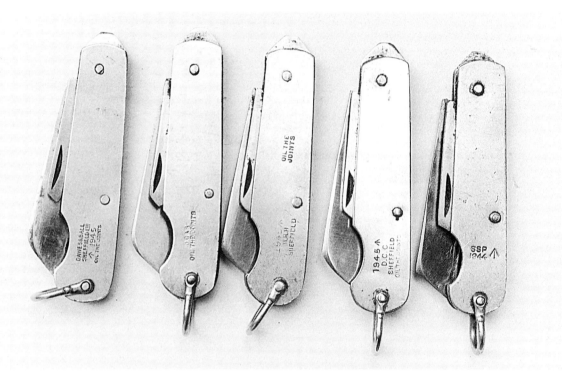

Plate 341

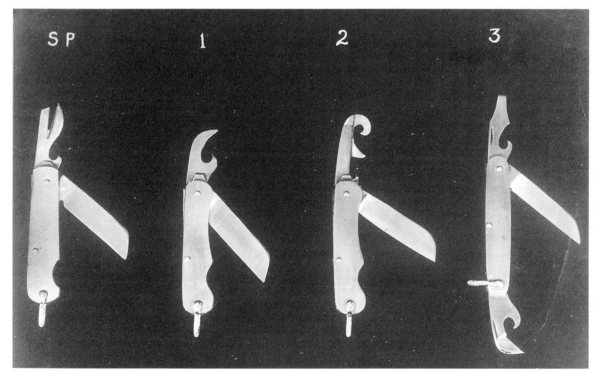

Plate 342

this time. Another interesting feature which appears on nearly all these knives is the OIL THE JOINTS marking which is still used today on stainless steel clasp knives.

340 & 341 The example illustrated at (340) is by Dawes & Ball and is dated 1945. (341) illustrates, along with the Dawes and Ball version, knives by J.C. & S. (John Clarke and Son), W.R.H. (W. R. Humphreys), D.C.C. (Davenport Cutlery Co.) and S.S.P. (Sheffield Steel Products). Average dimensions are: blade length 2.625 inches; overall length 6 inches.

342 From the Pattern Room photographs, this illustration shows four all-steel pocket knives. The two examples numbered SP and 1 are recognised patterns, but numbers 2 and 3 have never previously been recorded. While 2 bears the same general body shape and main blade as knife 1, the can opener is of a most unusual form. The body of knife 3 is more like that found on US military pocket knives but, unusually for a British military knife, is fitted with a can opener blade and a bottle opener/screwdriver blade. Note that the main blade is rather slim. These knives are possibly experimental or trials patterns; it is not known if any were ever issued.

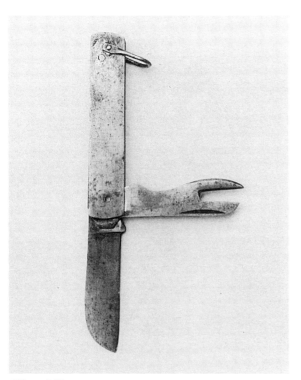

Plate 343

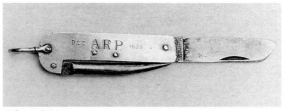

Plate 344

343 Only a few of this particular pattern of all-steel clasp knife have been observed. They are all unmarked and are of a completely different pattern to other all-metal clasp knives, but they are almost certainly World War Two in origin. All examples were found in batches of surplus World War Two knives and are fitted with typical period-style can openers. Blade length 2.5 inches; overall length 6.0625 inches

344 This all-steel clasp knife was officially issued to the ARP (Air Raids Precautions) personnel during World War Two. Although the ARP was a civil defence organisation rather than military, the knife is an interesting example of a wartime official issue knife. The knife is marked on the scales DCC ARP 1939. The DCC stands for Davenport Cutlery Company. The main blade is stamped SHEFFIELD ENGLAND.

345 This ARP knife was made by George Gill & Sons. The scales are marked

ARP

GG & S

1939

with the main blade marked GEO GILL & SONS.

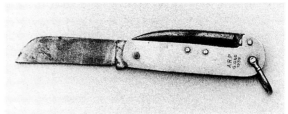

Plate 345

RAF ESCAPE BOOT KNIFE

346 to 348 What must be the smallest military knife ever issued was carried in a pocket in the World War Two RAF escape boots. The purpose of the knife was to enable the flyer to cut the stitching between the upper and lower part of the boot, thus enabling its conversion to a shoe. (346), copied

from an undated and unreferenced pamphlet, shows the escape boot and use of the knife. The construction of these knives is very simple, the body being formed from folded sheet steel with blued finish, fitted with a single bright finished blade. Two versions of the knife exist, both with different blades, and these are shown in the photo. (347) (left) has a 2.5-inch sheep's-foot blade and is 5.5-inches overall; (348) (right) has a 1.5-inch pen blade and is 4.5-inches overall. As one would suspect, these knives are unmarked but they were possibly made by George Ibberson. This is an assumption based on the similarity in construction with other Ibberson-made knives.

RAF Clasp Knife

In recent years a large number of these knives appeared on the surplus market but despite this recent apparent end to their service little is known about their history. The knives come in marked and unmarked versions, the marked examples bearing Air Ministry markings indicating issue to the RAF. However, no dated examples are known so the exact period of their

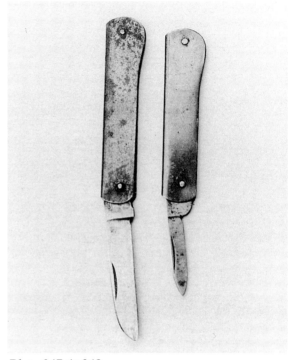

Plate 347 & 348

Plate 346

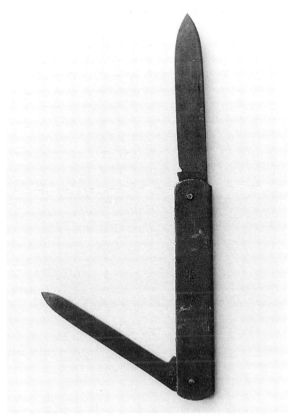

Plate 349

Plate 350

manufacture cannot be ascertained, but according to one letter in my files from the RAF Museum such knives were not general issue to the RAF until late in World War Two.

The unmarked examples have been the subject of much speculation; theories that they were packed in Red Cross parcels or that they were dropped to the Resistance have been put forward. Two USA sources have recorded these unmarked versions as being OSS/SOE survival kit knives.[36]

---

349 & 350 (349) shows a marked version, (350) the unmarked version. The hilt of the marked piece is stamped with a crowned AM mark along with

G.I. & CO

22P/11

'G.I. & Co' are the initials of the maker George Ibberson and Company. The folded sheet steel body is fitted with a 3.75-

inch spear-point blade and a substantial oblong section spike. Overall length is 8.5 inches.

A few examples of these knives with a saw edge applied to the spike have been noted. The origin of this feature is not known.

MISCELLANEOUS WORLD WAR TWO CLASP KNIVES

---

351 Unlike World War One, personalised pocket knives from the World War Two period are not very common, and even this example utilises a pre-war pattern knife. The knife was manufactured by Thomas Turner, with the scales engraved

T. BROWN

R.A.F. FORTINHALL 1943

---

352 to 354 While evidence exists to indicate that these knives were issued to the military during World War Two

they do not comply in style with any of the usual patterns. Although made by a number of different manufacturers they are not common today, possibly as a result of limited manufacturing effort.

(352) is by Wade & Butcher whose name appears on both main blade and can opener. The scales are of fibre and the marlin spike is stamped with a service number of 527401. Main blade is 3.25 inches and overall length is 7.625 inches. Another example made by George Wostenholm has its marlin spike marked with a W↑D stamp.

(353) was copied from the Maleham and Yeoman daybook mentioned earlier in this book, and shows this style of knife listed as the 'Army Knife', available with or without marlin spike.

(354), made by Joseph Allen and Sons, has the same scale material as (352) and is fitted with the same type of main blade and can opener. Like (352), this piece carries no indication of official issue. Blade length 3.0625 inches; overall length 7.25 inches.

COMMANDO LOCK KNIFE (?)

355 The question mark that accompanies the designation of this knife is there for a good reason: I do not really know what this knife is. The only reason I have called it a Commando Lock Knife is because an American collector claims that that is what it is. As will be noted the knife uses the same type of body as the SOE Tyre Slasher Knife but has no tyre slashing blade and the main blade is of the sabre spear type. The only markings to be found on the knife are a

↑

K

on the blade. Blade length 3.5 inches; overall length 8.3125

Plate 352

Plate 351

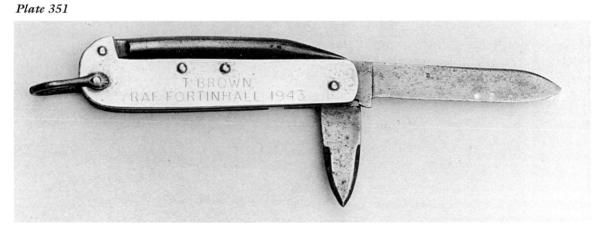

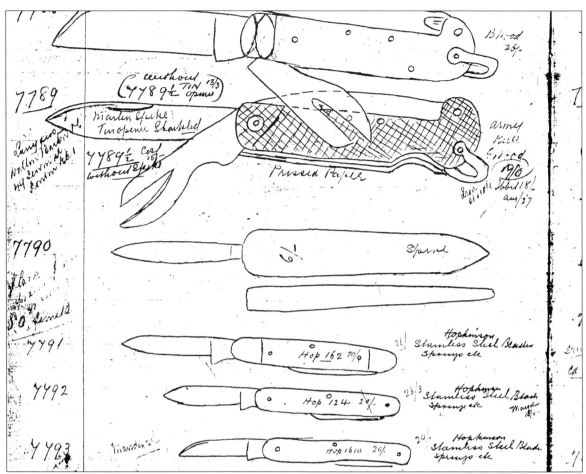

Plate 353

Plate 354

Plate 355

inches. Similar knives with the same main blade form as found on the tyre slasher have been noted, with the blades bearing the date of 1944.

POST-WAR ALL-METAL KNIVES

Around 1952 a slightly different pattern two-piece stainless steel knife was introduced. In this version the body shape was more contoured and it was fitted with a different style of can opener blade. Like its 1944–5 counterpart it carried the OIL THE JOINTS marking but it was also marked with the CC code of CC1286. These knives are also frequently found bearing a ↑ number inspection mark. Two finishes are found with these knives, either plain stainless or Parkerised.

151

356 This photograph shows a knife by Harrison Fisher & Co. Ltd which was manufactured in 1952.

357 These examples are by H. M. Slater, Myson, H. Rowbotham, and J.B.H. (J. B. Holland). Note the 450↑ inspection mark on the knives by Slater and Holland, and the 448↑ mark on the knife by Myson.

358 This photograph compares a 1979 version of this knife with one from 1952, and as will be noted, except for the markings the knife has been subject to no design changes over the years. The 1979 knife is by Joseph Rodgers and it carries the NATO Stores code of 7340-99-975-7402. These marks are etched onto the blade; the OIL THE JOINTS mark is, however, stamped.

Exactly when the three-piece all-stainless version was introduced is not known, but the earliest dated specimens are from the early 1950s. Like its

two-piece counterpart this pattern is still in use today.

359 A 1953 example made by J. R. Thompson (Cutlery) Ltd which bears the CC code CC1287 and the inspector's mark of 448↑.

360 Two recent versions of CC1287, the top piece by Joseph Rodgers, the lower by Hopkinson. These knives are described in Naval Stores catalogues under the Seaman's Clothing section as 'Knife, Clasp, New Pattern, VN 21307, NATO Number 7340-99-975-7403'. The VN number is an abbreviation for VOCAB number which is a number applied in naval circles to an item of Victualling Stores which includes clothing and personal equipment items. The designation of the knife is relatively recent; it was previously catalogued as 'Knife, Clasp, for personal survival packs

Plate 356

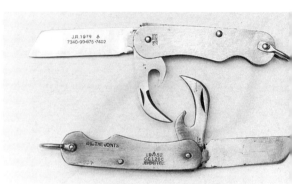

Plate 358

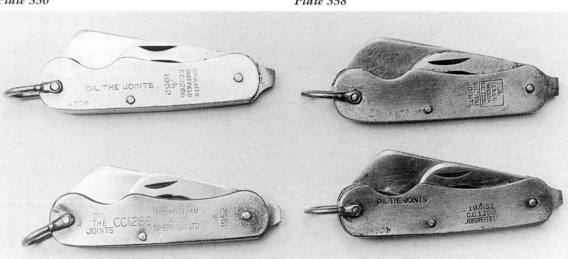

Plate 357

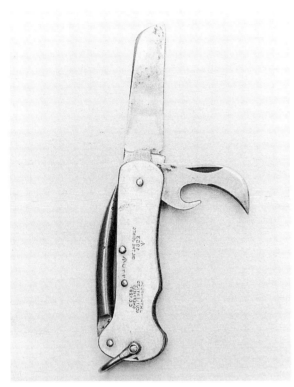

Plate 359

VOCAB number 47408' and listed under the Flying Clothing section. Examples by James Hall & Co. dating from the early 1970s and by Kutrite from 1986 have been noted. Blade length 2.625 inches; overall length 6.125 inches.

ROYAL NAVY SEAMAN'S CLASP KNIFE

This knife, the earliest known example of which

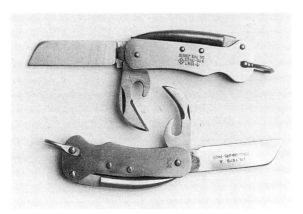

Plate 360

dates from 1940, was still in service up until 1986 when it was officially phased out under the authority of DCI RN 245/86, the text of which read:

245/86 Uniform – replacement pattern clasp knife (U)

{DGST(N)83A-D/ST83/314/1/3} 1. Knife clasp, RSN V021-99-571-3619, is to be phased out of Naval Service. The requirement that all Class II seamen ratings and all RM and RMR ranks maintain a folding knife in their compulsory kit remains unchanged however. The lighter and more compact in-service stainless steel knife, pocket, RSN V021-99-975-7403, is to be provided for this purpose once the small residual assets of heavy clasp knives have been exhausted.
Storekeeping instructions
2. Supply officers should ensure that unit stocks of knife, clasp, RSN V021-99-571-3619 are reduced to nil at the earliest opportunity by transferring current holdings direct to HMS Raleigh for use in kitting seamen ratings. Future demands for folding knives should be for the replacement pattern only. Accounting details are shown in the Annex to this DCI.
3. BR 81 (RN and RM Uniform Regulations) will be amended. In the meantime, a copy of this instruction is to be retained within the covers of BR 81, and is to be removed only when its contents have been incorporated in the text by the next routine amendments.

Historically it would appear that this type of knife is the successor to Admiralty Pattern 301, and as far as is known this type of knife has only seen service with the Royal Navy. With the exception of one knife (see 365) the design of these knives has remained unchanged throughout its life. They have a 3.25-inch sheep's-foot blade, chequered alloy grips with one side having a shield, screwdriver tip formed by the centre liner and a marlin spike. Overall length is 8 inches. Markings vary with the date from which the knife originates: early knives carry only the maker's name and the year of manufacture; later pieces carry either only the maker's name or the maker's name along with either a VOCAB or NATO stores number. Various other marks are occasionally found, such as a single number on the marlin spike, inspector's marks and names/service number on the shield.

361 A 1940 dated example manufactured by Joseph Allen which is fitted with a copper shackle. Scratched into the shield is the name F.A.H.RUDGE.

362 Specimens without formal stores marks are not uncommon, but these can be identified as having seen military use by added marks, usually the previous owner's name, in this case ERA A.G.HARDEN. The knife was made by Humphreys.

363 Manufactured by Rodgers this knife carries the VOCAB number 21306. The shield has been stamped PO 33105K DWR.

364 Dating from 1978 this knife by Rodgers has its stores number and year of manufacture etched on the blade, i.e. 1978 broad arrow 571-3619, and the VOCAB number 21306 stamped into the ricasso. The hilt is stamped in the shield HADKIN, along with the inspector's stamp of ↑462.

365 & 365A Although bearing the VOCAB number this is the only example of the heavy-duty RN clasp knife so far observed that is fitted with a can opener. Enquiries with the manufacturers, Rodgers, and within naval circles have failed to reveal the reason for this apparent anomaly. It is, however, known that this type of knife was available on contract from Rodgers (see extract from their circa 1975 sales brochure at (365A)). It was also used by the Canadians (see 457).

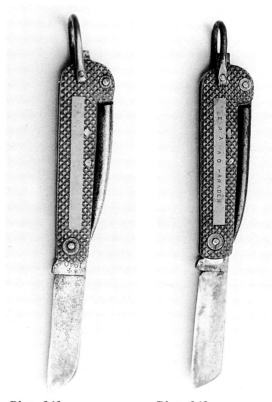

Plate 361   *Plate 362*

Plate 363

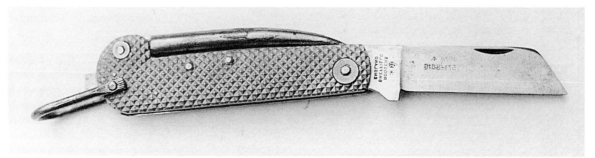

Plate 364

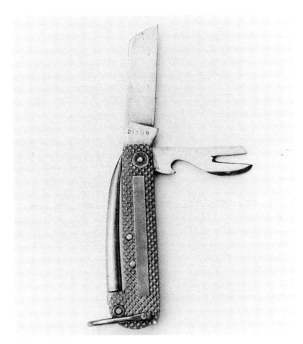

Plate 365

366 It is not known if this knife is an official or private purchase item but it was certainly carried by a member of the Royal Navy. The knife has plain stainless steel scales

which carry the inscription C.R.S. P. MCCOOEY. The 'C.R.S.' in the inscription stands for the naval rank of Chief Radio Supervisor. The knife carries no maker's or stores marks but is fitted with an RN issue lanyard. Blade length 3.25 inches; overall length 8 inches.

ELECTRICIAN'S POCKET KNIFE

Like other service pocket knives still in use today this knife has World War Two origins. The earliest dated specimen so far observed is dated 1943. The knife, unlike the American TL29, has the screwdriver, file edge and cutting edge all combined on one blade, although one example fitted with an extra blade is known. The hilt has a white metal bolster and scales made from an unidentified ebony/plastic material. No shackle is fitted. The quality of these knives is high, and the back spring on all examples is very strong, presumably to prevent the blade snapping shut when in use as a screwdriver. Blade length is 2.75 inches; overall length 6.5 inches.

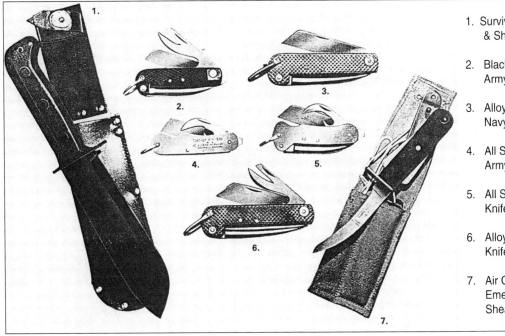

1. Survival Knife & Sheath.

2. Black handle Army Knife 3 pces.

3. Alloy handle Navy Knife 2 pces.

4. All Stainless Army Knife 2 pces.

5. All Stainless Army Knife 3 pces.

6. Alloy handle navy Knife 3 pces.

7. Air Crew Emergency Knife & Sheath.

Plate 365A

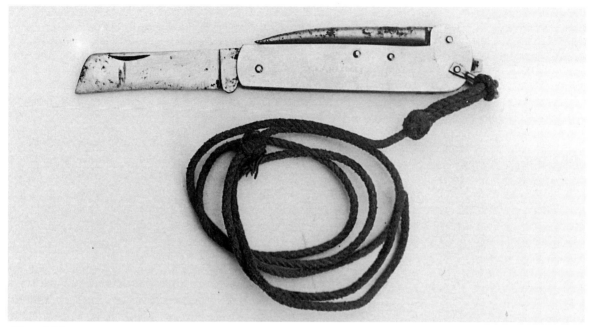

Plate 366

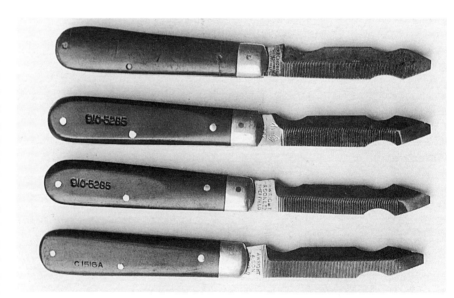

Plate 368

Plate 367

367 This knife was made by George Wostenholm and is dated 1943↑. It is not known if the lanyard hole is original.

___

368 This photograph illustrates, top to bottom:
(1) Another example by George Wostenholm. This knife carries no official marks but is stamped on the grip 91375.
(2) Piece made by Hopkinson in 1982 which bears the stores mark 910-5285 on the grip. The full stores number for this knife is 5110-99-910-5285, official description being 'Knife,

Pocket, flex stripping and cleaning, folding, (composite for use as screwdriver, file and stripper)'.

(3) A. Wright and Son were the contractors for this knife for many years. This example is dated 1979 and bears the stores number on the hilt.

(4) Another A. Wright example dated 1952. This piece carries the early stores mark of C1516A.

---

369 & 370 (369) shows a version by J. Thompson from 1961. This knife is marked on the bolster T13. The example on the right (370) is unusual in that it has two blades, one being the normal type associated with these knives, the other a small pen type blade. Both blades bear the name and IXL trademark of George Wostenholm.

LEATHERMAN SURVIVAL TOOL

---

371 Introduced into service for the Royal Marines as a survival tool under the authority of DCI RN 68/90, the Leatherman tool was developed in the USA by Tim Leatherman. Of all-stainless steel construction it comprises twelve separate tools and blades which fold away into a four-inch-long body. The full range of tools and blades carried by the Leatherman comprises long nose pliers, regular pliers, wire cutters, knife blade, imperial/metric scale, can/bottle opener, large screwdriver, small screwdriver, crosshead screwdriver , medium screwdriver, metal or wood file/saw and bradawl.

The official description of the tool as described by the DCI is Leatherman Survival Tool NATO Stock Number 5120-99-786-5369. The version issued to the Royal Marines is marked on the body 90 ↑ 786-5369. A more recent example has been noted marked 786-5369 ↑ 1993.

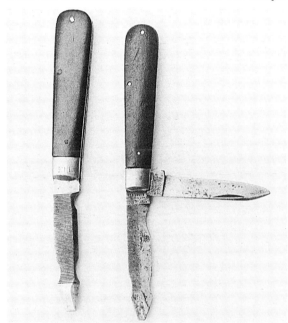

Plate 369/370

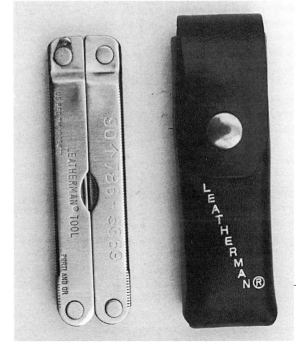

Plate 371

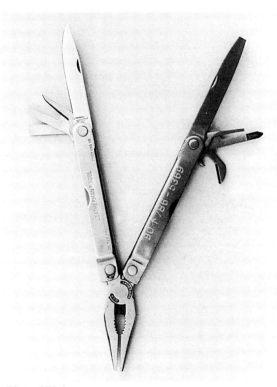

Plate 371A

PART TWO

AUSTRALIA

ustralia has produced a considerable number of different military knives for use by its armed forces. It was also responsible for the manufacture of several types of knife used by US troops who used Australia as a base during World War Two. Many of these knives also found use with Australian Forces. Nearly all the knives in this section date from the World War Two period; I have only been able to obtain details of one knife which dates prior to this, though others are likely to exist. Post-World War Two, the knives available to the Australian military appear to be limited to machetes, pocket knives and survival knives, the latter provided by buying in available commercial designs.

BILLHOOKS

372 Dating from 1916 this billhook is stamped on the blade G.H.BISHOP over 1916 and AUSTRALIA over a ↑. These knives were useful tools for clearing brush etc. This example has a one-piece wood grip. Blade length 10.375 inches; overall length 16 inches.

373 While bearing no date, this billhook dates from around the World War Two period. In this example the grips are two-piece, secured by three rivets. The only marks to be found are EG over a ↑ stamped into the grips. Another example marked with the Australian Department of Defence mark of D↑D, and W over a ↑, has also been noted. Blade length 10.125 inches; overall length 15.625 inches.

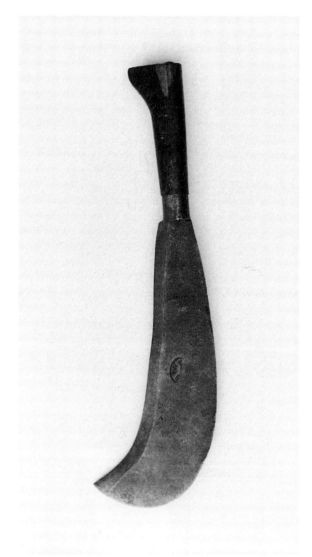

Plate 372

MACHETES

With the exception of the Aircrew Survival Machetes, the machetes used by the Australians both during and after World War Two have tended to utilise the same blade styles as are found on British types. The Australians, however, fitted these blades with different hilt forms.

374 This machete has a rather lightweight blade and is fitted with wood grips which are similar in shape to those found on the Canadian issue machete (see 447). The only marks borne by this piece are D↑D stamped on the blade. The example dates from World War Two. Blade length 14.4 inches; overall length 19 inches.

Plate 373

Plate 374

375 Having a much heavier blade than the previous example, this machete is fitted with large chunky wood grips which are secured by three steel rivets. The blade is stamped SCOTT TROJAN over the D↑D. Blade length 14.375 inches; overall length 20.25 inches.

---

376 & 377 Officially known as 'Matchet, 15" Blade (Aust) with Lanyard', this piece was introduced into service via MGO (Military General Order) Equipment Memorandum No. 16, June 1945, a copy of which is reproduced at (377). The grips of this example are similar in shape to those encountered on the previous piece, but in this case they are made of plastic secured by brass rivets. The blade is marked

D↑D over DC-45. The latter marking is presumed to be a reference to the date i.e. 1945 and maker. Blade length 14.625 inches; overall length 20.25 inches.

---

378 Made by Gregsteel, this blank has never been assembled into a full machete. It was obtained by an Australian collector from the Gregsteel factory when it closed down a number of years ago. It bears some features not noted on the previous examples. The back of the blade is straight rather than being upswept towards the tip, the end of the blade is very nearly round almost in a bolo fashion, and there is a short back edge. The only marks to be found on the knife are

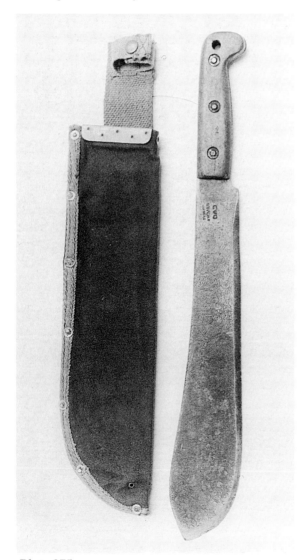

Plate 375

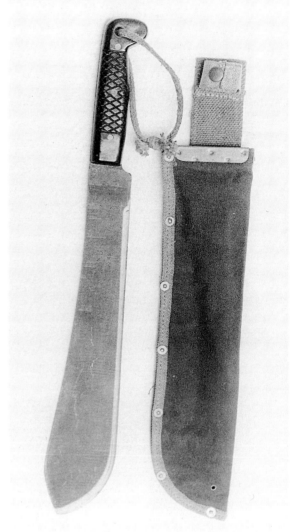

Plate 376

GREGSTEEL

AUST

Blade length 14.25 inches; overall length 20 inches.

All the previously described machetes came with the same type of sheath which has a green canvas body reinforced down its edge with khaki webbing, and fitted with a khaki webbing belt loop. The throat of the sheath is strengthened by a brass strip. The backs of these sheaths have a maker's

Plate 377

25. MATCHET, 15" BLADE (AUST.) WITH LANYARD

A well-balanced Matchet made from tempered steel (carbon 0·6%, manganese 0·9%) with a plastic handle incorporated in the design, has now been developed.

The blade, 15" long and 3" wide at the maximum width, is punched from steel sheet, surfaced to the required thickness of 12-gauge, hardened, tempered, and with a black finish. The cutting edge is then ground sharp.

The handle, consisting of two pieces of cotton filled Phenolic moulding with indentations to provide a sure grip, is secured to the blade with three brass rivets.

A cord lanyard made from 30" of ¾" rotproofed braided flax is looped through the handle for attachment to the wrist.

The total weight is 1 lb. 5 oz.

A lightweight canvas sheath for use with the matchet has been introduced into service and is described and illustrated in M.G.O. Equipment Memorandum No. 11.

PLATE 36

Matchet, 15" Blade (Aust.) (with lanyard)

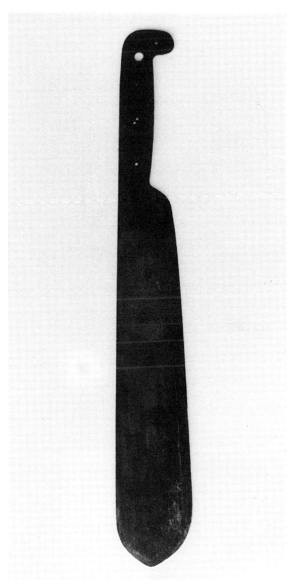

Plate 378

mark but in all cases this is scuffed and unreadable. The date stamp of 1944 is, however, clear. These sheaths were introduced via MGO Equipment Memorandum No. 11, April 1944, a copy of which is reproduced at (379). It will be noted that the text of MGO No. 11 indicates that this style of sheath replaced a leather (presumably British style) sheath and that it is photographed with the same type of machete as shown in (375).

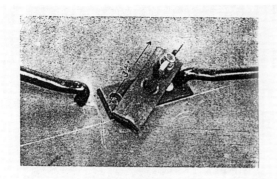

PLATE 23

Forms, Dining Tent

Showing stay rod clip

18. MATCHET 15" BLADE (AUST.)—SHEATHS CANVAS

The existing leather matchet sheath has been replaced by a new lightweight tropic proofed canvas sheath, designed to effectively carry the 15" matchet. Material used in construction is 18 oz., olive drab canvas duck rot and mildew proofed, and a 2" wide web loop enables attachment to the belt. The matchet is held firmly by the handle with a ½" web strap clipped with a brass fastener.

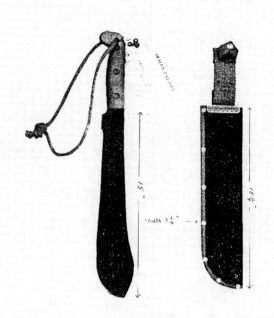

PLATE 24

Matchets 15" Blade (Aust.)—Sheaths Canvas

Plate 379

Plate 380

WHITTINGSLOWE
ADELAIDE

over D↑D. Blade length 19 inches; overall length 25 inches.

---

381 Vietnam period machete of a type which is still believed to be in use. This machete is styled on the British issue golok but has a larger blade and a hilt made of resin-impregnated wood secured by four alloy rivets. The only marks to be found on the knife are MA65 stamped into the grip. The MA mark stands for Munitions Australia. The sheath is of olive green webbing, and is fitted with a pouch for a stone. The back of the sheath is marked with an ink-stamped rectangle containing partially erased marks, possibly a stores number. Blade length 12.875 inches; overall length 18.75 inches.

381A & B These photographs illustrate a more recent version of the above machete. The hilt of the machete is only marked

380 Made by Whittingslowe during World War Two this style of machete has not as far as I am aware been previously recorded. Having a black finish blade with bright cutting edge, the grips are of light-coloured wood secured by three brass rivets. The blade is marked

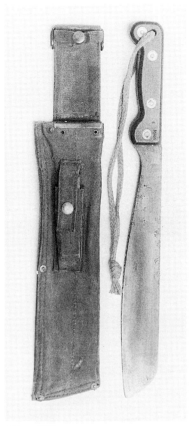

Plate 381   *Plate 381A*   *Plate 381B*

Plate 382

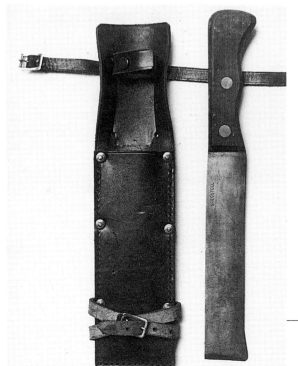

with a letter H and the number 9. The reverse of the sheath, which is made from what appears to be a waxed canvas, is marked as follows:

8465-66-011-5820

↑

CANTAS

88

Note the use of NATO style stores numbering for the sheath. Besides the machetes illustrated and described, I have in my collection a British machete made by Martindale which is stamped D ↑ D on the hilt.

---

382 to 385 The alloy-hilted version of the Air Force Survival Machete is the same as those listed by Cole as being used by the USAAF during World War Two, and even though the examples shown by him bear US marks they were in fact made in Australia.[1]

(382) by Gregsteel is somewhat unusual in that it has wood

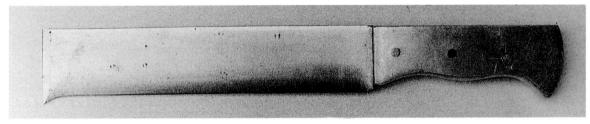

Plate 383

grips – alloy is the norm. The single-edged blade is 7.687 inches in length and is marked only GREGSTEEL. The leather sheath is designed for attachment to the belt or the leg and is provided with both belt slot and leg straps. The sheath is stamped on the belt flap BONNEY & CLARK. Overall length 12.813 inches.

(383) is an alloy-hilted version of this knife. This example, although unmarked, is virtually identical to those illustrated by Cole. The same type of sheath that accompanies (382) goes

Plate 385

with this knife, but in this case it is unmarked. Blade length 7.75 inches; overall length 12.1875 inches

(384) is of the same design as 383, with the blade marked

EAST BROS.

SYDNEY

The sheath is stamped

GOLDSEAL

1944

SYDNEY

Blade length 8.437 inches; overall length 13.125 inches.

(385) is a short-bladed example of the aircrew machete, the blade being only 7.125 inches in length.

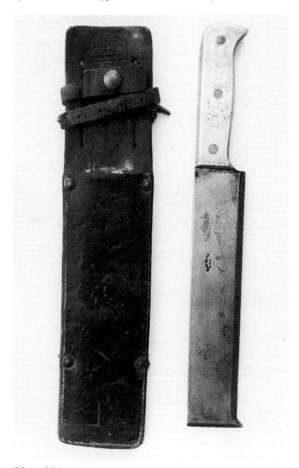

Plate 384

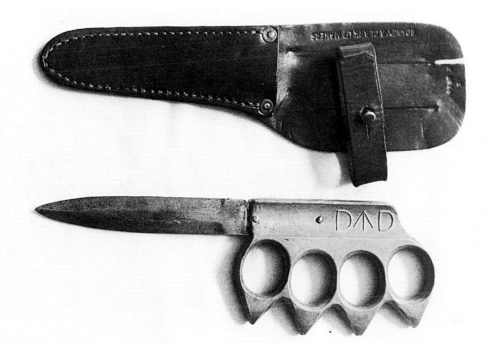

Plate 386

KNUCKLE KNIVES

386 & 386A This very rare knuckle knife made in Australia during World War Two was according to Hughes made in very limited numbers for members of X, Y, and Z Force.[2] Very little information is available on this knife, but its official description as given in MGO Equipment Memorandum No. 8, October 1943, was as follows:

KNIVES, FIGHTING (AUST)
1. This knife was recently introduced into service for special purposes (October 1943). It consists of a 4½″ blade riveted to either a brass or Mazak knuckle-duster handle grip. Finger holes are all of the same size to enable the knife to be used for upward or downwards stab.
2. Limited quantities are available for operational area for the purposes of special patrols or close fighting operations.

The reference to a brass knuckle is very interesting, and the existence of such a variation has as far as I am aware not been previously recorded in a book. However, such examples do exist and unlike their alloy counterparts they are not marked. The reference to 'Mazak' is presumably about a type of alloy. The example of this knife illustrated is extensively marked. Moulded on the hilt is the Australian Department of Defence mark of D↑D, on the other side of the hilt there is an engraved

Plate 386A

↑C mark (see 386A) and a stamped mark of ↑ over 788. The blade tang is stamped 446 and the hilt palm piece is stamped

3

X1614

The leather sheath also carries this mark but without the line between the two rows of figures. The sheath is also marked with the name of its manufacturer: BONNEY & CLARKE LTD MAKER.

This example differs from the official description in that the blade length is 5.875 inches rather than the 4.5 inches quoted, and the blade tends to swell rather than have parallel sides. Overall length is 9.5 inches.

387 A rare example of the brass-hilted version of this knuckle knife. Note that the finger holes are not all the same size.

388 shows two rare knuckle knives recorded by Hughes as being of Australian origin and having been made by Gregsteel.[3] This identification is supported by Silvey[4] who illustrates one of the smaller versions with its hilt marked

GREGORY STEEL PRODUCTS.

MADE IN

AUSTRALIA

Both knives utilise the same hilt form, but the top specimen has a 8.25-inch double-edged blade and the lower a 5.5-inch single-edged blade. One unusual feature of the top specimen is that it is marked with only a ↑ on the blade – most Australian-made knives of the period usually carry the D↑D mark. One Australian collector does, however, have a similar example which in addition to the ↑ is also marked on the blade

GREGORY STEEL

PRODUCTS

AUSTRALIA

(388A) illustrates part of the hilt casting for the top knife shown in (388).

Plate 387

Plate 388A

Plate 388

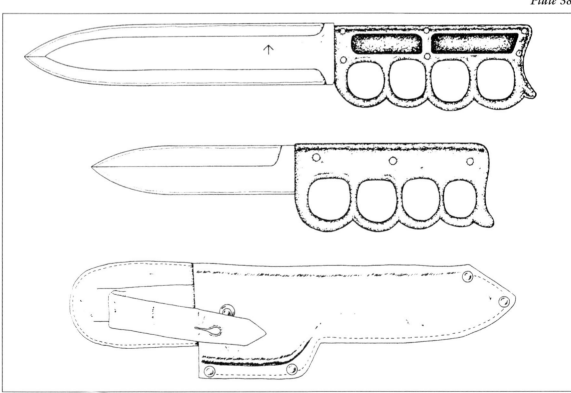

389 Recorded by both Hughes and Stephens as being of Australian origin, no other details have been forthcoming about these knives, but assuming the identification is correct they presumably date from the World War Two period.[5] The alloy knuckleduster hilt is cast onto a 6-inch double-edged blade, with the knuckles being painted dark green, though examples painted black have been noted. An example with an 8-inch blade is recorded by Hughes in his *Primer Part 2* (knife 135). No sheath is available for study. Overall length 10.5 inches.

390 The so-called US 'Rangers' Cog Wheel Knuckle Knife. These knives generally but erroneously associated with the American Rangers were in fact made in Australia during the war for private purchase. These knives come in two sizes, the one illustrated being the larger version. The knife has a brass hilt with 'cog wheel' style knuckle bow and a V-44 style blade. This example, originally illustrated by Hughes, was once owned by Alan Simpson, an Australian collector, who had it stolen from his home some years ago. As will be noted the scabbard of this knife had the original owner's name stamped on the back. Research by Jeff Cossum traced Mr Sanderson, who provided the following information:

I purchased the knife in Brisbane during a transit stop early in 1944 and the description that it is rather crude is correct. My reason for purchasing the knife was as an emergency weapon, but mainly for slashing undergrowth as the blade was quite large. I sold the knife after about a month to six weeks because I found it cumbersome and not really suitable for my purpose. Also its appearance was rather ostentatious and I was subject to a certain amount of ribbing. I am almost sure that Trooper Wally Simpson, who was also in the 2/9th Armoured Regiment, purchased the knife from me.

Blade length 9.475 inches; overall length 14 inches.

391 A number of examples of this type of knife, similar to the American Everett Knuckle Knife, were illustrated in the Australian arms magazine *Caps and Flints*.[6] These knives all have cast aluminium hilts which have been blackened and blades made from shortened Pattern 1907 bayonets. The sheaths are likewise made from cut-down 1907 scabbards.

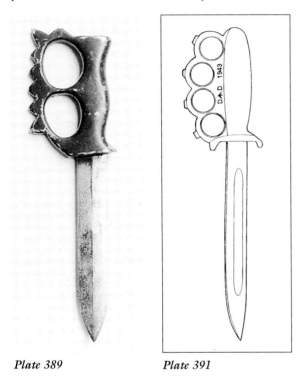

Plate 389

Plate 391

Plate 390

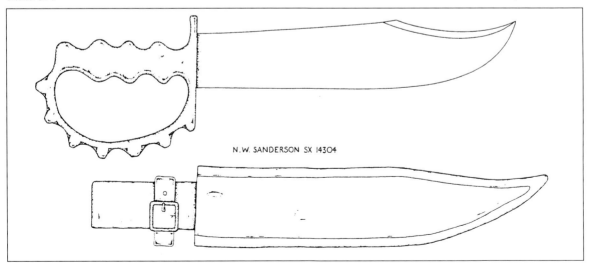

N.W. SANDERSON SX 14304

The only markings to be found are D↑D 1943 stamped into the hilt. Blade length varies between 7 and 9 inches with an overall length of between 11.625 and 13.5 inches. There is a possibility that these knives may not be correct.

392 This knuckle knife was illustrated in an American auction catalogue and was described as having a 5.5-inch double-edged blade, and alloy knuckles that were marked with the Australian D↑D mark.[7]

393 Dating from the Vietnam period this knife was made by the custom knife maker Gary Swinnerton. The knife has a 8.25-inch double-edged blade marked

G SWINNERTON
MELBOURNE

The hilt has a very large alloy knuckle guard and a wood grip with five finger grooves. The pommel nut is cone-shaped to form a skull crusher. The sheath that accompanies the knife is that from an Owen bayonet shortened to suit the knife.

Very little information is available on Swinnerton. Apparently he was a technical school teacher who made knives during the 1960s and 1970s. He produced a variety of knives which he displayed at militaria shows. His work is now highly sought after, a Bowie knife of his recently being on the market for 850 Australian dollars. Blade length 8.25 inches; overall length 14.25 inches.

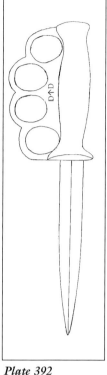

Plate 392

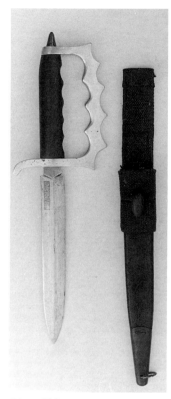

Plate 394

Plate 393

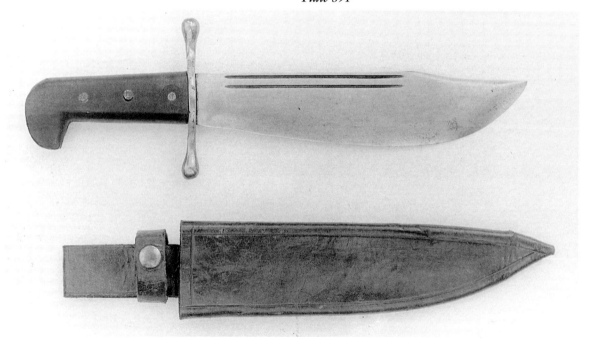

AUSTRALIAN V-44S

Generally thought of as an American knife, the V-44 was also made in Australia during World War Two both as a private purchase weapon and for both the US and Australian military. The knife is certainly known to have been used by the Royal Australian Air Force (RAAF) as a survival weapon.

I should mention that from a purist point of view these knives are not the true V-44. However, over the years this name has stuck to these large-bladed Bowies, and consequently it is the term I have used.

---

394 An extremely fine example of an Australian-made V-44. The quality of this knife is very high, similar to examples made by Case. The knife is unmarked but the sheath, which is different in style to those which accompany US-made knives, provides the main clue to its origin, the inside of the

snap fastener being marked AUSTRALIA. The hilt is of black plastic secured by three rivets and the crossguard is of brass. Similar examples to this knife have, however, been noted bearing ↑ letter stamps on the crossguard. Blade length 9.25 inches; overall length 13.875 inches.

---

395 A rare Australian V-44, in this case manufactured by Gregsteel (Gregory Steel Products). The blade of this version does not have fullers and the brass crossguard is of a form not recorded on any other model of V-44. The hilt is of dark wood secured to the tang by a nut recessed into the pommel. An example of this knife illustrated by Cole bears US Army Air Force markings, but this example is unmarked.[8] Blade length 9 inches; overall length 13.75 inches.

---

396 Similar to (394), this example is stamped on the blade

MARSDEN

SYDNEY

Blade length 9.375 inches; overall length 14 inches.

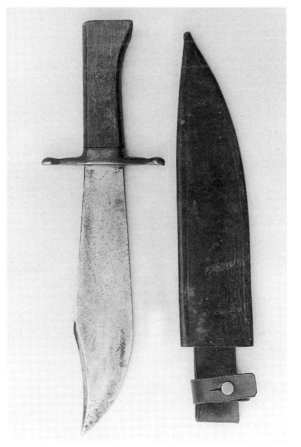

Plate 395

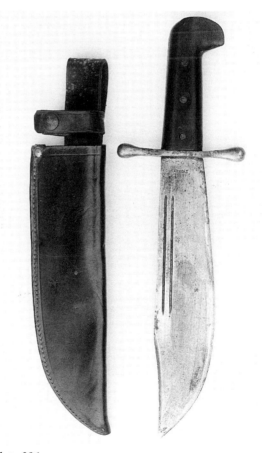

Plate 396

397 This V-44 is stamped on the blade

MARS

MACHINE TOOLS

BRISBANE

The very heavy leather sheath has a large broad arrow stamp on the front, although it is thought that the sheath is a later replacement.

---

398 This fine example of a Marsden V-44 has

MARSDEN

PRODUCTS

cast in raised letters on the underside of the crossguard.

---

399 A previously unrecorded variation of a Marsden-made V-44. This knife, which is stamped MARSDEN LTD SYDNEY on the underside of the brass crossguard, has a black plastic hilt the shape of which is almost identical to that found on the Collins-made, Canadian issue machete shown in (447). Blade length 9.25 inches; overall length 14.187 inches.

---

400 This rather crude V-44, made in Australia during the war, comes in several minor variations all of which exhibit the same low standard of manufacture. The wood grips can be found in one or two pieces secured by two rivets. The sheaths come with hilt straps fitted with snap fasteners or buckles. No example bearing any form of maker's mark has been recorded. Blade length 9 inches; overall length 14.5 inches.

Plate 398

Plate 397

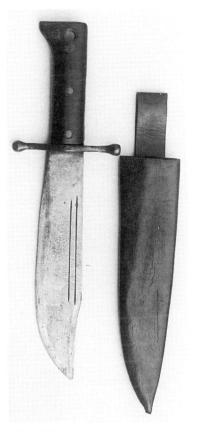

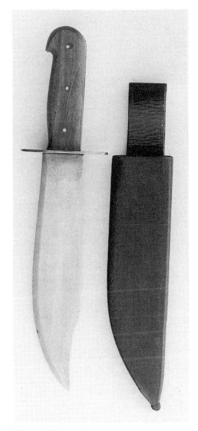

Plate 399   *Plate 400*   *Plate 401*

Plate 402

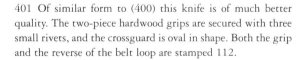

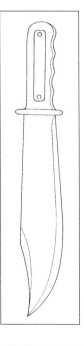

401 Of similar form to (400) this knife is of much better quality. The two-piece hardwood grips are secured with three small rivets, and the crossguard is oval in shape. Both the grip and the reverse of the belt loop are stamped 112.

402 With a blade similar to that found on (400) this V-44-style bowie has a most unusual hilt. The alloy hilt has been cast onto the tang in such a way that it leaves a cut-out through which a portion of the tang is visible.

403 A V-44 in wear by a member of the RAAF during the war. This photo is a selective enlargement from a larger photograph which shows pilots of 76 Squadron RAAF lending a hand in pushing the aircraft of Squadron Leader Truscott back into its dispersal bay. The photo was taken at Milne Bay, Papua New Guinea, September 1942. (AWM 026648)

Plate 403

AUSTRALIAN COMMANDO KNIVES

The Australian issue Commando knife made by both Whittingslowe and Gregsteel is rather unique in design. These knives, while retaining a square shank ricasso, have a longer more tapering blade than that found on British Commando knives. The crossguard is of steel and the cast alloy hilt is secured by the top of the tang being peened. The blade length of these knives is 7.5 inches and overall length is 12.625 inches.

Four types of sheath are known to have been made for these knives, one made from cut-down bayonet sheaths, two versions made from leather, and a fourth made from canvas.

404 This photograph shows an example made by Whittingslowe which, in addition to the marks shown, is also stamped with a I over ↑ mark. This mark has been noted on other examples and the use of a mark normally associated with Indian Government issue is interesting. It would appear to indicate that although manufactured in Australia the knife was inspected and issued in India. The sheath is manufactured from a cut-down bayonet scabbard, the associated frog being clearly marked DENZIL DON over 1942 along with a D↑D mark and the inspector's mark of ↑ over B.

405 This photograph illustrates three examples of this knife along with the issue leather sheath. The knife on the left is unmarked but was in all probability made by Gregory Steel Products. The centrepiece is marked on the ricasso

GREGORY

STEEL

PRODUCTS

and the example on the right is a further example by Whittingslowe. Interestingly, the hilt of the Gregory-manufactured piece is painted blue, this being the colour used by the Australians to denote training weapons. The leather sheath, which comes in both tan and dark brown leather, has a number of holes both on the belt flap and main body. These are thought to be to allow the sheath to be tied to various items of kit or uniform. The belt flap is marked with the maker's name R.G.BROWN, the date 1943 and the D↑D mark. The reverse of some sheaths bears a broad arrow letter code inspector's stamp such as

↑

HB

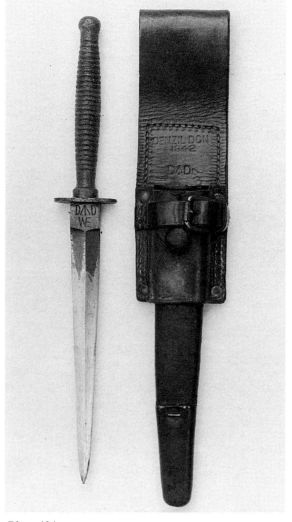

Plate 404

406 A wood-gripped version of the Australian Commando knife. The grips are of the same form as the previous two examples but in this case made from a hardwood. The knife was made by Gregory Steel Products.

407 & 408 These two Commando knives have unusual hilts. (407) has an alloy hilt which is cut with three grooves. The knife is unmarked. The hilt is undoubtedly a replacement. (408) has a steel hilt which is also probably a replacement. The blade and hilt of this piece have a phosphate-type finish.

409 Australian Commandos with the Whittingslowe/ Gregsteel stilettos in wear. Close examination of this photograph shows that the sheaths being used are the now rare canvas type. (AWM122554)

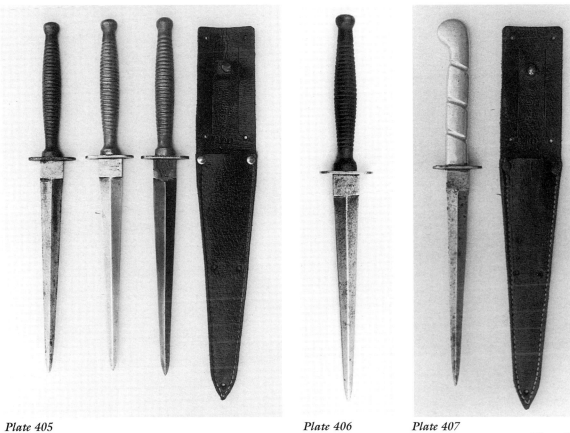

Plate 405

Plate 406   Plate 407

Plate 409

Plate 408

WOOD-GRIPPED COMBAT KNIVES

Several versions of this knife are known but most follow the same basic pattern of a single-edged spear-point blade, steel crossguard and wood grips secured by three rivets. Besides use by the Australians, Cole states that they were also made under contract for US forces based in Australia during the war.[9] Some of the examples illustrated by Cole bear a US stamp. The known makers of these knives are Gregory Steel Products, East Brothers, Whittingslowe and Barker.

410 This example was made by Whittingslowe, and besides their trademark on the blade this knife is marked with a ↑ over I on the crossguard. The sheath that accompanies this piece is not the correct pattern, but is a cut-down version of the type associated with Chindit combat Bowies. Blade length 6 inches; overall length 11 inches.

411 This example was made by East Bros and is marked on the grip with the Australian inspection mark of EW over ↑. The sheath is the correct pattern for this type of knife and is marked on the back HB over ↑, and within a rectangle

GOLDSEAL

1942

SYDNEY

Blade length 6.125 inches; overall length 11.125 inches.

412 A fine specimen made by Gregsteel. The grips of this knife are made of a lighter-coloured wood than that found on the previous specimens. No other marks are to be found on the knife but the reverse of the sheath is marked with a

↑

S

Blade length 6 inches; overall length 11 inches. A further variation of the last three knives has been recorded by Van Dyk, an example with a composition hilt with chequered finish.[10]

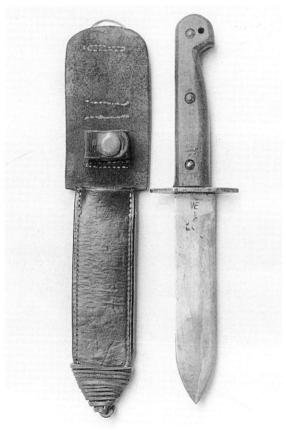

Plate 410

Plate 411

Plate 413

Plate 412

413 This photograph shows a version with an unusual hilt shape. This particular example has had the blade misshapen by sharpening; the correct blade form is of the same type shown in (410) to (412). The knife illustrated is unmarked, but another example which has its crossguard marked ↑ over I and the blade marked

GREGORY STEEL PRODUCTS

MADE IN AUSTRALIA

has been noted.

Miscellaneous Australian Knives

414 & 415 This very interesting derivative of the knives shown at (410) to (413) was patented in 1943 (see 415), and while registered as a hunting knife the period and the similarity of the knife to the wood-hilted combat knives must

Plate 414

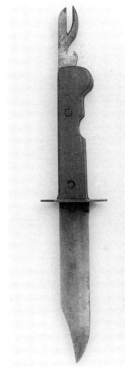

Plate 414A

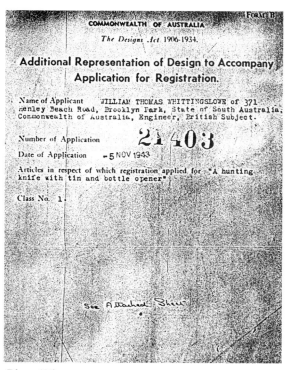

make military usage via private purchase or military contract highly likely. The knife shown is almost identical to the original patent design except for the fact that the blade is Bowie-tipped. The blade is 5.875 inches and is marked

WHITTINGSLOWE

46

RD.21403

PRODUCT

the Whittingslowe being stamped in an arc. As will be noted from both the original design drawing at (415A) and the photo the hilt contains a tin and bottle opener. Overall length 11 inches.

---

416 Two examples of a knife which utilises the same type of blade as (414), but with hilts like that found on (410). Both knives are unmarked.

---

417 This interesting combat knife appears to have been made from the same blade stock as used on the knuckle knife shown in (388) and is of a type not previously recorded. The cross-guard is of thin sheet metal and the grips are of alloy. The blade is stamped with a D↑D mark at the ricasso and there is

Plate 415

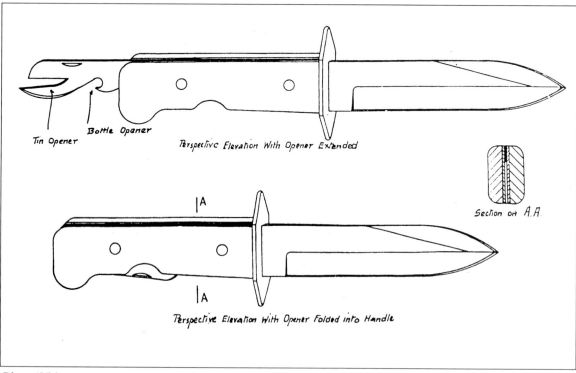

Plate 415A

a small C mark on the hilt. The sheath is made of olive green canvas which is stiffened internally by a fibre insert. The reverse of the sheath is marked

↑

AC

Blade length 5 inches; overall length 10.125 inches.

418 These two blades were recovered from the Gregsteel factory when it closed down a number of years ago. Neither piece

has ever been assembled into a complete knife. However, it is known that completed knives were used during the war, with one Australian collector having one which saw service in New Guinea. Both the examples shown are doubled-edged, and have curious 'waisted' ricassos. There is some dispute among Australian collectors as to whether or not Gregsteel actually made these blades. Although they were found in their factory there is a suggestion that the blades were actually made by Ernst Brothers.

Plate 417

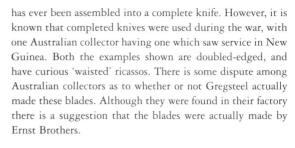

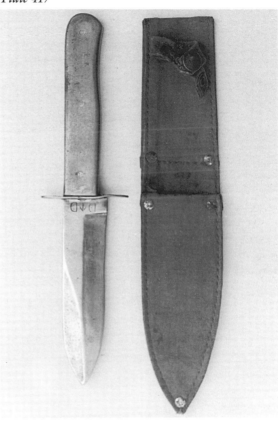

Plate 416

Plate 418

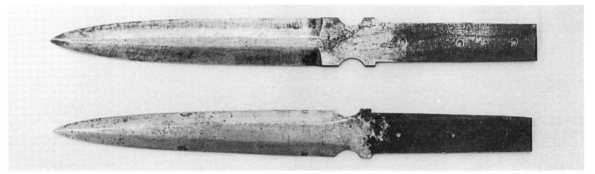

419 A complete knife which utilises one of the blade types shown previously. The knife has well-shaped hardwood grips and a thick brass crossguard. The saw teeth are a private addition. The knife does not carry any marks. Examples of complete knives with the waisted ricasso blades are very rare and were probably made towards the end of the war in small numbers.

420 Almost certainly from the same manufacturer as (402), this knife has the same type of hilt but with a short, rather plain blade. The leather sheath, even though it has been personalised, is thought to be the correct pattern for this knife. Blade length 6.75 inches; overall length 11 inches.

421 Taken from a larger photograph, this illustration shows Gunner A. C. Thynne of C Troop 2/3rd Australian Light Anti-Aircraft Battery wearing one of the knives illustrated in (420). The photo was taken at Godowa, New Guinea in November 1943. (AWM 060426)

422 This 'Ram's-head' push dagger is reputed to have been made in Australia during World War Two by Bruce Hand. The knife has a 4-inch spear-point blade with an integral push dagger hilt which is held by the first three fingers of the hand. The knife bears a '&' trademark. This maker is also supposed to have made other clandestine blades.[11] Both of the references to this maker are American and could be in error. When

Plate 421

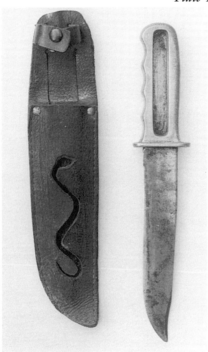

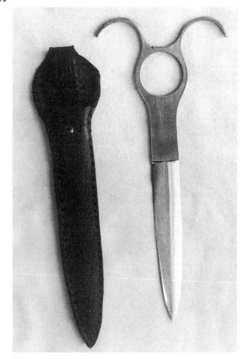

Plate 419   *Plate 420*   *Plate 422*

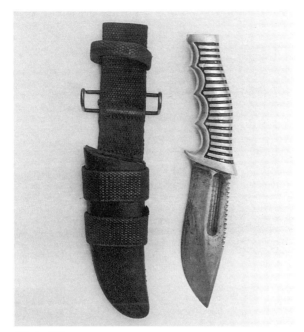

Plate 423

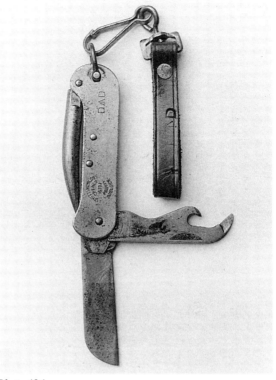

Plate 424

collectors in Australia were contacted about this maker no information or corroborative evidence was forthcoming even to support his existence.

423 This knife was issued to an Australian helicopter pilot during deployment in Vietnam. Having a short stubby blade with saw-toothed back edge and grips of alloy the knife would have been issued as a survival rather than combat weapon. The sheath is of a black plastic material and is fitted with a webbing frog which has been modified by the addition of a belt hook. Blade length 4.625 inches; overall length 9.125 inches.

POCKET KNIVES

424 & 425 Australian manufactured and issued pocket knife by Whittingslowe utilising the same canoe-shaped body that is found on (337). The main blade and marlin spike are quite standard but the can opener is rather unusual in shape. The body of the knife is marked

WHITTINGSLOWE

OPENER

15737

PAT APP

ADELAIDE

along with the D↑D mark. The knife is accompanied by its leather belt loop which also carries the D↑D mark. Blade length 2.5 inches; overall length 6.125 inches.

This pattern of knife was listed in MGO No. 18, July 1945 under 'Knives, Clasp' along with a description of how to use the can opener. (See 425)

426 This illustration shows four other Australian issue pocket knives, three being of Australian origin and one of British origin.

(1) Left bottom. World War Two knife with typical British-style can opener which is marked with the Whittingslowe mark of a joined WE over a ↑.

(2) Left top. Same as (424) but manufactured by Sterling. Another similar example made by Carr Fast has been noted.

(3) Centre. Same type as (359), this 1977 dated knife is marked ↑ 5110-66-013-1930 on the scales. The can opener is marked STAINLESS STEEL and the main blade JAPAN and STANLEY RODGERS. According to Don Lawrence, Stanley Rodgers and Son of Victoria, Australia were awarded the contract for the supply of pocket knives between 1975 and 1979.[12]

1945 JULY 1945 M.G.O. NO.18

21. BOOTS, CANVAS AND RUBBER SOLED

Experience has shown that standard boots AB Universal or half heavy, slip on wet or oily wood or metal surfaces. Boots AB canvas and rubber soled have therefore been designed for issue to tank crews of Armd. Units, Sea-going personnel of Water Tpt. Units, personnel of Docks Op. Coys. employed on Ships, and personnel of Tpt. Pls. A.A.S.C. and Amphibious Veh. Increments operating vehs. D.U.K.W.S.

Boots, AB, canvas and rubber soled are constructed as follows :—

Uppers . . . . . . Chrome tanned leather.
Soles—Insole . . . Chrome re-tan leather.
Through Sole Chrome re-tan leather, wax filled. This sole is screwed and blake-stitched to the insole.
Outer Sole . Made from five layers of 36-oz. canvas impregnated with re-claimed rubber, thus forming a laminated material ¼" thick.

Chrome tanned leather retains its pliability when subjected to constant wetting and drying. Chrome re-tanned leather also has those properties, but the final bark tanning which it undergoes gives the additional substance needed in sole leather.

Scale of issue is to be published in an M.G.O. Equipment Order.

22. KNIVES, CLASP

A knife of improved design is now being manufactured with the following features :—

(a) All parts are dull nickel plated as a rust preventive.
(b) Marline spike, screw driver and tin opener are made of tool steel.
(c) Newly designed tin opener gives clean cut instead of the ragged cut produced by the tin opener on the knife at present being issued. The tin opener functions by being drawn toward the user, the lower jaw "A" hooking under the beaded edge of the tin and acting as a fulcrum for the cutting edge "B" which is levered down and cuts the tin close to inside of the rim. The tin opener can also be used as a bottle opener.

Priority of issue will be to troops in or proceeding to tropical areas outside Australia.

50

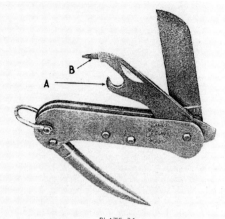

PLATE 34

Knives, Clasp
(showing newly designed Tin Opener)

23. KNIVES, FORKS AND SPOONS, LIGHTWEIGHT, FS

Experience has shown that troops serving in tropical areas outside Australia require knives, forks and spoons which will be as light as possible without impairing their serviceability, and short enough to fit into Tins, mess, rectangular.

Satisfactory designs have been evolved, the main features of which are :—

(a) Spoons and forks . . . Each 6" long and made from nickel silver 18% hard.
(b) Knives . . . 6" long, the blade being made from best cutlery steel and the handle die-cast of aluminium.

There is a saving of over 50% in the weight of Knives, Forks and Spoons, lightweight, FS, compared with standard issues.

51

Plate 425

Rodgers had the knives made in Japan. Another knife of the same pattern marked with the same stores number along with SHELHAM 8/1983 on the scales, and SHELHAM 3099 on the blade, has also been noted.

(4) Right. Two-blade pocket knife of the same type as 356. The scales are marked

7340-66-013-1930→

JOSEPH RODGERS

SHEFFIELD ENGLAND

1/1970

Strangely this knife, like the previous specimen, is marked 013-1930 despite being a different pattern.

---

427 Although this knife has unfortunately had its marlin spike removed it is obviously of the same pattern as the RN jack knife (see 361). The main blade is marked:

GREGSTEEL

MELB

Plate 426

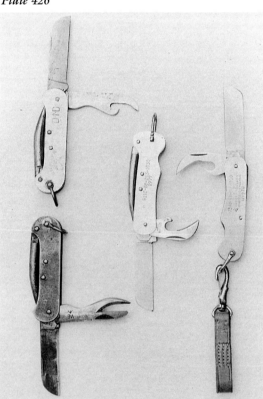

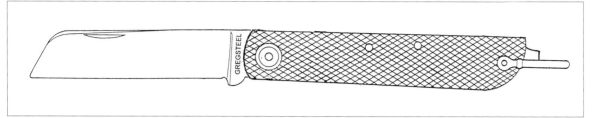

Plate 427

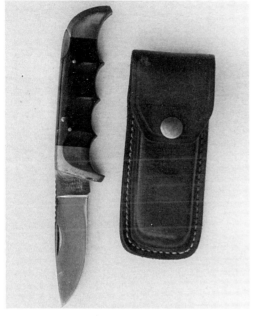

Plate 428

RAAF LOCK KNIFE

428 to 430 (428) shows a commercial lock knife procured for use by the RAAF. In the publication *Commonwealth of Australia Gazette* No. G46, 27 November 1984, which lists Australian government contracts, there is a reference to survival knives being provided by Angus Smith Sports Store, Townsville, Queensland. The appropriate extract is reproduced at (429). Enquiries with Angus Smith reveal that the knives in question were provided to the Royal Australian Air Force and that they were a commercially marketed lock knife. Angus Smith kindly provided a photostat illustration of the maker's brochure (see 430) and the model which they provided is the 4-inch blade Model 1050. Despite the fact that Kershaw is an American company it is, according to Bernard Levine, a wholesale importer of Japanese-manufactured knives.[13]

Commonwealth of Australia Gazette No. G 46, 27 November 1984		Government departments	5079
Reference	Description of supplies	Value ($)	Contractor
34526959	Paint remover	2 260.00	Turco Aust. Pty Ltd, Eagle Farm, Qld 4007
34527337	Jeweller's swivel knob screwdriver set	2 859.00	Pauls Merchants Pty Ltd, Bankstown, N.S.W. 2200
34526633	Solid rubber sheet	2 460.00	Qld Rubber Co. Pty Ltd, Zillmere, Qld 4034
34526705	Abrasive grain	2 050.00	Hoey Fry Pty Ltd, Spring Hill, Qld 4000
34526983	Brazing alloy, silver and electrode, welding	8 346.00	Strata Consolidated, St Leonards, N.S.W. 2065
34526991	Plastic rod	2 373.00	Cadillac Plastics (Aust.) Pty Ltd, Mayne, Qld 4006
34527396	Cartridge, respirator, air filtering and respirator, air filtering	1 143.00	MSA Aust. Pty Ltd, Albion, Qld 4006
34527716	Corrugated fibreboard	4 808.00	Triwall Containers Pty Ltd, Archerfield, Qld 4108
34527978	Cleaning gun	1 097.00	Godfrey Engineering Pty Ltd, West End, Qld 4101
3452817+	Paint remover	4 460.00	Turco Aust. Pty Ltd, Eagle Farm, Qld 4007
34526406	Socket wrench handle	1 330.00	Broughton Industrial Agencies, East Kew, Vic. 3102
34521584	Muff cup	2 323.00	Protector Sureguard Ltd, Bowen Hills, Qld 4006
34521621	Electrode, welding	2 040.00	Strata Consolidated, St Leonards, N.S.W. 2065
34522245	Timber, fir, 25 x 50 mm, timber, softwood	6 003.00	Wildmans Timber Ind. Pty Ltd, Toowoomba, Qld 4350
3452710+	Survival knives	1 680.00	Angus Smith Sports Store, Townsville, Qld 4810
34523440	Tablecloth	1 850.00	Hannas, Toowoomba, Qld 4350
34525681	Felt sheet	3 723.00	P & S Textiles Pty Ltd, Smithfield, N.S.W. 2164
34526780	Conditioner, paint, latex	2 955.00	Redic Industries Pty Ltd, Brisbane, Qld 4000
34526799	Paint, latex	4 470.00	Redic Industries Pty Ltd, Brisbane, Qld 4000
3452680!	Sealer, surface	3 032.00	Redic Industries Pty Ltd, Brisbane, Qld 4000
34524187	Plastics sheet, laminated, copper clad, black	1 368.00	Cadillac Plastics (Aust.) P/L, Mayne, Qld 4006
34525091	Mower, lawn, power	2 075.00	Rover Scott Bonnar Ltd, Eagle Farm, Qld 4007
Tasmania			
611 Supply Company, Dowsings Point			
LP4/84-85	Gymnasium equipment	1 079.20	Health Equipment, Hobart 7000
DEPARTMENT OF DEFENCE SUPPORT			
DEFENCE PURCHASING REGIONAL OFFICE			
Victoria			
05/75206F	Relay armature	11 599.75‡	Promark Electronics (Vic.) P/L, Nunawading, Vic. 3131
05/63475U	Beef and beans, canned, 450 gm	27 786.00	Unifood Services Pty Ltd, Sydney, N.S.W. 2001
05/63472Y	Pork and beans, 110 gm can	41 838.24	Unifood Services Pty Ltd, Sydney, N.S.W. 2001
04/63110H-1	Servo amplifiers	45 376.00	Zephyr Electronics Pty Ltd, Moorabbin, Vic. 3189
07/63357C-2	Tents, three adult capacity	2 978.63	Wyett Manufacturing Co. Pty Ltd, Geelong, Vic. 3220
07/63357C-1	Tents, family and marquee	23 116.00	Pickers Canvas & Plastics, Moonah, Tas. 7009
07/74518U-1	Cloth, cotton/polyester	15 327.00	Bradmill Textiles Operations, Yarraville, Vic. 3013
08/63057T	High pressure stainless steel fittings and valves	24 541.97	Victoria Fittings & Valves, East Brunswick, Vic. 3057
02/63591N-1	Sea water condenser	12 413.00	Starkstrom Control Gear (Aust.), Hawthorn, Vic. 3122
08/63057T-1	High pressure stainless steel fittings and valves	1 794.00	Prochem Pty Ltd, Villawood, N.S.W. 2163
07/61800U-2	Cloth, wool, barathea	750 600.00*	Macquarie Worsteds Ltd, Sydney, N.S.W. 2000
04/22501H-8	Attenuators	1 120.00‡	Warburton Franki, Noble Park, Vic. 3174
07/74707M-1	Cloth, cotton/polyester	35 685.00	Bradmill Textiles Operations, Yarraville, Vic. 3013
04/75164X	Disk turbine	28 390.38‡	P. & W. C. Services (A'asia), Tullamarine, Vic.
* Estimate ‡ Duty free			

Plate 429

kershaw
Knives

Folding Hunting Knives

Shaped and balanced to fit your hand naturally, each Kershaw hunting knife is precision crafted to provide you with a quality tool in the field. The high carbon stainless steel blades (AUS 8A) lock firmly into place and will not break away even under the roughest use.

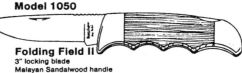

Folding Field
4" locking blade
Rugged phenolic handle with finger grooves
Shipped with leather sheath
Model 1050

Little Stud
2" hollow ground locking blade
Durable Thailand Water Buffalo bone handle
Model 2105

Folding Field II
3" locking blade
Malayan Sandalwood handle
Shipped with leather sheath
Model 1040W

Honcho
2½" hollow ground locking blade
Durable Thailand Water Buffalo bone handle

Macho
3" hollow ground locking blade
Durable Thailand Water Buffalo bone handle
Model 2120

Folding Field II
3" locking blade
Durable Thailand Water Buffalo bone handle
Shipped with leather sheath
Model 1040B

KERSHAW Leather Pocket Sheaths

GUARANTEE
We guarantee Kershaw Knives to be shaving sharp when they come from the factory. If a Kershaw Knife ever proves defective under normal use, return it directly to us, and it will be repaired or replaced without charge. Naturally this simple guarantee does not cover intentional misuse or neglect.

KERSHAW Leather Belt Sheaths

Key Chain Knife / Model 6500
1½" blade, nail file, scissors

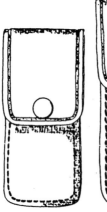

Model 2456
Fits Stag, Rancher, Stockman, Macho

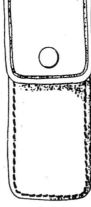

Model 2070S
Fits Big Foot

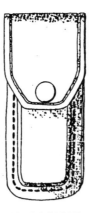

Model 1050S
Fits Folding Field

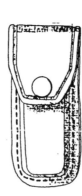

Model 1040S
Fits Folding Field II

kershaw by kai 6024 JEAN RD. LAKE OSWEGO, OR. 97034 (503) 636-0111

11/81

Plate 430

PART THREE
CANADA

The Canadian military appears to have procured many of its military knives from other countries. This is rather surprising as the Ross bayonet certainly indicates that the Canadians had the manufacturing capability to make their own edged weapons. During World War One military pocket knives were obtained from both the USA and Britain, and during the next war period issue machetes were obtained from the USA. In the post-war period knives are obtained from commercial sources.

431 In the book *War Underground* by Alexander Barrie, which deals with the activities of the mining and tunnelling units of the First World War, there is an interesting reference to a brass dagger carried by the tunnellers of the 2nd Canadian Company. Extensive correspondence with the Royal Engineers Museum and the Canadian Military Engineers Museum failed to locate an example of the actual knife described. However, in 1989 Barrie donated to the Royal Engineers Museum the material he had gathered while researching his book. To quote from these papers and the personal memories of a John Westacott who served with the tunnellers, 'the best weapon of all for underground working was a specially made knife with a blade about five inches long which was fitted to a brass frame over our hand and strapped to our wrist so when our fist was closed the knife was at right angles to your arm. We were all trained how to use it in such confined spaces'. In other papers donated by Barrie including a sketch of the knife, Westacott states: 'The knife connected to a leather thong and when you had your hand open like this, it lay up there and you flicked it down and enclosed it and it came out at right angles. Very handy, especially when raiding galleries.' The illustration is a drawing interpreted from Barrie's original notes and sketches, and whilst the described method of use is somewhat unclear it is obvious that the knife

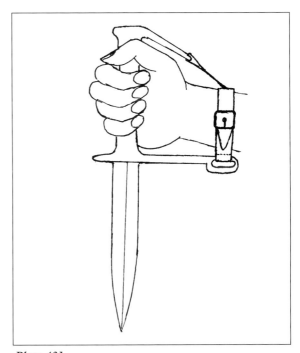

Plate 431

was a valued item amongst these men.

ROSS BAYONET CONVERSION

432 & 433 The well-known Ross bayonet conversion was produced on both an official and commercial basis. At some stage during World War Two it would appear that in order to meet the needs for a good sturdy knife the Canadians converted surplus stocks of Ross bayonets and scabbards. Little evidence exists about these official conversions but one Canadian collector does have one with reported usage by a Canadian Commando.

these can be identified by the method used to secure the cross-guard: the Mk I has its crossguard brazed in place, the Mk II used double rivets. The conversion to fighting/hunting knife resulted in the original 10.25-inch blade being altered to a 7.5-inch Bowie blade. The release button was ground down, the muzzle ring and crossguard finial were removed and the scabbards shortened to suit the shorter blade. Two versions appear to have resulted from the conversion: (432) has a blued blade and an oak russet-coloured scabbard which carries both acceptance and mustering-out-of-service marks; (433) has a bright polished blade and is in a black finish scabbard which, according to Dupuis, identifies the piece as being one of the commercial conversions.

The whole subject of identifying the official from commercial variations is, however, shrouded in confusion. Both Dupuis and Hughes state that the official versions have mustering-out-of-service marks stamped over the release button alteration, indicating that it must have been applied after the

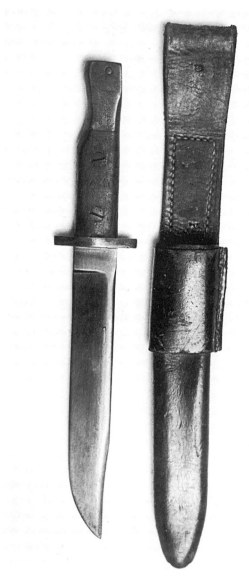

Plate 432

Plate 433

On the commercial front, and according to Frank Dupuis,[1] due to a shortage of hunting knives some Ross bayonets and scabbards were converted for this purpose. In March and April 1944 some 2,209 bayonets and 1,963 scabbards were declared surplus and sold to William Margolin of Montreal. These bayonets and scabbards were then shipped to the PAL Cutlery Company, Holyoak, Massachusetts and altered.

The Ross bayonet was manufactured by the Ross Rifle Co. of Quebec, and their name is found stamped on the pommel. Two marks of the bayonet were made, and in conversions button was removed. Dupuis also states that the commercial versions bear no mustering-out-of-service marks, yet both my examples bear such a mark, but not stamped over the ground-down release button. Also, the example mentioned earlier which was obtained from a Canadian Commando bears no mustering-out mark. Blade length 7.5 inches; overall length 12 inches.

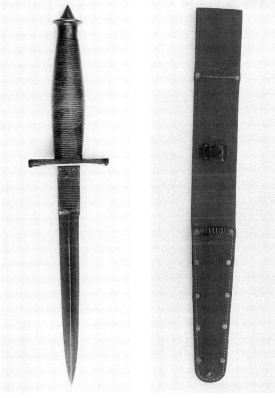

Plate 434   *Plate 435*

1ST SPECIAL SERVICE FORCE V-42 STILETTO

434 Despite its American manufacture the V-42 was issued to the Canadian element of a unique unit. The 1st Special Service Force was a combined US/Canadian unit formed in 1942 for snow and mountain warfare operations in Europe. Despite becoming fully integrated as a fighting unit the Canadians retained their own rates of pay and were still administered by their parent army. (For those interested in reading a full unit history I suggest you consult *The Black Devils* by Ray Routhier, privately published in 1982.)

The knife has a 7.25-inch blued stiletto blade with grooved recess at the ricasso, which provides a thumb grip when thrusting. The crossguard is of thin steel backed by a thick piece of leather. The hilt is made up from leather washers grooved to improve the grip which are secured to the tang by a steel 'skull crusher' pommel. The blade is marked CASE above the thumb recess and some specimens also carry a serial number. Overall length is 12.5 inches. The sheath design was somewhat unusual in that it was some 20 inches in length (see 435). W. R. Case and Sons state that approximately 3,200 of these knives were made, and assuming that about half went to the Canadian element of the force it must rank as one of the rarest knives issued to Canadian forces. (A full and detailed history of the V-42 can be found in *Allied Military Fighting Knives* by Robert A. Buerlein.)

1ST SPECIAL SERVICE FORCE POCKET KNIFE

436 Another knife issued to the force and presumably to its Canadian members was a small pocket knife designated the Mountain Pocket Knife, manufactured by the Ulster Knife

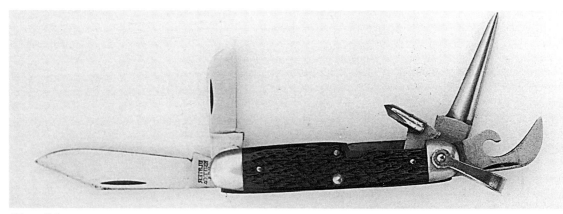

Plate 436

Co. These knives apparently had a stock number of 74-K-75 and were first shipped to the quartermaster's store in 1942. Cole records three patterns of this knife, although (436) appears to be an example of a fourth pattern unrecorded by Cole.[2] Despite these variations all patterns follow the same general style having either a main blade of the type shown in the illustrations or a sheep's-foot type, small pen blade, awl/hole punch, can opener and Phillips screwdriver blade. On one variation this latter feature is attached to the shackle, and this blade was apparently for adjusting the metal rails on Army issue skis. The grip material is gouged bone. Blade length 2.375 inches; overall length 5.75 inches. (Other Canadian issue pocket knives are covered later in this section.)

Plate 437

Plate 438   *Plate 439*

PARATROOPER STILETTO

437 to 439 This knife is usually identified as the American USMC Raiders stiletto, but was also issued to members of the 1st Canadian Parachute Battalion who undertook jump training at Fort Benning in the United States during World War Two.

The normal USMC issue stiletto was etched USMC within a scroll on the blade along with the maker's name CAMILLUS. The finish of the USMC version was a green hilt and bright blade. The version issued to the Canadians has an all-black finish and was unmarked. As will be noted the major difference between the USMC stiletto and the standard Commando knife is the fact that the hilt of zinc alloy is cast directly onto the tang.

The example shown at (437) shows signs of blackening on both blade and hilt and exhibits no signs of the maker's name or the USMC scroll. Many knives do, however, have these features worn off so it is difficult to fully identify the piece as Canadian, but the signs are that it could be. The sheath (see 438), similar to the US M6, is a variation which as far as I am aware has not been previously recorded.

(439) is an almost mint example of this very rare knife. The original black finish is virtually intact, and in keeping with the known facts the knife is unmarked. Blade length 6.75 inches; overall length 11.875 inches.

CANADIAN ISSUE F-S KNIVES

The following two illustrations, while not showing the whole knife, give a graphic representation of two known examples of F-S knives marked with Canadian acceptance marks.

440 This shows the pommel portion of a First Pattern F-S stamped with the Canadian acceptance mark of a ↑ within a C. This mark also appears on the crossguard, and additionally the piece is marked 69E on the pommel.

441 This shows a standard Third Pattern with a very small ↑C mark stamped on the edge of the crossguard.

PRINCESS PATRICIA'S CANADIAN LIGHT INFANTRY PARACHUTIST KNIFE (?)

442 to 444 The existence of these knives first became apparent as a result of one appearing in auction in 1980 with the auction illustration being reproduced in the 1981 edition of

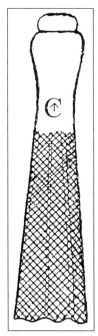

Plate 441

Plate 440

Plate 442

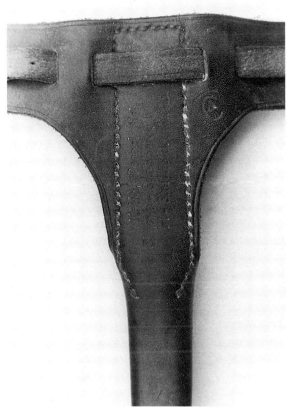

Plate 444

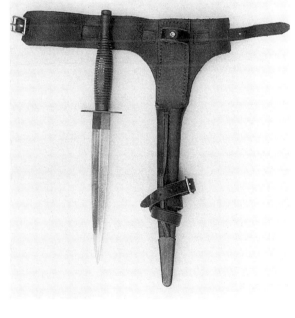

Plate 443

the *Lyle Official Arms and Armour Review*. The knife was then subsequently written up by Hughes, Buerlein and Thompson.[3] As a result a lot of collectors including myself put this 'rare' Commando knife and its associated sheath on their list of wants.

The published information describes a knife of the Third Pattern with a standard style hilt which has been painted green. These Third Patterns all seem to be of post-war manufacture having thin crossguards which in some cases bear the William Rodgers name. The top portion of the blade may be found also painted green with the remainder of the blade bright. The examples recorded by Thompson and Buerlein bear different markings: one is marked on the blade P.P.C.L.I. (Princess Patricia's Canadian Light Infantry) and on the crossguard the Canadian ↑C acceptance mark; the other example is marked 1953, 197 along with a maple leaf emblem. The piece illustrated, in addition to carrying the William Rodgers name on the crossguard, is marked P.P.C.L.I. on a flat on the hilt; along with electric pencil marks of 1953 and a maple leaf emblem on the blade (see 443).

The sheath is reputed to have been designed to allow it to be carried on the forearm. The finish is in green, though black versions are reported to exist and the reverse of the sheath is marked

KNIFE, PARACHUTIST

SLEEVE – SCABBARD, MK 1

H – SHEFFIELD, M45

along with the ↑C mark (see 444). Some sheaths are also supposed to be marked either Mk I* or Mk II.

The previous writers on this knife record usage not only by the PPCLI, who incidentally operated in an airborne role from 1948, but by British, French and Belgian SAS and British Paratroops. In 1992 Thompson produced an article in which he stated the first sheaths of this type were produced by Cogswell and Harrison for private purchase during World War Two and that only about 100 of these were made.[4] There is a suspicion amongst some collectors that these sheaths are not correct, and that the markings on the knife are spurious. Undoubtedly some readers will disagree with this view.

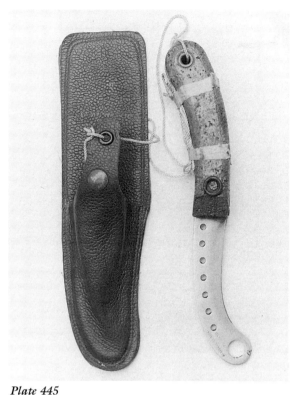

Plate 445

Plate 446

DINGHY KNIFE

---

445 This Dinghy knife is stamped

NATIONAL CUTLERY

TORONTO

While it does not bear any official military marks it is very likely that this knife was used by Canadian forces.

BILLHOOK

---

446 & 446A This massive billhook is accompanied by a sheath which has no means of securing it to a belt. It is assumed therefore that the piece was intended to be carried in a pack or as part of vehicle equipment. The blade is marked WALTERS 1942. The blade and hilt have been painted green overall. The sheath is marked inside the flap:

CECIL SPRIGINGS

MONTREAL – 1942

The sheath is also stamped with some small, almost indistin-

Plate 446A

guishable acceptance/inspector's stamps. These are a P over ↑ and another ↑ mark which is not totally clear. Blade length 11 inches; overall length 17.25 inches.

MACHETE

447 & 447A This American-manufactured machete was made for the Canadians during the war. This example, which still bears its original wrapping, was made by Collins and carries their LEGITIMUS trademark on the blade and the original Collins trade label under the wrapping. The blade is of the British form and the hilt made from black plastic is the same shape as used on (374) and (399). The hilt is still fitted with its original wrist thong and the blade is marked with the date 1943 and the Collins pattern number of 1250. While this

Plate 447A

piece lacks it, examples are frequently found with the Canadian ↑C mark stamped into the hilt.

According to the late D. E. Henry, who studied the works of Collins, these knives were officially known by the Canadian Army as 'Knife, Bush'.[5]

The leather sheath is the same as the British pattern and, as will be seen from (447A), is marked on the back of the belt loop

H. CARSON CO. LTD

OTTAWA 1940

along with the ↑C mark. The firm of Carson is known to have made scabbards for the Ross bayonet. Blade length 14.875 inches; overall length 19.75 inches.

RUSSELL BELT KNIFE

448 Issued to the Canadian Paratroop Regiment in the 1960s as part of their survival kit this small hunting-style knife was designed by D. H. Russell of Pictou, Nova Scotia. The single-edged blade is 4 inches in length and the hilt has rosewood grips secured by three brass rivets and is pierced with a thong hole. The blade is marked with an S (for stainless) within a circle and

D.H.RUSSELL

BELT KNIFE

CANADA

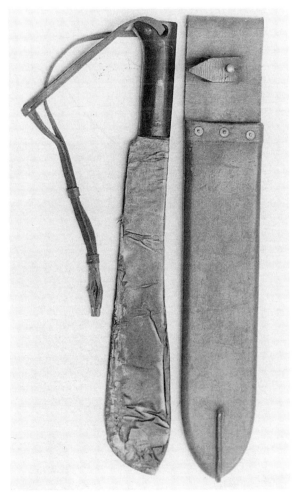

Plate 447

Plate 448

The brown leather sheath is of the pouch type which totally encloses the knife.

The actual manufacturer of the knife is something of a mystery. Levine lists Russell as a maker in his own right, noting that he operated around the 1970s.[6] However, one Canadian collector states that while the knife was designed by Russell it was actually made by Grohmann Outdoor Knives. It is understood that Russell-type belt knives are still supplied to the Canadian Armed Forces. Overall length 8.25 inches.

449 A Russell knife in wear by a Canadian para during winter manoeuvres, *circa* 1960.

POCKET KNIVES

Like many of the foregoing knives the procurement of pocket knives for the Canadian forces was also from non-Canadian sources, either American or British.

450 & 451 Of the same pattern as (309) these two knives were made by Thomas Turner. (450) is marked on the grip

M & D CANADA

1914

The 'M & D' mark stands for Militia and Defence, a government mark that according to Don Lawrence was used *circa*

Note — enclosed copy of Photo showing Cdn Trooper Russel Knife on Winter manovers 1960's

all the best

Jim

Plate 449

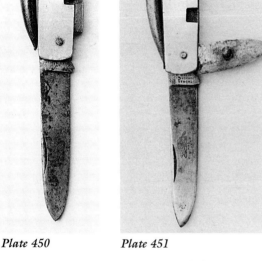
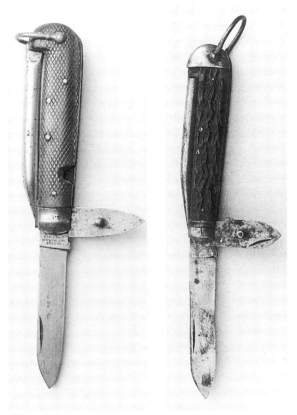

Plate 450   *Plate 451*   *Plate 452*   *Plate 453*

1895 to 1900 before being replaced by the ↑C mark, though its use obviously continued in parallel with the ↑C well into the World War One period.[7]

(451) is marked with a beaver and M & D CANADA on the blade along with the ↑C on the grip. The lack of a date may indicate this piece pre-dates World War One.

---

452 This fine World War One period knife by George Wostenholm bearing their IXL trademark on the blade is the same pattern used by the British (see 304). The knife has chequered green horn grips and bears the ↑C mark on the marlin spike. Blade length 3.5 inches; overall length 8.375 inches.

---

453 This example was made by Schatt and Morgan Cutlery Co. of Titusville, Pennsylvania around 1915. The grips are of jigged bone and the Canadian acceptance mark is stamped into the marlin spike. Somewhat unusually the knife has a double metal bolster, a feature which is rarely found on military pocket knives. A similar version made by Camillus Cutlery Co. of New York has been noted with the date 1915 stamped on the tang and the Canadian acceptance mark on the marlin spike.

CASE M346

The history of the Case M346 is rather involved and much of its background, particularly the variations in marks, has been untangled by the Canadian collector Don Lawrence. There appears to be four manufacturing series for the M346: those made in the US during World War Two for the US Navy; those made in the US during World War Two for the Canadians; those made in Canada in the early post-war years; and those made in the US post-World War Two.

The World War Two period US Navy knives were made by W. R. Case and Sons Cutlery Co., Bradford, Pennsylvania, USA between 1940 and 1942 and bore the mark CASE XX on the blade. The knives made by Case during the war for the Canadians carried the CASE XX METAL STAMPINGS LTD mark. Only knives with the alloy scales appear to carry this marking and they were made between 1942 and 1945. The early post-war Canadian-made knives were produced between 1948 and 1949 by the Case subsidiary W. R. Case and Sons of Canada Ltd, Pictou, Nova Scotia. These knives bear the M.S.LTD XX mark. The fourth and final batch date from the 1950s onwards were purchased by the Canadian government from Case. The knives are marked

CASE XX

STAINLESS

– a mark that was used up until 1965.

While this style of knife is generally associated with naval use there is reported usage by the Canadian Army, and Voyles and Kelly record an example marked R.C.A.F. (Royal Canadian Air Force).[8]

The Case M346 has a sheep's-foot blade, can opener, marlin spike and flat metal scales. Three types of scale material have been noted: alloy, steel and stainless steel.

---

454 This knife has alloy scales which have been stamped with the owner's name of L.J.PARDON P.O. and also bears a faint ↑C mark. The tang is marked

CASE XX

METAL STAMPINGS LTD

---

455 This photograph shows four variations of the knife which are, right to left:

(1) Alloy scales marked PAT LATIMER. Note the acceptance

Plate 454

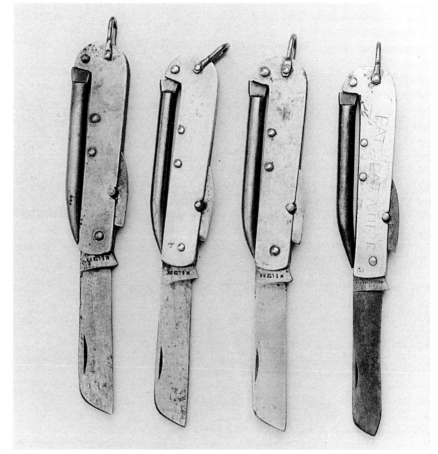

Plate 455

192

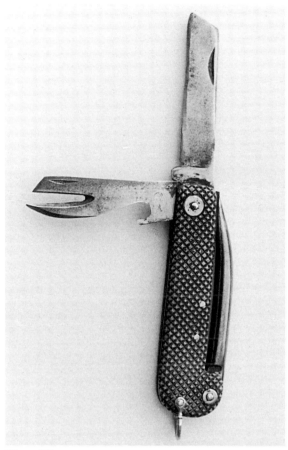

Plate 456   *Plate 457*

mark near the tip of the marlin spike. The blade markings are as on (454).

(2) Steel scales, with brass rivets. The blade is marked M.S. LTD XX.

(3) Stainless scales, blade marked as above.

(4) All-steel construction, blade marked as previous two examples. Blade length 3.625 inches; overall length 8.375 inches.

---

456 There was another maker of the M346 – at least it certainly appears so. Lawrence, in his *Canadian Military Folders of World War One*, records and illustrates an example marked OMF within a rectangle with pointed ends, along with the Canadian acceptance mark. To date, the origin of this trademark has not been established. An example is illustrated here, although the mark looks more like DMF.

---

457 This knife, of the same style as (365), is marked PREMIER within an oval on the can opener, and ENGLAND on the tang of the main blade. According to research undertaken by Lawrence, these knives were made for the Canadian Armed Forces during World War Two and up until about the 1950s. The knives were apparently made by Wostenholm under contract for the Premier Cutlery Co. of Toronto. While not bearing any official marks, this knife and two other examples are marked with servicemen's numbers on the shield.

PART FOUR
INDIA

Probably the knife most associated with the Indian sub-continent is the famed and feared kukri. Found in several design variations, the kukri was not only used by the Gurkhas but also found widespread use among other Indian and Allied troops. Besides the kukri, many other military knives were made in India, particularly during the World War Two period when a wide variety of combat knives and machetes were made for the war against the Japanese.

KUKRI

458 to 461 (458) and (459) show typical World War One specimens of the kukri, with (460) and (461) showing the Indian government inspection marks on the blades. In addition to the marks shown in (461) this piece is marked on the other side of the blade with a large capital E above the name

E BOOTA SINGH & SON

RAWALPINDI

Both pieces have exactly the same form of construction with a blade some 13.25 inches in length and two-piece wood grips secured by two rivets. The base of the hilt has a metal ferrule and the hilt is surmounted by a metal butt plate. Overall length of both examples is 17.75 inches.

Note that (459) is accompanied by a typical kukri sheath which consists of leather over a wooden former. There is a brass chape and the ridge on the sheath is to secure the frog which, as with many specimens, is missing.

462 This kukri is believed to date from World War One and is unusual in that it has an alloy hilt. These are reputed to have been made for a regiment of troops raised by the

Plate 458

Plate 459

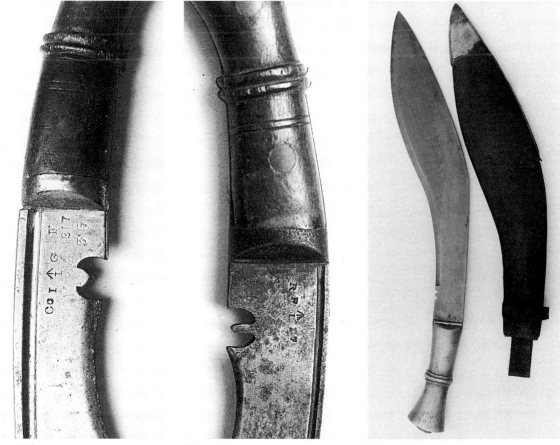

Plate 460   *Plate 461*   *Plate 462*

Maharaja of Jodhur. The blades of these kukris have a different profile to that found on more traditional examples, and some variations do exist between examples: some have blued blades, some are stamped with a crest, others have no blade notch, and some are stamped with a serial number. The sheath that accompanies this pattern is also somewhat unusual in that it is designed so that the knife is withdrawn from the side. Blade length 13.5 inches; overall length 18.25 inches.

463 A First World War soldier carrying one of the alloy-hilted kukris.

464 This large and heavy kukri exhibits a couple of unusual features. Unlike (458) and (459) the hilt is of one piece with the tang peened over at the pommel. The other unusual fea-

ture is that the markings,

CO I ↑ G 1915 FW
23

are stamped along the back edge of the blade. The sheath is marked 714 at the throat. Blade length 13.75 inches; overall length 17.75 inches..

465 to 467 These kukris are a complete mystery with regard to the unit/troops they were made for, though I have seen a photograph showing these being worn by British troops in India between the wars. They are also unlike other kukris in that they can be used in a stabbing mode and are accompanied by a sheath of a different design to the norm. As can be seen

Plate 463

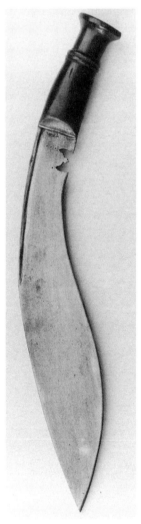

Plate 464

Plate 465

from (465) the blade is very plain with no notch or fuller and has been hand-forged, the hammer marks clearly visible on close examination. The blade is marked

COI ↑1921

I

and the grips are secured by three rivets; it is stamped 5 over 148. Blade length 12.75 inches; overall length 17.5 inches.

(466) and (467) show a kukri complete with its sheath and it is of better quality than (465). The knife is totally unmarked but the heavy-duty leather sheath, secured down one side by copper rivets, is marked at the front c↑15, and Co 20 at the throat. Blade length 13 inches; overall length 17.625 inches.

468 Dating from World War Two this kukri is almost iden-

tical to (458) except that the hilt lacks the ridges. The blade is marked

PIONEER

CALCUTA

43

The sheath is of the same pattern as shown in (459) and is marked co 1944 over c↑644. Blade length 13.25 inches; overall length 17.5 inches.

469 This kukri is of the same pattern as (468) and is just marked on the blade with an M over 43. The sheath that accompanies this example is shown at (470); it is covered with black leather rather than the brown normally found, has no chape, and the frog has two belt straps and lace-up fastening. Blade length 13 inches; overall length 17.5 inches.

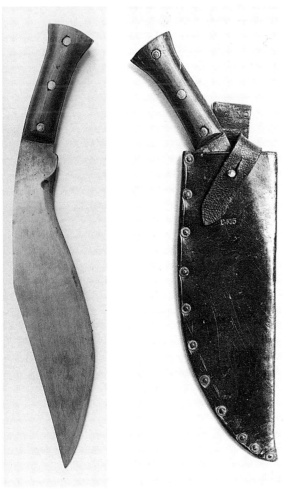

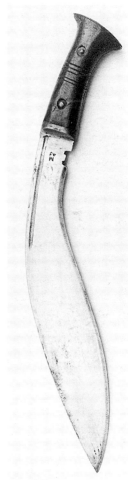

Plate 466   *Plate 467*   *Plate 468*   *Plate 469*

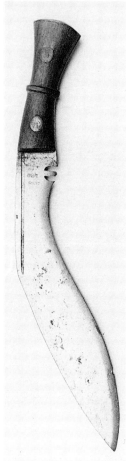

Plate 470   *Plate 471*   *Plate 472*

471 Several of these World War Two kukris have been observed with the original ordnance marks overstamped INDIA. The original marks have been almost erased by this overstamping, but appear to be L168 over I↑D. The grip is plainer than found on many other kukris and is secured by two steel rivets. The overstamping on these knives was in likelihood added after the war when the kukris were sold as souvenirs. Blade length 12 inches; overall length 16.75 inches.

472 Very few of these kukris have been observed. As will be noted the blade has no fullers or blade notch and the grips are very basic. This example is stamped on the blade SIRAJ 43 and the hilt is stamped with very small letters s over 177.

473 This kukri is of the same pattern as (472) but is unmarked and accompanied by a most unusual scabbard. This is made of wood with the throat strengthened with brass and fitted with a leather belt loop.

474 Four specimens of this small kukri have been noted, and while not bearing any official markings they do bear the mark CMW, which is the same mark as is found on (495). One example also has the CMW mark on the front of the sheath, and this particular example has associations with the RAF and may well have been carried as a survival knife. Blade length 8.625 inches; overall length 12.5 inches.

475 While of more usual shape, this kukri is also of small dimensions and comes in a pouch-type sheath. The knife is unmarked but has the overall appearance of being an issue military item. It is thought that, as with the previous example, this too was made as a survival weapon. Blade length 8.5 inches; overall length 13 inches.

476 The date of this kukri is unknown but it is possibly postwar. Both hilt and blade are similar in style to World War One examples but the only marks on the blade are the num-

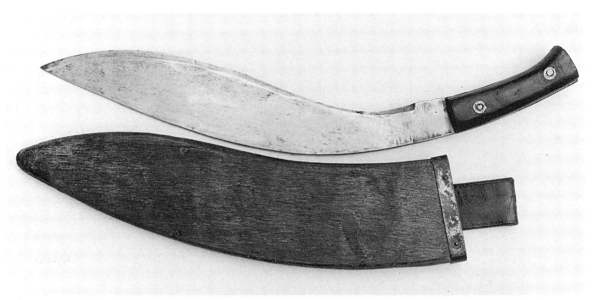

Plate 473

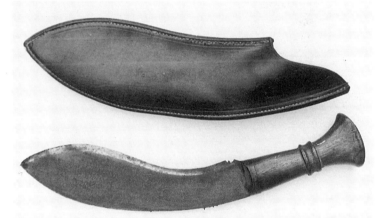

Plate 475

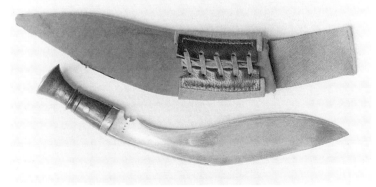

Plate 474

Plate 476

bers 3441. The black leather sheath has been overwrapped with olive green cloth and is fitted with a webbing frog which is marked with a ↑. Blade length 12.5 inches; overall length 16.25 inches.

---

477 An example of the style of kukri which is still current issue. The blade is somewhat smaller than World War One and Two versions and the hilt is of black horn with the tang peened over at the brass pommel cap. The black leather sheath has a laced frog accompanied by the two small knives. An article published by the National Army Museum states that current issue kukris are not marked.[1] This piece is, however, stamped on the blade

ORDEP

NEPAL

7/80

Another similar example has been observed marked

DHARAN

NEPAL

87

Dharan is the Gurkha recruiting base in Nepal.

INDIAN MACHETES

To meet the needs of the forces in India, large numbers of crude but effective square-pointed machetes were locally made during World War Two. These machetes, all of which utilised the same type of blade and scabbard style, come with a wide variety of hilt designs. In addition to these

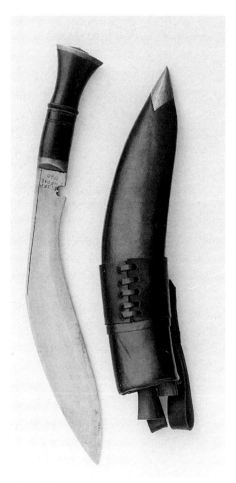

Plate 477

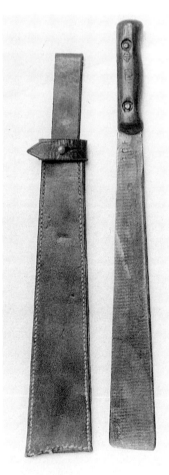

Plate 478

Plate 479

locally made pieces machetes made by the Americans also saw service in India.

---

478 & 479 These photographs show a typical example of the square-pointed machete along with its side opening sheath. The example shown has a 14.125-inch blade which has been very crudely ground, and is fitted with wood grips secured by two rivets. The blade is marked GCF over 45 and the hilt is marked

I ↑ C
I

within a diamond and 197 within an oblong. On the other side of the grip 134 is stamped within a diamond. The heavy leather sheath is marked on the back CO 1943 over C↑645 along with 15 at the base of the belt loop. Overall length 19.125 inches.

---

480 This photograph shows typical hilt styles found on these pieces. The marks found on these three variations are:
(1) Left – on blade 421 within a diamond along with

MACH MKIII
M.L. 45

(2) Centre – on blade KCG, on sheath CO 1943 over ↑840
(3) Right – is the hilt of (478).

481 Two further examples of these square-pointed machetes with unusual hilts. The right example has a 12-inch blade and is 16 inches overall. The lefr specimen is 20 inches overall and has a 14-inch blade.

---

482 A very unusual presentation version of this type of machete. Very similar to the right specimen in (481) the hilt of this piece is of black horn with plated ferrule and pommel cap. The circular crossguard is of alloy and the plated blade is engraved

PRESENTED BY
ALL OFFICERS
1ST BN THE ASSAM REGT
TO
LT COL E H M PARSONS DSO

Lt-Col Parsons was the Commanding Officer of the 1st Battalion of the Assam Regiment from February 1945 to June 1947. The piece is accompanied by the standard sheath. Blade length 12.125 inches; overall length 16.625 inches.

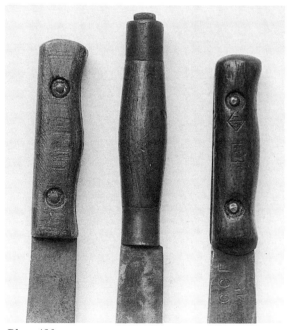

Plate 480

Plate 481

Plate 482

483 This Chindit machete has a blade of much better quality than the other specimens observed; its accompanying sheath also exhibits some unusual features. The blade is 13.5 inches in length and 3 inches wide at the tip. The crude specimens are generally only about 2 inches wide at this point. The sheath has a belt loop fixed by a buckle which allows its length to be adjusted, and there is a fixing front and back for a tie-down strap. Overall length 19.875 inches.

484 This short version of the square-ended machete is believed to be Chindit and/or Indian paratrooper issue, the sheath being designed for attachment to the leg. The machete has a 10.5-inch blade with a very short and cramped hilt which has its ferrule soldered into place. The sheath is similar in style to that which accompanies (478) except that it has no belt loop provided; instead it has two (one is missing in this example) leg straps. The piece has no official marks but has the name J.PRIMROSE (see also 493) on the front of the sheath. Overall length 14.375 inches.

485 This machete, while US-made, is accompanied by a sheath made in India. Its use by Indian troops is also supported by photographic evidence. Made by the American Fork and Hoe Co. of Geneva, Ohio, the 18-inch blade bears their trademark of TRUE TEMPER along with the marks U.S. and TT-18-B over the year 1943. Examples with the same marks are known to have been used by US troops during World War Two but the examples recorded by Cole have an olive-green plastic hilt rather than the black plastic in this example.[2] The sheath is of tan leather and is stamped on the back with the date 1944 and c↑544.

Several examples of these US-made machete/Indian-made sheath combinations have been noted, and it would appear that the machetes were shipped to India to be paired with locally made sheaths. Blade length 17.75 inches; overall length 23 inches.

COMMANDO KNIVES

Both Hughes and Thompson list these knives as Australian; Stephens, however, states that they are

Plate 483   Plate 484   Plate 485

Indian, and I support this identification.[3] The standard of workmanship and the type of sheath which accompanies these knives all indicate Indian origin. These knives usually have rather poorly finished brass hilts with brass crossguards which are soldered onto the tangs.

486 This knife has a bright finish blade some 6.75 inches in length with an overall length of 11.375 inches. The sheath is correctly made for the knife and not a cut down bayonet scabbard as sometimes reported.

487 This example has a blued blade 6.75 inches in length. The sheath is more traditional in design but has a very long chape. The hilt retaining strap with press-stud is a replacement. Overall length 11.375 inches.

488 This Commando knife has a thicker crossguard than either of the two previous specimens and also has a blade only 5.5 inches in length. Close examination of the blade indicates that it was either made like this or has been very professionally reground. Overall length 10.25 inches.

PARATROOPER KNIVES

These wood-gripped combat knives have over the years gained the designation of Paratrooper knives, but it is not known if they were specifically made for issue to such troops. However, examples which have a specially made webbing leg strap attached to the sheath have been noted. Several variations are known, all of which follow the same design of a double-edged blade with central fuller, square shank ricasso, oval crossguard and wood grips cut with three grooves and secured by two steel rivets. Various marks can be found on these knives, and those marked M.I.L. are believed to have been made by Metal Industries Ltd;

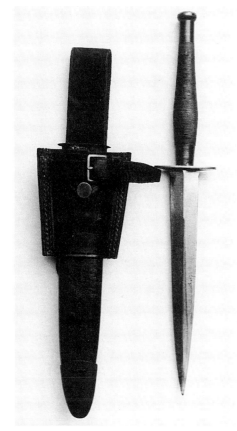

Plate 486

Plate 487

Plate 488

although some authorities state that it stands for Metal Industries Lahore. I have, however, seen an Indian-made Bowie knife marked METAL INDUS-TRIES LTD, which seems to confirm the meaning of the stamp. Another example has been noted marked with ATD over 43 for Army Traders Dhuran and the year 1943.

---

489 This shows the three versions illustrated by Hughes in *Primer Part 1*.

---

490 This example is marked on the ricasso MK.I.42 over M.I.L. with the hilt stamped

IG

20

The sheath of the same type which accompanies (486) is marked on the front

SA

20

The crossguard of this example is made of steel. Blade length

6.75 inches; overall length 10.75 inches.

---

491 This fine example of the Paratrooper knife has a white metal crossguard rather than the steel found on the previous example. It is also marked on the hilt and on the reverse of the sheath M & CO. The hilt is also stamped with the mark of SA over 251.

---

492 This example is totally unmarked and has a brass crossguard.

COMBAT BOWIES

These knives were manufactured in India during World War Two. They are generally known on the UK collecting scene as Chindit Bowies, and come in a number of variations. Examples (493) to (496) have wood grips, examples similar to (496) have been noted with horn grips.

---

493 This specimen belonged to J. Primrose (see 484). The knife has a 7.5-inch Bowie blade, thin white metal oval-shaped crossguard and wood grips secured by three steel riv-

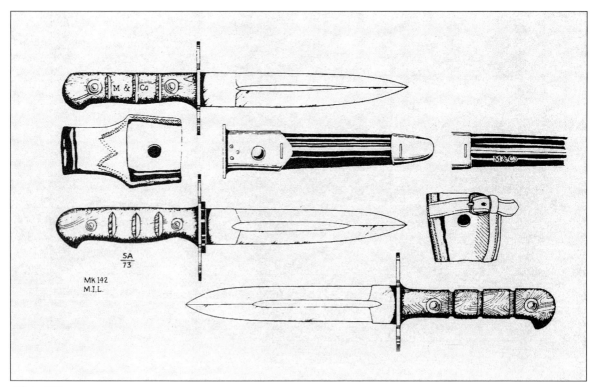

Plate 489

Plate 490   Plate 491   Plate 492

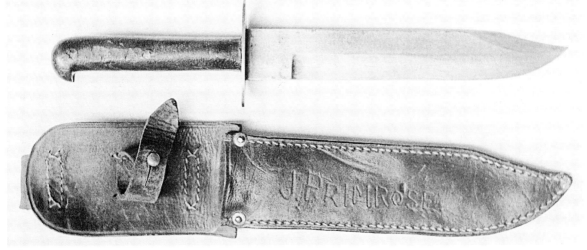

Plate 493

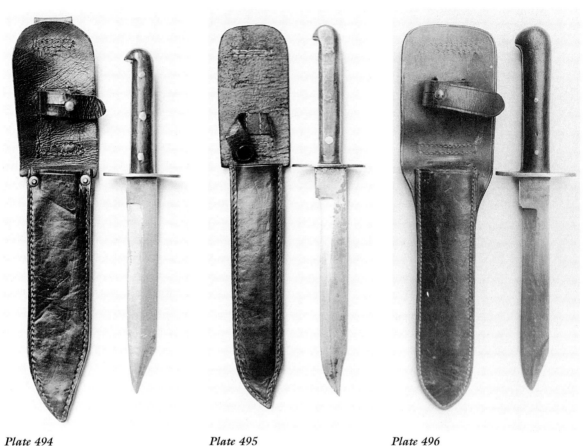

Plate 494 *Plate 495* *Plate 496*

ets. The leather sheath exhibits similar workmanship to that found on other Indian-made sheaths and has a hilt retaining strap with brass pillar stud. Other than the name on the sheath there are no other marks. Overall length 12 inches.

494 This is virtually a scaled-down version of (493). The style of the blade tip is somewhat unusual but could be attributed to bad grinding. The hilt is smaller than (493) and the crossguard is of brass. Blade length 7.875 inches; overall length 11 inches.

495 A variation with narrow blade and steel crossguard. The grips are made of a different type of wood and are secured by three brass rivets. The grips are also rather flat, not rounded as in the previous specimens. The sheath also differs in that it is made of black rather than brown leather and is of an all-stitched construction with no rivets. The hilt retainer has a press-stud rather than a pillar stud. This knife and others like it are the only versions of these combat Bowies which are marked. This example is marked on the tang C.M.W. and Hughes records an example marked GMW 1943.[4] Blade

length 7.375 inches; overall length 11.875 inches.

496 This variation has a crossguard made from 0.125-inch thick white metal. The sheath is also unusual in that it appears to have been made for a double-edged blade, but I have never seen or heard of one of these knives with such a blade. Blade length 6.75 inches; overall length 11.25 inches.

497 Two Chindits with the 'Chindit Bowies' in wear. Also note the square-pointed machetes, one thrust through the belt, the other held.

INDIAN-MADE V-44

Obviously copied from the American V-44s these generally crudely manufactured knives are attributed as Chindit issue, though it is likely they could have been used by aircrew as the V-44 was originally designed by the Americans as an aircrew

Plate 497

survival knife. These knives are rare and are virtually never found in anything like good condition. All the examples illustrated have wood grips, but examples are known with grips made from horn.

498 This Chindit V-44 has a 9.75-inch blade made from heavy stock. The large oval crossguard is of white metal, and the grips are cut with three grooves and secured by two rivets. The leather sheath is a scaled-up version of the type that accompanies (493). Overall length 14.5 inches

499 The blade of this piece is 8.5 inches long, the oval crossguard is of brass and the one-piece wood grip is cut with three grooves and secured by a single rivet. Overall length 13.375 inches.

500 Almost identical to (499), the crossguard of this version is of white metal. The knife is accompanied by a sheath which

Plate 498

Plate 499

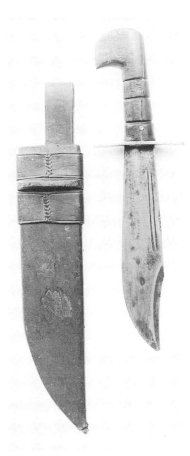

Plate 500

is far too long for the blade. It could, however, be of a type designed for these V-44s. Constructed in the same manner as a kukri sheath, i.e. leather over a wooden body, it is fitted with a leather frog. Blade length 9.25 inches; overall length 14.25 inches.

501 A rather interesting variation of the Indian V-44 which has several features not observed on the other examples. The hardwood grip is not grooved, the brass crossguard is of the same shape as that found on US-made V-44s, and the blade has virtually parallel edges. The sheath is made of leather over a wooden body and has a ridge which is presumably to secure a frog. The ridge is also fitted with a pillar stud which may have been for securing a strap which wrapped across the crossguard. Blade length 9.125 inches; overall length 14 inches.

KNUCKLE KNIVES

502 The American collector/author Adrian Van Dyk lists these knives as 'Gurkha Paratroop issue'.[5] While I do not know what evidence Van Dyk had to support this identifica-

tion, these very heavy knives were certainly made for the non-Caucasian hand. The Middle East Commando knuckleduster hilt has finger stalls which would only be suitable for someone with a small hand. The interesting feature of this knife is its large double-edged bolo-type blade similar to that found on the Australian machete bayonet. The knife is unmarked and no example with a correct sheath has yet been observed. Blade length 10 inches; overall length 15.125 inches.

503 Again, this Middle East Commando-style hilt has small finger stalls. While the sheath is similar in style to that which accompanies the Middle East, the workmanship is like that found on other sheaths of Indian origin. Only a few examples of this pattern of knife have been noted. Blade length 6 inches; overall length 11.125 inches.

504 & 505 Three variations of this knife have been noted: two are recorded here, the other having a plain brass hilt. The correct pattern of sheath for these knives is illustrated by Hughes, and this again is almost certainly of Indian origin.[6] (504) has an alloy hilt with chequered pattern. (505) has a

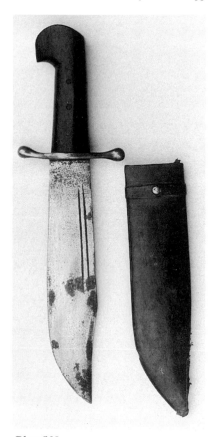

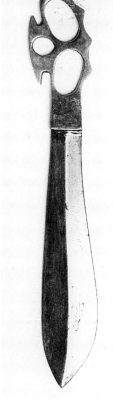

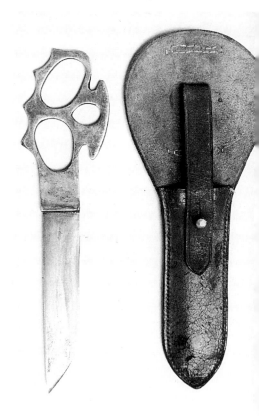

Plate 501 *Plate 502* *Plate 503*

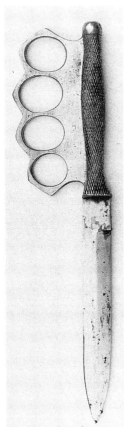

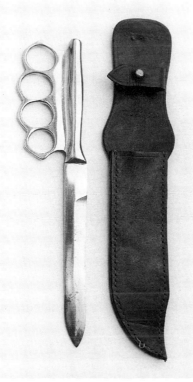

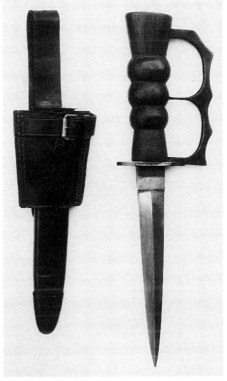

Plate 505

Plate 506

Plate 507

Plate 504

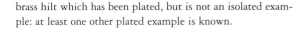

brass hilt which has been plated, but is not an isolated example: at least one other plated example is known.

506 Almost certainly made in India for Allied forces during World War Two, the Commando-type blade is almost identical to examples illustrated by Buerlein.[7] The knife has a large oval crossguard and chunky wood grip. The interesting aspect of the hilt is, however, the brass knuckle guard. This has almost certainly been added as an afterthought but is contemporary with the knife. The guard is fixed to the crossguard by two pins while the other two junctures with the hilt are simply recessed into the grip. The knife is unmarked. The sheath is made from the same scabbards which are used with (489) to (492). One other example of this knife is known to exist. Blade length 7 inches; overall length 12 inches.

507 More ceremonial than combat, this knife does help confirm the Indian origin of (502) and (503). Except for the finish, which is nickel-plated, the hilt is identical to that found on these two pieces in respect of size. The hilt is stamped on one side JODHPUR CITY VOLUNTEER CORP No (there is no number) along with a crest, which is presumably that of the city

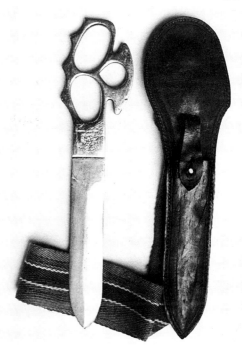

of Jodhpur. The other side of the hilt is marked

AUSPICIOUS

WEDDING

PRINCESS JODHPUR

APRIL 22ND 1950

The blade is double-edged and is riveted to the hilt. The sheath is of very poor quality and is provided with a coloured cloth sash. Blade length 6 inches; overall length 11 inches.

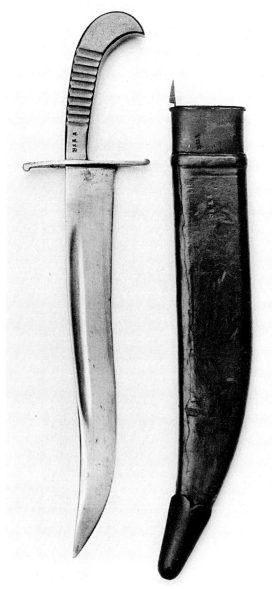

Plate 508

MISCELLANEOUS KNIVES

508 Believed to be styled on the Indo-Persian khanjar, this knife is almost certainly of Indian military origin. The sheath construction is very similar to that associated with kukri sheaths and the piece bears a four-digit serial number like that found on (476) The knife is all-metal construction with a 9-inch recurving blade which has fullers on both sides. The crossguard has a hole in it which mates with the catch on the sheath, and the ribbed hilt is stamped 3111. The sheath is of leather over a wooden body and is fitted with metal chape and top mount. Both top mount and sheath body are marked 3111. The sheath has a ridge to hold the frog and the top mount is fitted with a catch which latches into the hole in the crossguard. Overall length 12.625 inches.

509 A scarce example of the Chindit wrist dagger or Orde knife. These knives were reputedly made for escape and evasion use by the Chindits of Orde Wingate's 77th Infantry Brigade. It is believed that these knives were also used by the SOE when they operated in the Far East. The knife has a 5-inch double-edged blade, white metal crossguard and black horn hilt. The sheath is described by some authorities as being a shortened Commando knife sheath.[8] However, while it is reminiscent of the lower part of such a sheath it is in fact correctly made for the knife. The arm or leg strap is attached to a stitch tab and the blued chape is smaller than that found on a Commando knife. The knife is held in the sheath by an internal leather rib which firmly holds the blade. Overall length 7.25 inches.

510 The factory-manufactured sheath almost certainly indicates that this conversion from a sword/cutlass is official. The blade has been shortened to 11.625 inches and the knuckle guard or bowl removed. The blade retains its original marks of WILKINSON on the back edge and ↑ over 1915 IG, and ↑ over ID on the ricasso. Despite the World War One origins of the blade the conversion probably dates from World War Two. Overall length 16 inches.

511 A very plain combat knife almost certainly made in India during World War Two. The knife has a double-edged blade, a steel crossguard of exactly the same form as that found on (490) and wood grips held in place with three brass wood screws. The knife is unmarked. Blade length 5.625 inches; overall length 10.25 inches.

512 The blade of this knife appears to have been taken from an Indian No.1 Mk II Bayonet. The blade has been shortened to 8 inches, fitted with an oval crossguard and wood grips which are secured in place with two screwbolts. The sheath

Plate 509

Plate 510

Plate 512

Plate 511

has been cut down to suit. The conversion is almost certainly World War Two period. Overall length 12.375 inches.

POCKET KNIVES

Despite the large volume of production of pocket knives in Britain during World War Two it would appear that those for the forces in India were manufactured locally. The quality of these Indian-made knives is generally low, especially those with the red fibre grips. The later patterns with horn grips are more substantial.

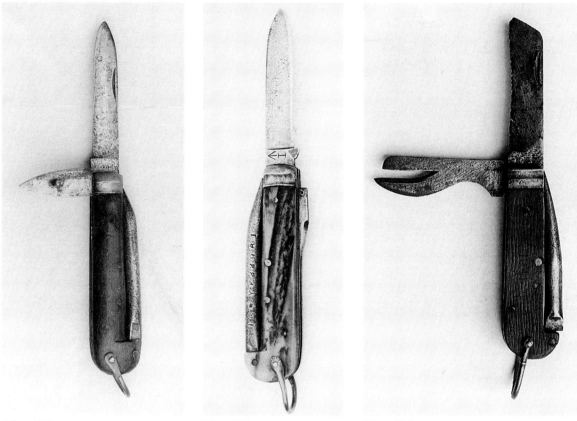

Plate 513   Plate 514   Plate 515

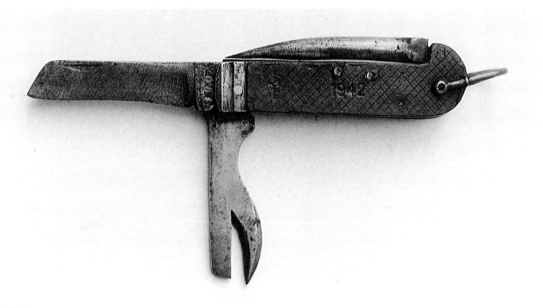

Plate 516

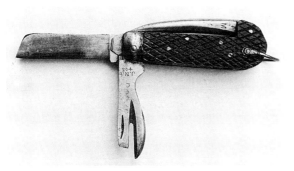

Plate 517

513 This Indian-made pocket knife could date any time from World War One up until and possibly including World War Two. The knife is the same type as the British 6363/1905 pattern but has wood grips. The main blade is marked nizamabal.

514 This example of Pattern 6363/1905 has staghorn grips and is marked on the blade with a large $\uparrow$I stamp. The marlin spike is marked 1GR YK22961 (1st Gurkha Rifles?). The knife was made by George Butler and Co. Blade length 3.625 inches; overall length 8.5 inches.

515 This pocket knife has red fibre grips which have a simulated staghorn pattern. The grip is stamped 1941 and the blade NKF. Blade length 2.75 inches; overall length 6.25 inches

516 This example is also by NKF and is dated 1942. It has a light criss-cross pattern on the grips.

517. This pattern is more substantially made, and has grips of crudely hand-chequered horn. These knives are usually very well-marked, the example shown being marked on the can opener

JNB

+45

along with what appears to be P broad arrow 2/0. The marlin spike is marked with a M. Marks noted on other examples include ASR broad arrow 49 and F.45, NDUD over 42 with P broad arrow 5, and JAYNEROY over 1943.

518 From the Maleham and Yeoman daybook comes this illustration of a knife described as 'Clasp Knife for Orderly's Dressing Case, Indian Stores Pattern 5328'. The knife has a single sheep's-foot blade and flat nickel silver scales marked with a $\uparrow$ over I.

Plate 518

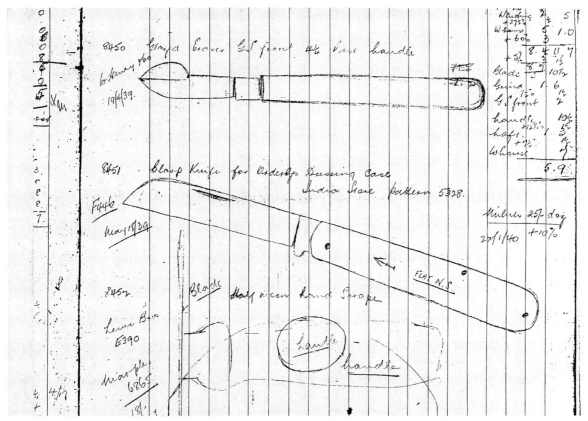

PART FIVE
NEW ZEALAND

O ther than the few knives illustrated I know of no other native New Zealand military knives although it is likely that others do exist. It is also very likely that the New Zealand military used or use knives made elsewhere as some limited photographic evidence does exist to indicate that British machetes of the Golok type were used by the New Zealand SAS.[1]

I should also mention that some confusion does exist among various authorities regarding the origins of the alloy-hilted knives (519 to 523). Some examples have been classified by previous authors as Australian, but while some are unmarked others have New Zealand markings. As far as I am aware no examples bearing marks indicating Australian origin have been observed, so I believe that such knives are of New Zealand manufacture. These alloy-hilted knives come in a variety of forms but all have the same type of moulded chequering on the hilt. They appear to have been popular with American forces, Cole illustrating examples in his book on US military knives.[2]

519 This knife has a 5.75-inch Bowie blade onto which is cast an alloy hilt with integral crossguard. The blade is marked

NZ

CUTLERS CO

AUCKLAND

The sheath is made from a converted USMC Medical Corpsman's knife sheath. Overall length 10.5 inches.

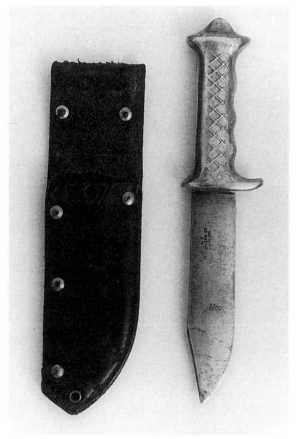

Plate 519

520 Of slightly different form to (519), this example is very interesting in that its blade is marked RNZAF (Royal New Zealand Air Force). The blade is some 6 inches in length and has a longer clip back to the blade than (519). Like the previous specimen the hilt is cast onto the blade but it has a longer, more upswept crossguard and does not have the bulge at the

Plate 520

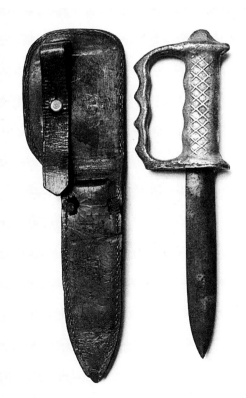

Plate 521

pommel. Overall length is 10.25 inches. As will be noted the sheath is correctly manufactured and not made from converted stock. The belt flap is well marked with a: 22B/N21, a crown stamp with AD within the crown, and a circle containing the marks

M

T   I

2

An American collector has a similar knife with the sheath marked RNZAF 22B/N28.

---

521 Utilising a similar type of grip but with the added refinement of a knuckle bow, this knife is fitted with a double-edged spear-point blade. The heavy-duty leather sheath is the correct pattern for this type of knife, which in this case has been painted green. Neither knife nor sheath bears any markings. Blade length 6.187 inches; overall length 10.875 inches.

---

522 This knife uses the same type of hilt as (521) but has a 6-inch Bowie blade stamped

NZ CUTLERS CO

AUCKLAND

Similar examples marked AKD REG and TUI REGD have been noted. A very rare version fitted with a large Bowie-style

Plate 522   *Plate 523*

blade with lengths varying between 9.5 and 10.75 inches have also been noted.

523 Members of the Royal New Zealand Air Force photographed during World War Two. Note the knuckle knife in wear. It is assumed that this is the same pattern as shown in (522) carried in a sheath like that shown in (520).

524 An example of this spear-pointed double-edged blade knuckle knife was reputedly obtained in New Zealand by a US serviceman during World War Two. The cast brass hilt has individual finger stalls with projections on the knuckles. The New Zealand origins of these knives is confirmed by the personalisation of this piece: the grip is marked with a KIWI and the initials NZ. Blade length 7 inches; overall length not known.

525 These knuckle knives are of crude construction and from information received from the Queen Elizabeth II Army Memorial Museum it appears they were provided by a local blacksmith in Auckland during World War Two for the NZ Home Guard. Approximately 100 were made. The knife shown has a 5.25-inch blade with half round wood grips secured by two rivets. The knuckle guard has been welded in place and the grip has two large leather washers which protect

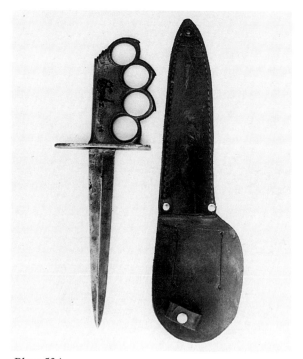

Plate 524

the hand. Variations with a longer blade and with a different form of guard have been noted.

526 An unusual Commando knife, possibly of post-war origin, which originated in New Zealand and has the brass crossguard marked NZ along with a ↑. The unusual feature of this knife is the fact that its Third Pattern-style hilt is made of brass which is fixed directly onto the tang, there being no pommel nut. The sheath that accompanies the knife is a commercial variety which is almost certainly post-war. The knife, when obtained, had a label affixed which stated: 'Rare special forces combat knife from Auckland NZ forces store Wythrou'. Blade length 6.785 inches; overall length 11 inches.

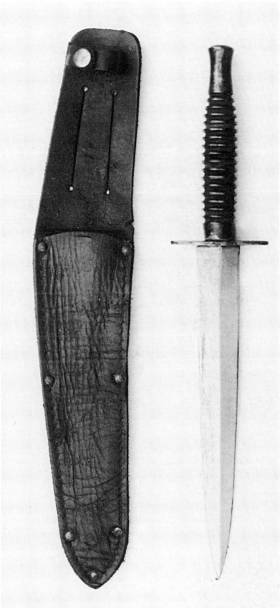

Plate 525

Plate 526

PART SIX
UNIDENTIFIED

The knives in this section are believed to be of British or Commonwealth origin but to date have not been positively identified. If a reader has any further information I would appreciate hearing from them.

527 This superb knife first illustrated by Hughes is of a quality which cannot be adequately shown either by my photograph or Hughes' line drawing.[1] The knife has a 10-inch double-edged blade, steel crossguard which is machined out on the underside, beautifully turned wood grips secured by a single screw bolt and a substantial blued steel pommel. Overall length is 14.125 inches. The sheath, which may provide some clues as to the origin of the knife, is very well made. The sheath has a metal throat piece or locket which has a projection which secures the frog. The style and workmanship are very similar to that found with some British 1903 Bayonet and Canadian Ross bayonet scabbards, and it is possible that the knife originated in either of these two countries.

528 Like the previous knife it is the sheath which may provide clues as to the knife's origin. The 7.375-inch single-edged blade appears to have been designed for hacking rather than fighting and would possibly indicate that the knife was designed for survival rather than combat. The hilt is fitted with grips made of a brown plastic-like material which are well-contoured to fit the hand and secured by three brass rivets. The overall length is 12.25 inches and the blade is stamped DHF. The sheath, of heavy leather with dark brown tan, exhibits similar workmanship to that found with the sheaths associated with some Indian-made knives. The press-stud on the hilt retainer is of the early Newey type that is found on the First Pattern F-S sheaths.

529 This bolo-type machete has a cast alloy hilt similar in shape to the wood hilt found on some of the British Type D survival knives and a very heavy blade which is made of

Plate 527

Plate 528

Plate 529

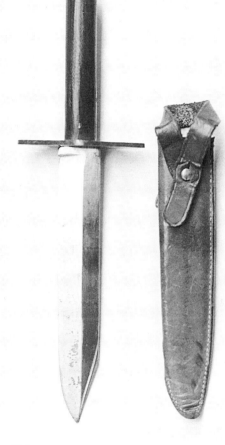

Plate 530

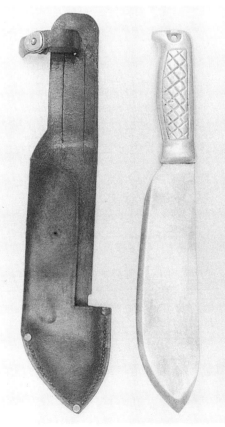

0.25-inch stock, 2.375 inches at its widest point. The blade is 9.25 inches and the overall length is 14.125 inches. The sheath is made of very thin leather which is cut away down one side to allow for easy withdrawal. The hilt retainer is fitted with a 'lift-the-dot' type catch like that fitted to some of the early patterns of Type D sheaths.

530 While no positive identification of this knife has been possible it is thought that it may be of Australian origin. The knife has a very high-quality blade some 7.125 inches in length, and a very large crossguard which provides considerable protection to the hand. The hilt is plain consisting of half round grips secured by two small rivets. For some strange reason the back of the tang has a hole drilled part of the way into it. The sheath is not unlike that which accompanies the Robbins shortsword, having a wrap-around hilt securing strap.

531 This Commando knife in the Third Pattern style has its brass crossguard and brass hilt soldered onto the tang in the same manner as the Indian pattern Commando knives. This piece came out of Australia and was accompanied by an Australian-style sheath; its true origins are, however, not known.

532 Although this knife has not been positively identified it is very likely that it is of Indian or Middle East origin. The roughly chequered brass hilt has been hammered onto the tang, and the thick brass crossguard is not soldered in place as on knives of known Indian origin. The blade is unusual in that it has a square shank style ricasso which is stamped TEST-ED over what appears to be RD. Blade length 6.5 inches; over-all length 11.25 inches.

533 This sheath purchased without a knife is obviously designed to take a machete of the standard British pattern (see 247). The sheath is made of green webbing with a hilt strap of green leather and the throat strengthened with a stiff fibre material. The front of the sheath is marked C.A.U.C. – 124255 but bears no other marks which would aid identification.

534 This knuckle knife is of almost certain Australian or New Zealand origin, but which is not clear. An example illustrated in an American magazine article on Australian/New Zealand knives does not identify the actual country of origin.[2] Although contemporary with the knife, the sheath, which is marked with the name of the Australian maker BONNEY & CLARKE, may not be original to the knife and cannot thus be guaranteed as a firm clue to the country of origin.

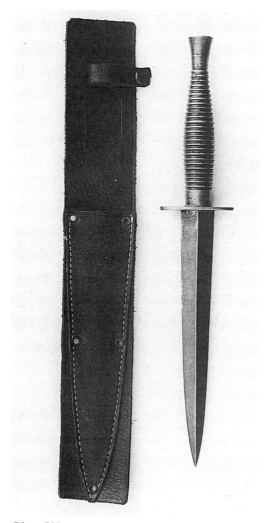

Plate 531

Plate 532

Plate 533

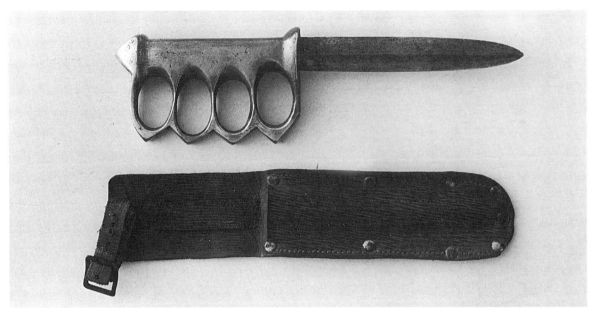

Plate 534

535 There are some indications that this large bolo-style knife may be Indian in origin. The serial number marked on the knife is similar to that found on some military kukris, and the sheath construction is also like that found with kukris. The sheath is also serial marked, but the numbers are not matching.

Plate 535

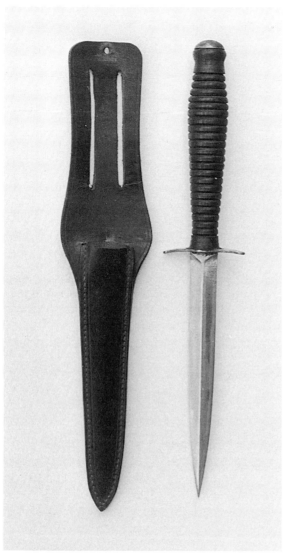

Plate 536

Plate 537

536 This and the following knife came out of Australia, but to date they have not been firmly identified. (536) is of very high quality with a turned wood hilt with steel pommel cap, steel crossguard and slim double-edged blade. The sheath likewise is of high quality and somewhat reminiscent in style of that which accompanies (272). The knife is devoid of a maker's marks. The only possible clue to its origins is an old sticker on the reverse of the sheath which states GREGSTEEL F/KNIFE AUST. However, enquiries in Australia have failed to identify this as a Gregsteel-made product. Blade length 6.125 inches; overall length 11.125 inches.

537 This massive V-44/Bowie-style knife is unmarked, but a military connection is found on the sheath which has a faint broad arrow mark over what appears to be 40 on the belt flap. The 10.75-inch blade is plain with no fullers, the crossguard of cast alloy is some 0.75 inches thick and the grips are secured by three hollow rivets. Note that the hilt shape is similar to that found on (376). Overall length 16.25 inches.

PART SEVEN
KNIFE PATENTS

Very few British or Commonwealth military knives have had their designs supported by a patent or registered design. Where the knife is well known, and where specimens have actually been available for study, these have been included in the main text. However, a number of designs are only known from the patent records, and these are described below.

538 An interesting combination weapon developed by M. Lesko and registered as Patent No. 122142 on 9 August 1918.

---

539 Although the designer, a Rupert Hughes, was an American citizen with an address in New York State, this design was registered as a British patent, number 134789, on 2 July 1919. The patent drawings are reproduced here, and the extensive text, running into some five pages, describes the weapon as a 'Trench Knife' which can be secured to the back

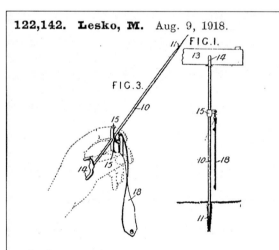

122,142. Lesko, M. Aug. 9, 1918.

Aiming-rests; carrying side-arms; daggers.—Consists of a combined arming-rest and weapon comprising a shaft 10 pointed at one end 11 and provided at the other with a fork 14 adapted to support the gun 13, as shown in Fig. 1. A forwardly-directed fork 15 is secured to the shaft a short distance from the end to serve with the other fork as a hand-grip when the device is used as a weapon, as shown in Fig. 3. A strap 18 is provided for securing the device to the belt or the like.

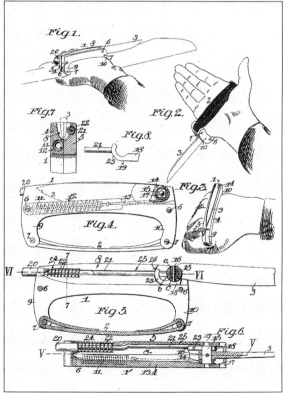

Plate 538

Plate 539

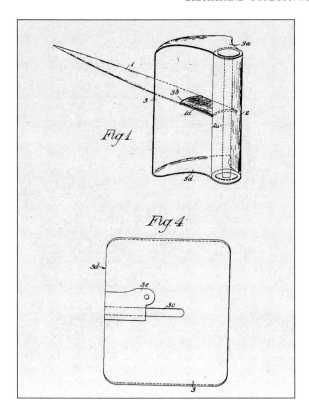

Fig.1.

Fig.4.

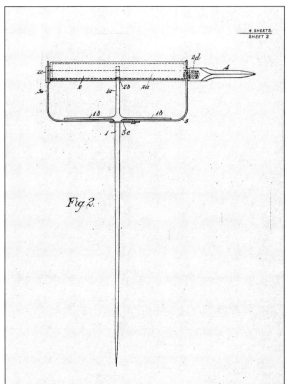

Fig.2.

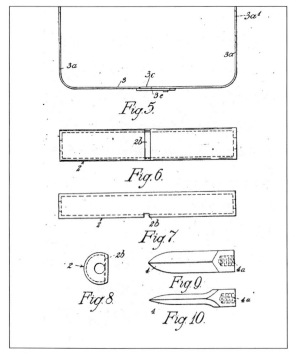

Fig.5.

Fig.6.

Fig.7.

Fig.8.

Fig.9.

Fig.10.

All Plate 540

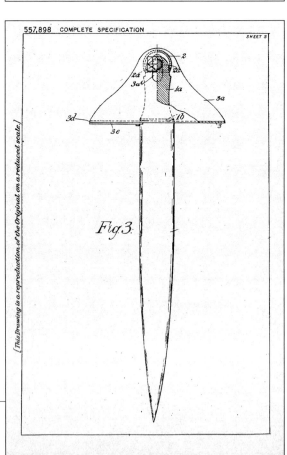

557,898 COMPLETE SPECIFICATION

SHEET 3

Fig.3.

[This Drawing is a reproduction of the Original on a reduced scale.]

of the hand by a strap and thus leave the palm of the hand open with the fingers free to grasp an object. Another object of the invention is to provide a trench knife which may be instantaneously opened by striking an extension thereon against any convenient member, such as the stock of a gun or the knee of the wearer.

---

540 This patent specification No.557898 was accepted on 9 December 1943. The design was registered by a Sydney Temple Leopold McLaglen. McLaglen's design specification runs into some six pages of text; this extract from the text illustrates his thinking in producing this design:

The principal aim of the invention is to provide a thrusting dagger such that while it is still retained in the hand freedom is afforded for the fingers to perform a variety of manipulative actions without material inconvenience and enables other offensive weapons such, for example, as a revolver or a rifle, to be used in the one same hand.

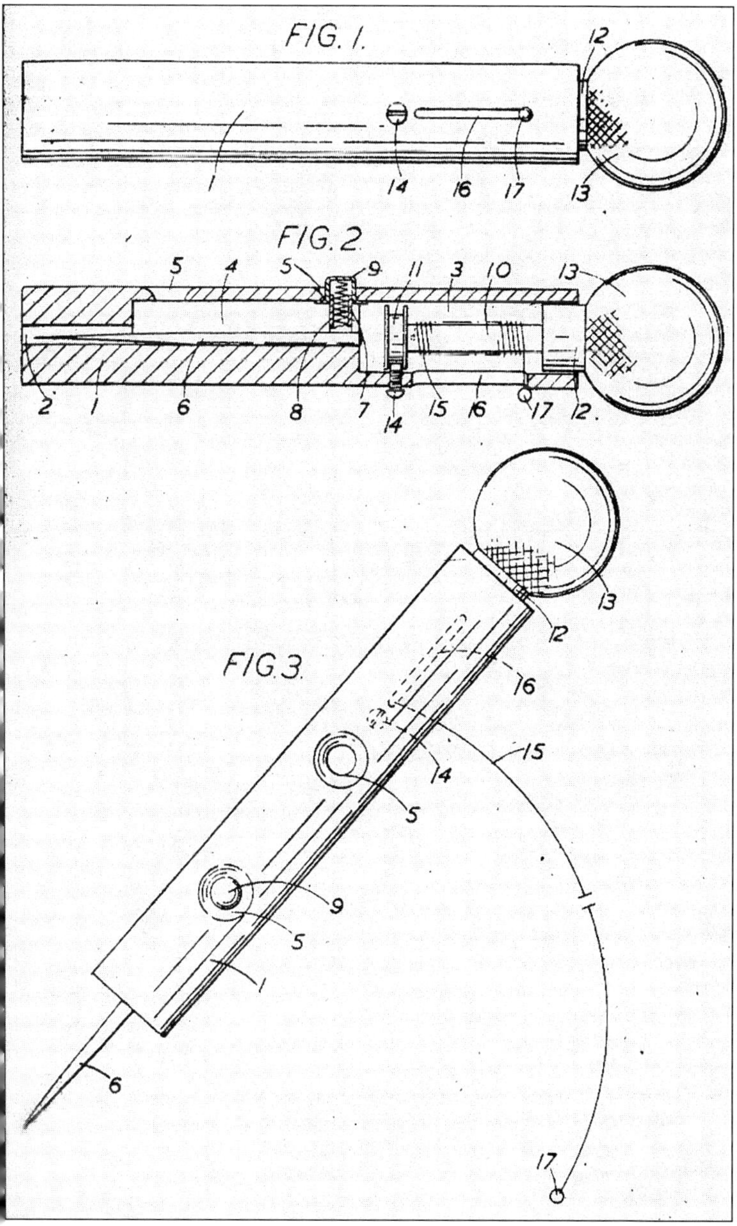

---

541 Specification 559747 was accepted on 3 March 1944, and while a number of specimens have appeared in collecting circles, it is a possibility that they may be of recent manufacture. Designed by John Edward Peskett and Sydney Temple Leopold McLaglen, this is a combination weapon rather than a pure knife. The weapon comprises a cosh, garrotte and retractable spike blade.

FIG. 1.

FIG. 2.

FIG. 3.

Plate 541

542 A further combination weapon, designed by G. D. B. Puckle in 1943. In this case the knife is attached to the hilt of a pistol or revolver in a housing which also forms a knuckleduster. A variation on this design was covered by Patent 559146.

543 A copy of the registered design drawing for a knife similar in form to the SOE Escape Knife shown in (98) and (99). In Cole's book on US military knives, one of these knives, which is of Joseph Rodgers manufacture, is illustrated under the description 'Pilot's and Engineer's Knife'.

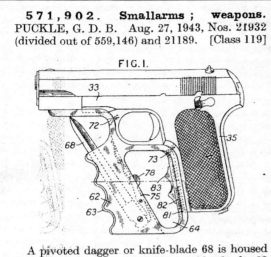

571,902. Smallarms ; weapons.
PUCKLE, G. D. B. Aug. 27, 1943, Nos. 21932 (divided out of 559,146) and 21189. [Class 119]

FIG. I.

A pivoted dagger or knife-blade 68 is housed in a channel formed between the side-cheeks 62 of a fitting which is attached to the frame 33 of a pistol or revolver. As shown, the fitting is fixed by two screws 72, 73, but it may be attached by one screw and by rearwardly-extending spring sides, projections on which are sprung into the open sides of the butt 35 in place of the usual side-plates shown. The front edges 63 of the channel-shaped housing 62 are of knuckle-duster formation. The fitting has a fingers-opening 64 into which projects the end 78 of a spring-pressed detent lever 75 which holds the blade in either the housed or the operative position. If the fitting covers the magazine finger-piece 81, a spring plunger 82 is mounted in the fitting so as to bear on the finger-piece and eject the magazine when the usual catch is released. The plunger may be operated by a slide 83 in the opening 64.

Plate 542

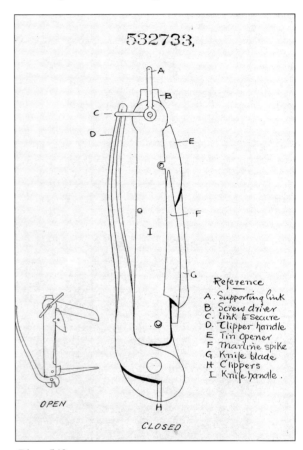

Reference
A. Supporting link
B. Screw driver
C. Link to secure
D. Clipper handle
E. Tin opener
F. Marline spike
G. Knife blade
H. Clippers
I. Knife handle.

Plate 543

PART EIGHT
LATE ENTRIES

The following knives appeared after the bulk of the text for the book was written. However, rather than rewrite the applicable sections, they have been added as late additions.

544 This knife by Robbins Dudley is of a pattern which has never previously been recorded. The knife has a double-edged blade some 6.625 inches in length and 1.1875 inches wide; the crossguard is of a rather unusual shape (see 544A) and is pierced with a slot which accepted the securing strap. The alloy hilt is of an oval cross-section flaring out in the pommel area. The hilt bears the usual Robbins Dudley mark. The leather sheath is extensively worn, missing both the securing strap and belt loop. Overall length 11.375 inches.

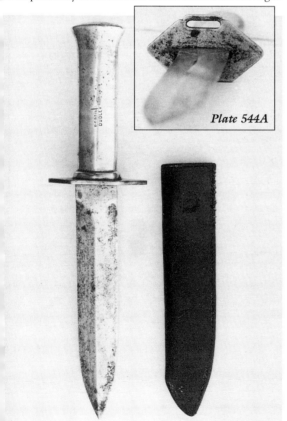

Plate 544A

Plate 544

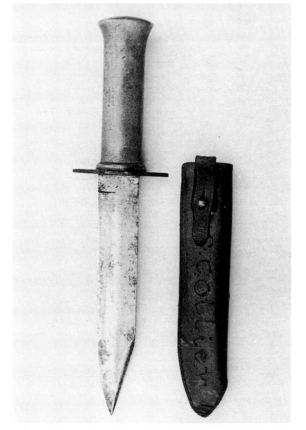

Plate 545

545 If not the twin of the previous example, certainly its brother. Utilising the same hilt crossguard and sheath styles this example has a 7-inch Bowie-type blade, giving an overall length of 11.5 inches. The front of the sheath is marked O.Collier. Like (544), this knife is of a pattern never previously recorded, and highlights, if all of Robbins work is to be properly recorded, the need to locate and preserve one of their catalogues.

546 A further (possibly spurious) example of a previously unknown design by Robbins. This illustration is taken from an American sales catalogue which describes the knife as being in the form of an ancient rondel-type dagger with a 6-inch double-edged blade and an overall length of 10.25 inches.[1] Without examination of the original it is impossible to say if this piece is authentic. If, however, it is original it represents yet a further unique design by this maker.

547 Two examples of a further variation of the wood-hilted Commando knife. The unusually shaped hilt is made in the example on the left from rosewood or similar wood, and in the example on the right from ebony. The grips of both knives are cut with five groups of rings and the tang is peened over at the top of the hilt. The crossguard on both examples is made from brass and the knives are totally unmarked. Note the larger diameter of the pommel area of the left-hand example.

Measurement of the example shown on the right are; blade length 6.75 inches; overall length 11.75 inches.

548 Five examples of this unusual knife with some features similar to an F-S knife have to date been located. Virtually nothing is known about their history or background, although there is one claim that they were made for 4 Commando. What is known is that Wilkinson have identified the etching plate used for the trademark as dating from the

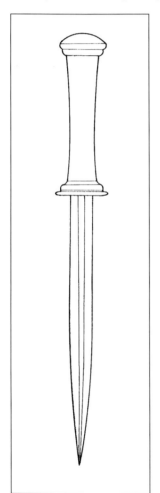

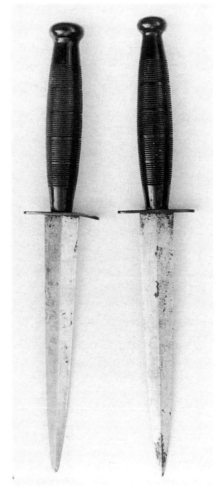

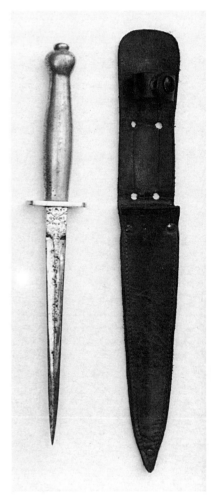

Plate 546   *Plate 547*   *Plate 548*

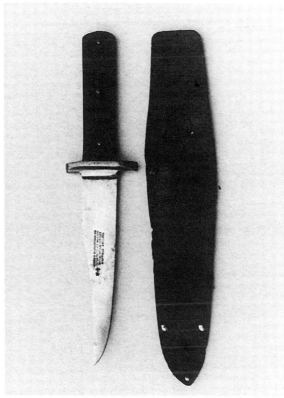

Plate 549

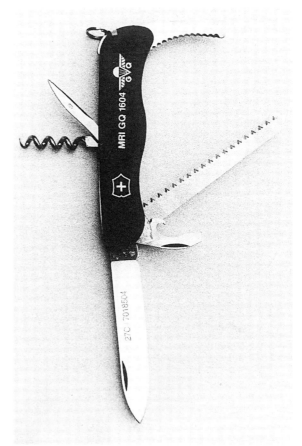

Plate 550

1930s and 1940s.[2] It would therefore seem, given the design, that the knife dates from the early 1940s.

The knife comprises a slim First Pattern-style blade some 6 inches in length, alloy crossguard and smooth alloy hilt. The square shank ricasso bears a simple trademark of crossed swords and WILKINSON SWORD CO. LTD. This is similar to that found on (178) and (179). The pommel nut is of the same type found on full scale F-S knives. The knife is accompanied by a flat, brown leather sheath. Overall length 10.125 inches.

---

549 This seemingly pure commercial sheath knife would appear to have no military origins. However, two examples have been observed, each with connections with Britain's World War Two Resistance Army, the Auxiliary Units. One example in the Dorset Military Museum, Dorchester is identified as having been issued to a member of the Auxiliaries who had subsequently donated his knife to the museum. The one illustrated has a recorded history of being issued to an Auxiliary member based in north Cornwall.

The knife has a 5.25-inch blade with long clipped Bowie back edge, cast crossguard and jigged bone scales to the hilt. The blade bears the name and trademark of Joseph Rodgers and Sons, along with CUTLERS TO HIS MAJESTY. The plain flat leather sheath, while contemporary with the knife, is possibly not the original.

As the Auxiliary Units were formed in early 1940, before the general issue of the F-S knife, the provision of an ordinary commercial item such as this is highly likely.

---

550 & 551 These two knives are provided to the British Ministry of Defence by GQ Parachutes as part of contracts for the provision of aircrew equipment. These items are, however, bought in by GQ in order to meet the contractual requirements. Grateful acknowledgement is made to GQ Parachutes Ltd for information and making available these two knives to photograph.

(550) is a Victorinox knife known as the Hunter pattern. The knife has a main locking blade, saw blade, corkscrew, punch, bottle opener/screwdriver, gutting blade, and the usual tweezers and toothpick. The scales are of the red plastic material now found on most Victorinox products, and these bear, in addition to the maker's trademark, the logo of GQ Parachutes and MRI GQ 1604. The main blade is etched

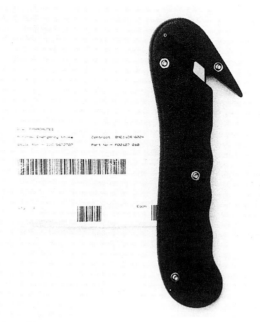

plastic handle which contains a guarded blade for cutting webbing etc. The blade can be slid out by about 0.25 inches to expose a point suitable for emergency deflation of a life-jacket or liferaft. The grip is marked:

GQ PARACHUTES LTD

22C/5670707

MRI GQ1581

MAY 1995

552 This is a V-44 with the style of hilt found on the Collins-made version. Despite the apparent US origins and hilt shape the knife is almost certainly Australian. The blade is unmarked and the general quality is not up to the same standards as found on an original Collins version. As with (339), which also uses a Collins-style hilt, it is interesting to speculate if there was some link between Collins and Australian V-44 manufacturers. Blade length 9.25 inches; overall length 13.875 inches.

553 A commercial divers' knife pressed into service with the Royal Australian Navy. The general style of the knife is similar to the Typhoon knife used by the Royal Navy (see 206), but in this case the knife is of Japanese manufacture. The knife has a black plastic hilt which has the moulded mark of PLAYRIGHT and a stainless steel blade which is marked STAINLESS STEEL JAPAN along with the etched mark of R.A.N. for Royal Australian Navy. The sheath bears the marks of the US Divers Co. Blade length 7.25 inches; overall length 12.5 inches.

554 Labelled by Silvey an Australian knife, this piece is, I believe, of New Zealand origin.[3] The blade is marked

Plate 551

27C/7018504.

(551) is a most interesting item which according to GQ has been introduced into service to replace the 'J' Knife, otherwise known as the 'Knife, Emergency Aircrew Mk 3' (see 227).

The example shown comes with its original MoD stores packet and, as will be noted, it is known as 'Aircrew Emergency Knife, Stock Ref. 22C/5670707, procured against Contract SMC11CR/6024'. The significance of the Part No. P00127 010 is not known.

The knife is a very basic implement, comprising a black

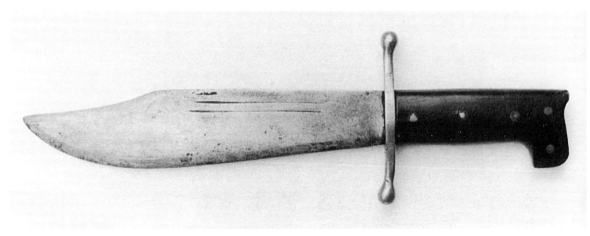

Plate 552

Plate 553

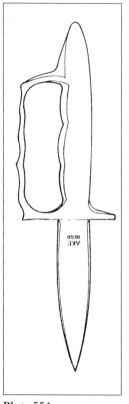

Plate 554

Plate 555

AKE/REGD. and similar marks are found on examples of (522). The knife has smooth alloy grips, a wavy D guard and a 4.625-inch blade. The blade is made from thin stock. Note the skull crusher pommel.

555 This unusual Indian-made machete is the only example of this particular pattern ever noted. It pre-dates the square-ended machetes shown in (478) and (479) the sheath being dated 1941. The piece has a 11.875-inch blade which is curved at the end in the manner of a billhook. The grip is one piece and of round section; scratched into it is the service-man's number of 1562999. The only marks to be found on the blade are the initials B.D.M. The side opening sheath has two side retaining straps rather than one as found on the type which accompanies (478) and (479). Besides the date the sheath is also marked c↑650. Overall length 17.75 inches.

556 This knife was previously recorded in my book *A Photographic Primer of Military Knives* as being of French ori-

Plate 556

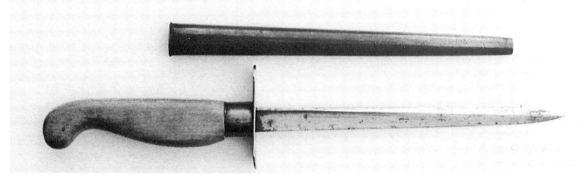

gin. This identification was based on the fact that the knife was made from a cut-down Gras bayonet blade. Since this identification was made two other examples have been noted, but additionally it has also been established that the knife is not recognised among French collectors as being of French origin. The theory has been advanced by one collector that the knife is in fact British, having been manufactured by W. W. Greener who made the Webley Pistol bayonet, which utilised the same portion of the Gras blade.

The knife uses the bottom 7.5 inches of a Gras bayonet blade fitted with an oval brass crossguard. The well-shaped wooden grip has serrations in the palm and finger areas and a brass ferrule at the junction of hilt and crossguard. The sheath, which has a copper finish, has no means of fixing it to a belt. Any information on this knife would be appreciated. Overall length 12.25 inches.

557 A very unusual Commando training knife with a retractable blade. Manufactured in the style of a Third Pattern, the bottom 2.5 inches of the blade retracts into the hollow blade when pushed against an object. The piston and spring part of the mechanism is contained within the hilt. The knife is very well made and in all probability dates from the World War Two period.

Plate 557

558 Exactly a month before this book was due for delivery to the publishers two knives were drawn to my attention which proved to be something of a major surprise. In (172) to (176) I wrote up what was then the known history of the post-war Commando knife and in particular the details of knives marked FR693. The existence of these two new knives has shown that this previous history is not totally complete.

The knife illustrated is a World War Two issue Third Pattern in unissued condition which has the common ↑B2 mark on the crossguard. The

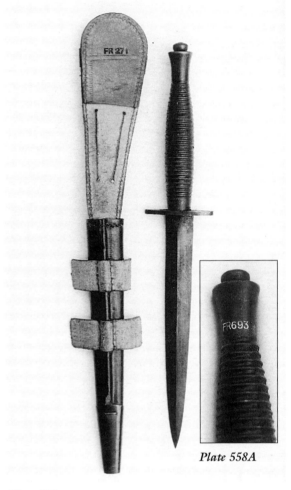

Plate 558

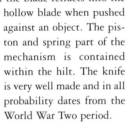

Plate 558A

knife is, however marked, around the pommel portion of the hilt FR693 (see 558A). The mark has obviously been applied with a correctly formed die stamp to match the curvature of the hilt. The accompanying World War Two period sheath is marked on the reverse FR271. The other knife referred to was a World War Two issue Second Pattern which is marked in a similar manner.

Quite where these knives fit into the FR693 story is not known but it is interesting to speculate that existing unissued stocks of wartime knives were marked up with the appropriate stores mark in the 1950s or 1960s. Bearing in mind the apparent date of use of the FR693 mark by the Royal Marines, this could be possible. It does, however, raise the interesting prospect of unissued Commando knives being in storage ten or fifteen years after the end of the war. Also, given the history of how these knives appeared in the late 1990s, some may still be held in store today!

APPENDIX ONE
FAKES AND REPRODUCTIONS

In the preface to this book I briefly mentioned the problems of fakes, and because of the extent of the problems that these cause I decided that the subject warranted an appendix in its own right. Indeed, in the area of Nazi collectibles a number of books have been written just on the fakes to be found in that field. Even though I have relatively few photographs on file of military knife fakes/reproductions, the notes and additional sketches will, I hope, aid collectors in protecting their money.

It is also worth a mention that from the point of view of this book the problems of fake military knives are generally limited to those whose origins are British. The problem is not as widespread among knives from the Commonwealth countries, but examples do exist. In general one of the best guides to avoiding the purchase of fake items is knowledge, whether gleaned from experience or from books. However, even the latter can be misleading in some instances as a number of knife books have included as original items which are patently wrong. Probably one of the best assessments I have read on fakes in general was produced by Skennerton and Richardson in their book on British and Commonwealth bayonets. Even though it is written around the subject matter of the book most of the points discussed apply equally to knives.

Now to the knives themselves. The following have been noted as being faked, or reproduced though it should be noted the list is not comprehensive

British
Welsh Sword – The blade of an original should give when flexed, fakes tend to be rigid with no give. The overall patina of fakes is also obviously artificially applied.

World War One Knuckle Knives – The type shown in (29) has been copied almost certainly in India or Pakistan. Blades are generally just marked CLEMENTS. These copies are very high quality and can be difficult to detect.

Other Ranks Pipers' Dirk – copies, again originating in the Indian subcontinent.

Robbins of Dudley Knives – These have been extensively copied. A general guide to recognising these is the manner of the lettering used in the name Robbins, and sheaths made from leather with incorrect type of finish. This should be similar to that found on a Sam Browne, but contemporary replacements can of course occur. Some examples also have incorrect dimensions, and spurious designs also exist. An example of a spurious Robbins knife is shown at (559). This knife exhibits all that is wrong with a fake Robbins: the

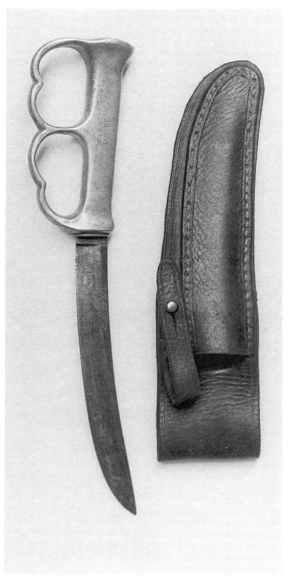

Plate 559

markings are incorrect, and there is incorrect leather for the sheath.

Middle East Commando Knife – Examples with steel grips are incorrect, as are those with sheath knife Bowie-style blades riveted in place and marked with W↑D. So that these are not confused with some original pieces which do have blades riveted in place, a sketch of what a fake looks like is shown at (560).

Smatchet – Very crude fakes appeared in the 1970s. These had cast steel pommels, grips made of softwood which had been stained, and blades that had no temper. More recently examples have appeared along with a curiously designed sheath. The knives themselves carry spurious marks.

SOE and other Clandestine Knives – The scarcity of original specimens of these knives makes the comparison of fakes with original pieces very difficult. Some of the nails and other spikes used by SOE/OSS have been very well copied and are very difficult to detect.

Lapel daggers, many with odd manufacturers and other markings, do occasionally appear. Some of these marks appertain to makers whose existence cannot be confirmed, such as JP for John Paisley, or '&' for Bruce Hand. A number of modern versions made in some cases from stainless steel have also been available from suppliers of survival equipment.

Besides lapel daggers, a small number of what are reputed to be agents' F-S knives have also been noted. Some of these scaled down versions of such knives were written up by Thompson in the Spring 1996 issue of the magazine *Tactical Blade*, and it is believed that Wilkinsons did make a very limited number of these small versions of the F-S, possibly for presentation purposes. However, some of these knives are highly suspect and one should treat with caution and if unsure seek advice before purchasing such pieces.

Although not typical of SOE fake knives, the knife shown in (561) appeared in an auction a number of years ago, and was described as an SOE lock knife. While extremely well made, the piece exhibited a number of features that indicated this was unlikely, and that it was of probably recent manufacture. The grips were made of softwood stained to a walnut colour, the bluing did not appear correct for the reputed period, and on close examination the metalwork showed numerous file marks.

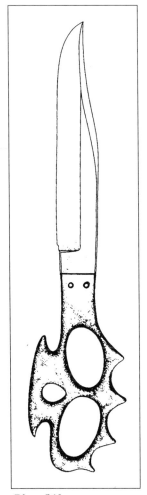

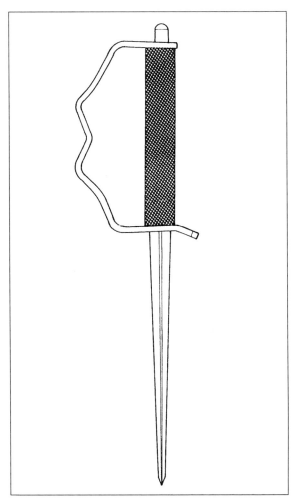

Plate 560   *Plate 561*   *Plate 562*

Fakes, fantasy pieces, spuriously marked items and rehilts all exist in the F-S and Commando knife area. It is my view that First Patterns with 2-inch crossguards have been reworked into versions with 3-inch crossguards. Copies of the smooth alloy hilt so-called Polish Paratrooper F-S exist, along with examples of the all-steel knife.

Third Patterns marked 1940 are obviously wrong, as are examples with Free French marks or the Cross of Lorraine applied to the hilt. More recently very well-made Second Patterns have been noted; these can detected by their rather thin crossguards and a ↑ acceptance mark which is applied with a wrongly sized stamp.

Crude, in comparison with the original, copies of the Cogswell Harrison push dagger (see 274) have also been noted.

(562) is a sketch of an all-steel knuckle knife, a number of which appeared in the early 1970s, and which occasionally still surface. These knives are marked W↑D and sometimes with the name DOWN LONDON. These knives are a complete fantasy.

Australian

The known fakes in this area were until recently restricted to some of the knuckle knives which were popular among American troops who served in the area, in particular the brass-hilted cog wheel

Plate 563

ranger's knife (see 390). Some of the fakes of these knives had incorrect blade forms along with the marking CASE XX. More recent copies have been observed which are true to the original design, along with those having alloy hilts.

A number of other knives have recently appeared on the US market which are reputed to be Australian-made versions of the US Special Forces SOG knives used in Vietnam, originals of which command very high prices. These so-called Australian SOG knives made by Bruce Hand, are in the opinion of advance Australian and US collectors spurious examples. Research into the existence of Walter Bruce Hand has failed to reveal any evidence to prove he actually existed.

Canadian

Not known to be a problem area, although the Canadian Paratroopers Arm Knife and sheath which I have written up in the Canadian section is in the view of some collectors spurious.

Indian

Copies of military knives from this area do not seem to be a major problem, though a very crude copy of the Orde knife has been observed. Also, the knife shown in (563) is a rework which uses an original Chindit Bowie blade. To this blade has been cast an alloy hilt which is marked on the reverse side BONNEY & CLARK. As the reader will know from the Australian section of this book, this company was a sheath not a knife maker.

NATO STORES NUMBERS

Thompson, in his book *Commando Dagger*, attributes a Commando knife marked on the crossguard

NATO NO
4658827
1976

to NATO issue. This assumption is only indirectly correct. While the knife is issued to the forces of one particular NATO country, it is not the case that it is general issue throughout the NATO alliance. The knife is in fact British issue, and to help the collector identify knives bearing NATO marks it may be useful to explain the stores nomenclature used by NATO.

Prior to and during World War Two the only branch of the British forces which placed stores marks on its knives as general practice was the RAF. The Army only rarely placed stores numbers on their knives, tending only to mark them with the date, a broad arrow, and occasionally an inspector's mark. Pre-World War Two the Royal Navy knives bore only the maker's name, but during the war the practice of dating knives appeared.

In the post-war years each service went its own way adopting totally separate stores identification systems. For example, Type D survival knives can be found bearing three different stores codes depending on the service for which it was made. Such a system was obviously not very efficient in terms of stores purchasing, and this, coupled with the formation of the NATO Alliance and Joint Command, created the need for a common supply language within NATO.

The system adopted works by allocating each item with a combination of figures in four groups, such as 8465-99-127-8106. The significant group in the NATO stock number from a collector's point of view is the two-figure group which indicates the nation code. This denotes that a particular country has identified the item and allocated the final seven-digit number. The nation code does not, however, necessarily identify the country of manufacture. Codes in current use are:

Country	Code	Country	Code
Australia	66	Belgium	13
Canada	21	Denmark	22
France	14	Germany	12
Greece	23	Iceland	24
Malaysia	34	NATO	11
Netherlands	17	New Zealand	98
Norway	25	Portugal	26
Singapore	32	Spain	33
Turkey	27	United Kingdom	99
United States	00, 01, 06		

Although several of the above countries are not part of NATO, many have adopted the system for convenience.

Unfortunately for the collector, not all knives bear the full thirteen-digit code; in most cases only the last seven digits are marked on the knife. However, by a little research via MOD departments it is usually possible to identify the origin of the knife. The essential point to remember is that because a knife may bear a NATO mark it does not mean it is general issue to all NATO countries. Transfer and supply of some items between NATO countries does occur (see 195), but such transfers are the exception rather than the rule.

APPENDIX THREE
KNIFE MARKS

Britain

↑ The well-known broad arrow or crow's-foot mark. Used to indicate government ownership. Primarily associated with British weapons but also used in a variety of combinations on knives from Australia, Canada and India.

W↑D, W↑D18 War Department acceptance mark. Although observed on other pieces of military equipment up until the mid-1950s, not noted on knives after 1939.

↑
56 A typical inspector's/acceptance mark. These broad arrow number and occasionally letter stamps are found primarily on Commando knives but also appear on other British military knives, particularly during the World War Two period.

↑B2 Only ever observed on Second and Third Pattern Commando knives.

455↑ Post-war period inspection mark, typically found on pocket knives.

C.O.S.D.2194 Central or Company Ordnance Supply Depot 2194. Only found on the British Gravity Knife, though the COSD has been observed on other pieces of military equipment.

FR693 and FR271 Royal Navy/Royal Marine Armament Stores codes found on Third Pattern Commando Knife issued from the mid-1950s to mid-1960s.

AP Indicates Admiralty Pattern, found in a number of different forms. Before the introduction of NATO numbers the Navy used a four-digit stores class group such as 0433. This was used with another four-digit number to provide a code such as AP 0433/1546. On some knives only the last four numbers are used, e.g. AP6260, and in some instances the AP is not used, e.g. 7587.

H1528, C1516A. Early post-war, i.e. 1950s, stores codes.

AM Air Ministry.
  CC
0532 Clothing Code. CC marks are found on some World War Two and early post-war pocket knives.

1B RAF and Army stores category for small handtools.

27C RAF survival equipment.

22C RAF aircrew equipment.

0274 Typical Royal Navy stores code used prior to introduction of NATO codes.

4320-99-523-9744 Typical thirteen digit NATO stores code. See Appendix Two for full explanation of this system.

Australia

D↑D Australian Department of Defence.

DC-45 Found on Australian machete, meaning unknown.

MA Munitions Australia, but some bayonet authorities state that this is a Lithgow Arsenal mark which is an abbreviation for Macharms.

↑   ↑EW↑
HB AC ↑ S Typical inspection marks found on Australian knives and sheaths.

7340-66-013-1930 Stores marking/pattern number which follows the NATO system. Note the 66 country code for Australia.

Canada

The standard Canadian government mark is a ↑ within a **C.**

M & D Militia and Defence.

India

The mark most closely associated with Indian weapons is the mark of

↑
I

It has, however, not been noted on any knife of known Indian origin but has been observed on Indian issue and manufactured bayonets. This mark is, however, found on many knives of Australian origin which date from the World War Two period, It has also been noted on two Commando Knives (126).

I↑G I↑D IG SA
 23   20 20 Indian Government ownership or inspection marks.

C↑15, C↑544, P↑5 Acceptance or inspector's marks.

New Zealand

22B/N12 Noted on the sheaths of alloy-hilted knives; meaning is not known.

APPENDIX FOUR
KNIFE MAKERS AND RETAILERS

Although some notes to the individual makers and retailers are written up within the main text of the book, this section provides, where available, brief notes on their operating dates and location. The information given regarding the latter is the last known address from which they operated.

As I mentioned in the preface the demise of the Sheffield cutlery industry has resulted in only sparse records being available for a large number of English cutlers. Even when a company name and trademark has been taken over the new owners know little of the history of the original company. It is also the case that the name of the company can live on under new owners who have no connection with the original, generally family-based, company. For example, Richard's bought the Rodgers–Wostenholm Group. Richard's was then sold to Imperial of the USA, and Imperial eventually sold to a group of businessmen.

I have not attempted to give information on those companies associated with the periphery of the cutlery trade. For example, C. E. Heinke's main activity was diving equipment, even though the company had knives available as part of this business.

Where I have been unable to locate any firm information on the name, details of the knife or knives on which its name are found are given.

For those interested in further reading on manufacturers, Geoffrey Tweedale's *The Sheffield Knife Book* provides an excellent reference to the history of the Sheffield cutlery industry. The information contained in Richard Washer's book on Sheffield Bowie makers should be treated with caution and only relied on if backed up by further research. Bernard Levine's *Guide* and John Goins' *Encyclopaedia* provide some basic data listing names, dates, location, some trademarks and information on makers and retailers from around the world (see Bibliography).

Joseph Allen – 1810–1959: Used a number of premises, finally settling in Oak Works, New Edwards Street, Sheffield. Originally a razor manufacturer but by the end of the First World War was listed as a razor and cutlery manufacturer. Used a number of trademarks, the one usually encountered being NON-XLL.

ANCSL (Army & Navy Co-operative Society Ltd): Established in 1871 by a group of Army and Navy officers who decided that wine was too expensive and that they would reduce cost by ordering it by the case at wholesale prices. Membership of the Army and Navy Co-operative Society was restricted to Officers and Non-Commissioned Officers, their families and friends introduced by them. The subscription was five shillings for the first year, then half a crown annually. The society acquired premises in Victoria Street, London and eventually had branches in Bombay, Delhi, Calcutta and Karachi; in Plymouth, Chatham, Aldershot and Southsea. It provided every conceivable service to its customers and its products were contained within a large cloth-bound catalogue. Its co-operative status ended in 1922 when membership tickets were issued free without introduction. The name of Army and Navy does, however, live on in some of the branches of one of the major department store chains.

From a knife perspective ANCSL did not manufacture their own but bought them in from the Sheffield trade. However, knives bearing their name are sought after by collectors as examples representing the heyday of the British Empire when an officer would have outfitted himself with a good-quality knife for duty in the colonies, or even on the Western Front.

Atkinson Bros – *circa* 1876 to 1985: Located Milton Street, Sheffield. Merchant and manufacturer of cutlery.

Baxter: Probably W. & J. A. Baxter Ltd, Congo Buildings, Trippett Lane, Sheffield. Little is known. Made the NAAFI knife and listed in the Sheffield telephone directory for 1981.

J. & J. Beal, (also Joseph Beal and Son, or J. B. & S.) – 1850s to 1956: Operated from a number of addresses, settling in Corporation St, Sheffield after the Great War. Listed in early directories as a manufacturer of butcher's, Bowie, hunting, table and pocket knives. Used a number of trademarks, ENDURE being the most commonly seen.

A. H. Bisby: Listed in the 1963 directory as being located at Carlisle Street, Sheffield. Not listed in the 1971 directory and no earlier history known. Name found on World War Two RAF folding machete and post-war period pocket knives.

E. Blyde – 1854 to date: Little London Road, Sheffield. Cutlery and electroplate manufacturers.

J. Blyde – 1841 to *circa* 1970s: Clintock Works, Milton Street, Sheffield. Used the mark of SATURN above the word GENIUS, as found on some wood-gripped Commando knives.

Brades: Name noted on an experimental (?) machete along with a paper label showing a Pagoda trademark. Period is probably World War Two.

Brookes & Crookes – 1858–1957: Atlantic Works, St Philips Road, Sheffield. A small company which produced a very high-quality product. Used the 'Bell' trademark.

John Brookes: A John Brookes was one of the founders of Brookes & Crookes, but there is no record of a separate company operating after this. The name is, however, found on a pocket knife dated 1946.

Abraham Brooksbank – 1849–1965: Brooksbank took over a W. Hoole's business, a merchant and maker of files, saws and cutlery. The company added machine knives, farrier's knives, pen and pocket knives to its range. Located at Malinda Street, Sheffield until 1932, then taken over by Eye Witness Works in Milton Street.

Bullock Bros: Listed in directories as Bullock Bros (Edged Tools) Ltd, The Plant Edge Tool Works, Landywood Lane, Cheslyn Hay, Walsall. Made the British Golok-style machete. The firm still exists but has not responded to enquiries about its history.

W. & S. Butcher/Wade & Butcher – 1819–1947: Formed by two brothers, William and Samuel, and was a company that made a major play for the US market. As their New York office was headed by a man called Wade, some products were marked WADE & BUTCHER. When Butcher died the firm was sold, but the name continued to be used; it did not, however, appear to survive the early post-war years.

George Butler – 1861–1993: The company trademark of a key dates back to 1681, Butler's acquiring the rights to use it in 1861. Located in Eyre Street, Sheffield. Bought out by Arthur Price in 1993.

Clarke Shirely, *circa* 1870s to ?: Boston Works, Sheffield. Apparently taken over by Harrison Fisher. Name noted on naval square-ended knife from late 1800s /early 1900s period.

John Clarke & Son – 1848–1983: Mowbray Street, Sheffield. Acquired the William Rodgers name and trademark around 1873. Made razors, table knives, pocket and sporting knives, Bowies, all of high quality. An examination of a 1942 Clarke-made Commando Knife will show the quality of their products.

Charles Clements: London retailer, obtained some of its knives from manufacturers such as Ibberson.

Cogswell Harrison: Well-known London-based gun maker. Certainly marketed some knives during the war; whether they were made by Cogswell Harrison or were bought in is not known.

Wm Cooper (HT) Ltd, Sheffield: Name found on post-war, *circa* 1970s, Rigger's Knife. The HT in the name almost certainly stands for Hand Tools.

Davenport Cutlery Co. (DCC): Standedge Works, Maltravers St, Sheffield. Listed in 1963 directory, but no other details known.

Dawes & Ball. 1935 to *circa* 1962: According to Levine only made pocket knives after 1935. Name noted on two-piece all-metal knife dated 1945, and two-piece knife with steel bolster and Bexoid grips.

Deane & Co.: Name found on a square-pointed jack knife dated 1878.

James Dixon & Son – 1805–1990s: Cornish Place, Sheffield. In its heyday one of Sheffield's biggest firms, it was not primarily a knife maker, most of its trade being in pewter, electroplate and Sheffield plate.

A. Dobson, 1835 to *circa* 1940s: Hollis Croft,

Sheffield. Found on two-piece knife with steel bolster and Bexoid grips dated 1940.

E & C. S.: Found marked on World War Two RAF folding machete.

Edwards & ?: The second part of the name is unreadable, but is accompanied by the name LUCAS within a scroll along with a blacksmith at an anvil trademark. These marks are located on a *circa* 1900s machete.

Thomas Ellin & Son – 1797–1933: Sylvester Works, Sheffield. In its prime produced table cutlery, working knives, pocket, pen and Bowie knives. Factory taken over by J. Elliot who also acquired rights to Ellin's marks.

Joseph Elliot – 1795–1990: Pre-World War One. Primarily a table knife manufacturer. Bought the marks and business of Allen and Son, expanding its range to cover pocket knives and tableware. Obtained rights to a number of company names and marks during the 1930s and survived the early post-World War Two years better than most. Bought by W. D. Slater in 1972.

Elwell: Made the current issue British Golok-style machete.

George Gill: Made World War Two period pocket knives, with name being noted on a three-piece pocket knife with bexoid grips and moulded bolster dated 1942, and the ARP knife dated 1939.

F. Graves & Son: Marked on 1940 dated two-piece, moulded bolster pocket knife.

R. Groves: 34 Victoria St, Sheffield. Marked on 1941 dated two-piece, moulded bolster pocket knife.

Hale Brothers – *circa* 1871 to *circa* 1970: Used horse's head trademark. Name found on both First and Second World War period pocket knives.

James Hall: A Jas Hall is listed in the 1963 directory under 'Pen, Pocket and Sportsmen's Knife

Manufacturers'. Located at 51 Athol Road, Sheffield.

Harrison Brothers & Howson – 1840–1960s: With an early pre-history the main company was established in 1840. Became a major force in the industry during the 1890s. Originally located in Norfolk Street, Sheffield, relocated to Carver Street in 1900.

Harrison Fisher – 1896 to date: Eye Witness Works, Milton Street, Sheffield. Primarily specialising in table knives, expanded over the years with the take-over of other companies including Dawes and Ball and Taylor's Eye Witness. Now makes a range of cutlery, pocket knives, kitchen, trade knives and scissors.

Hibbert & Son: World War One period knuckleduster knife.

Hill & Son – late Victorian to pre-World War One period?: 4 Haymarket, London. It is not known if they were retailers or manufacturers, but the quality of their product is very high. Given the nature of the pieces made by them it would indicate that they operated during the period given.

J. B. Holland – *circa* 1940s: Made World War Two period pocket knives.

Holtzapffel & Co. – 1794–1928: Started by a John Jacob Holtzapffel who came to England in 1792 from the Alsace and set up business in London in 1794 specialising in the manufacture of turning lathes. He died in 1835 and was succeeded by his son Charles, who died in 1847. His son John Jacob (the second) was an infant at the time and his widow carried on until John Jacob took over. He died in 1897. Firm then carried on under a nephew, George William Holtzapffel Budd, until 1924 when his son, Col G. H. Budd, took over. All engineering activity ceased in 1928. During the company's history they made Bowies and folding and hunting knives along with tomahawks and engineering equipment.

F. E. & J. R. Hopkinson – 1949 to late 1996: Seems to have appeared on the scene in 1949 when the company is reputed to have bought John Nowill and Son. However, its name appeared in the 1963 directory, not in the 1970 Sheffield directory, but did in the 1981 edition. Its first venture into the military knife market seems to have been around this time when its name appeared on a RN diver's knife. Also made Type D survival knives and all-metal pocket knives. Used an H within a diamond shape trademark. The company ceased operation in late 1996 or early 1997.

W. R. Humphreys – 1880–1970: Latterly located at Randall Street, Sheffield. Used the trademark RADIANT. Took over the J. Wragg business in 1900.

Hunter: There is a M. Hunter listed by both Levine and Washer, but it is not possible to confirm if this is the same name as found on both the AP301 Naval Jack Knife and a Boer War period knife.

George Ibberson – 1700–1980s: Rockingham St, Sheffield. Made the usual range of cutlery but was particularly noted for its high-quality sportsman's knives. Especially noted in military knife circles as the manufacturer of the British version of the German Paratrooper Gravity Knife.

J. Ireland & Sons, Contractor: Name found on a square-pointed naval jack knife. No details known, but must date from the late Victorian period.

Christopher Johnson – 1836–1956: Western Works, Sheffield. A firm of high repute producing a large range of cutlery products. Around mid-1950s bought by Wostenholm.

Robert Kelly: Liverpool retailer whose name is found on World War One knuckle knives. The business existed until the 1960s.

Samuel Kitchen, also S. & J. Kitchen – 1737–1957: Broadfield and Saxon Streets, Sheffield. Originally made table and butcher's knives, but later extended its products to pocket knives, razors, Bowie and hunting knives and machetes etc.

Kutrite: Still listed in directory but have not responded to enquiries. Made current pattern three-piece stainless steel pocket knives with examples dated 1986 noted.

Walter Locke: Possibly not a manufacturer; name found on Baldock Knife Spear. However, the marking on the knife indicates that it was made by Dixon for Locke.

Lockwood Brothers – 1767–1933: Sylvester Street, Sheffield. Originally tool manufacturers but in the late 1800s started selling cutlery. Used among its trademarks is C:X, and the company was well-known for making Bushman's Friend knives. Trademark acquired by Elliot.

H. G. Long – 1846 to early 1990s: Now part of H. M. Slater. Name noted on Boer War period jack knife.

Lowe: Name found on World War One style knuckle knife, but no trace of a company or maker called Lowe operating in that period has been located. A Herbert Lowe did, however, operate in the 1970s in conjunction with Freddie James, an ex-Wostenholm employee who started his own business and who was the source of a number of spurious Bowie knives marked with the IXL trademark and Wostenholm name. Knives marked JAMES AND LOWE are known, and James is known to have made knives under his own name. It is possible that Lowe did likewise.

Maleham & Yeomans – 1876–1970: Produced fine quality pocket cutlery and also seems to have been a steel merchant in the 1880s. Was located at Bowdon Street, Sheffield for much of its life but moved to Pond Street in the mid-1960s after its take-over by Rodgers.

Mappin Bros – 1810–1920s: Queen's Cutlery Works, Bakers Hill, Sheffield. This firm was the forerunner of the well-known Mappin and Webb jewellery and silverware company. Started by a Joseph Mappin in conjunction with another partner and manufactured pen, spring, sporting and table knives and razors. The firm was renamed Mappin Bros in 1851. While the cutlery side deteriorated another member of the family had been successful in the electroplate business, operating under the name of Mappin and Webb. This arm bought out Mappin Bros, and after World War One the cutlery side was slowly discontinued.

W. & I. Marshall (Marshalls Cutlers Ltd) – 1888 to present: St Enoch Square, Glasgow. Started by Alex Marshall and described in the directories as a 'Plane, Saw and Edge Tool Maker'. Run by his son W. Marshall from 1913 to 1934. William and Ian Marshall succeeded in business after their father died in 1935. According to information received, the company traded as J. and I. Marshall from this period up until 1950. From 1935 onwards listed as merchants or retailers. The high-quality F-S knife bearing their name was made by John Clarke and Sons.

Ralph Martindale & Co Ltd – 1869 to present: Alma Street, Birmingham. Ralph Martindale bought the sword factory of a Horace Chavasse in 1869. In 1873 the company was in trouble and Ralph Martindale was forced to sell the business to a consortium, although he retained some shares. He died in 1879 but his name was retained. Over the years the company acquired Robert Mole and Sons, J. and J. Beal, and S. and J. Kitchen. Although at various time they have manufactured swords, bayonets, axes, tools and many kinds of knife, their main business has always been machetes. The well-known CROCODILE trademark was first registered in 1876.

J. McClory – circa 1870 to 1970s: Herries Road, Sheffield. Name appears in the 1970 directory but not in that for 1981.

W. Mills & Son – 1921 to circa World War Two:

Willis Mills was a spring knife maker with Thomas Turner and he was joined by his son, Ernest, for his apprenticeship between 1914 and 1921. In 1921 both father and son started their own business in Napier Street, then Edgerton St, Sheffield. The war finished the partnership and Willis died in 1947.

John Milner – 1848 to late 1960s: Arundel St, Sheffield. Early history not known. Used the mark of INTRINSIC and made pen and pocket knives, razors, table knives, scissors and surgical instruments.

C. Myers: Made pocket knives during World War Two period.

Myson: Name observed on two-piece all-metal folding knife of pattern made late 1940s/early 1950s, the particular example being dated 1955.

Needham Bros – 1868 to circa 1950: Matilda Street, Sheffield. Used the mark REPEAT and made pen, pocket and sports knives. The REPEAT mark was acquired by Slater.

John Nowill & Sons – 1700 to present: 87 London Road, Sheffield. The well-known trademark of Nowill, the D and star, was granted to a Thomas Nowill in 1700. The second mark of crossed keys was acquired in 1842 and the company had not only a London office but also agents in Greece, Turkey and Egypt. The company was bought by Hopkinson Ltd around 1950. Trade knives and Bowies were still made under its name in the 1960s, and even though its name was still in the directories in 1995 it does not appear to be active in the knife field.

Albert Oakes: Name noted on two-piece pocket knife of the type with flat grips, no bolster and chequering covering total area of scales. Knife is dated 1940.

A. & F. Parkes: A Birmingham-based company that used the trademark BIPED along with two feet. Name found on 1916 dated billhook.

Parkin & Marshall – 1846 to circa 1920: Telegraph Works, Furnival Street, Sheffield. A William Parkin took over the existing business of Smith and Moorhouse and in 1846 took a William Marshall in as a partner. They made steel and files, machine knives, table and pocket knives. It was bought by M. Hunter before World War One but went into decline after the war.

John Petty & Sons – 1868–1986: Garden St, Sheffield. Started as a maker of oyster and farrier's knives. Expanded so that in the early 1900s made a complete range of trade knives, pocket and sportsman's knives. Used the trademark of a barrel.

R. P. & C.: Probably the Rockingham Plate and Cutlery Co. Noted from a 1940 dated two-piece, moulded bolster knife.

Richards or RBS – 1932–1983: Moore St, Sheffield. Started by a German, Stephan Richartz, who came over to repeat the success of the German operation by making knives for the lower quality end of the market. The company was registered as Richards Bros and Sons, a title which gives rise to the marking found on some knives of RBS, and they used the same lamp-post trademark as Richartz in Germany. They also had use of a tent trademark. Achieved rapid growth in the 1950s and 1960s. The company was sold several times in the 1970s and 1980s but became insolvent in 1983 and closed.

Robbins & Co. Ltd, Dudley (ROBBINS DUDLEY): One of the most enigmatic makers of knives during the World War One period. They seem to have been founded in 1876, being described in the trade directory as 'Fender Makers' with an address in Constitution Hill, Dudley. The directory of 1879–80 gives their trade as 'Brass and Iron Founders, Fountain Works'. The directory for 1911–12 gives their address as Fountain Street. In 1921 the nature of their trade is given as 'Fender Manufacturers', and in 1924 and 1928 as 'Grate

Makers'. There is no entry in the 1932 local directory. Dudley Library has an undated catalogue of 'Select Designs of Cast Iron Mantel Register etc. for Tenement and Building Schemes' which is by Robbins and Co. Ltd, Metal Founders and Craftsmen, Manufacturers of Interior Hob and Dog Grates, Curb Suites and Coal Boxes, Electrical Fittings, Door Furniture and Knockers, Wrot Gates and Fencing, Stairs, Balusters and Balconies, Grilles, Street Signs and Weather Vanes.

Herbert Robinson – *circa* 1873: This is the only information located in print, the name being listed by Levine. However, a 1940 dated two-piece, moulded bolster knife has been noted.

Joseph Rodgers & Sons – *circa* 1724 to 1975: Pond Hill Works, Sheffield. The premier name in the history of the Sheffield cutlery industry. So much has been written about Rodgers it is difficult to condense the history of this firm into a few lines. During the 1800s and early 1900s the maker of very high-quality Bowie and folding knives with an extensive market in America. In the mid-1800s due to the American demand became the largest knife factory in Sheffield. The First World War, however, took its toll, as did foreign competition, and the 1920s and 1930s were difficult years for Rodgers. After a slight up-turn during World War Two the company was again hit in the 1960s by overseas imports. It was sold in 1975 to Richards, though its famous trademark of the star and Maltese cross was obtained by the Eggington Group.

William Rodgers – *circa* 1830 to 1873: Little is known about the history of this company other than that the name and I CUT MY WAY trademark was acquired by John Clarke in 1873. Clarke obviously used the name for some of the lower quality products, as it is frequently seen on poor-quality post-World War Two Commando knives.

H. Rowbotham: Listed by Levine as *circa* 1954,

this general date would be supported by dated knives. A three-piece moulded bolster with Bexoid grips knife dated 1949 and a two-piece stainless steel knife dated 1952 have been noted.

S. & H.: Name marked on RN Rigger's Knife dated 1977.

W. Saynor – 1865–1958: Carlton Works, Furnace Hill, Sheffield. Started out as a horticultural and table knife manufacturer. In the early 1900s began making, in addition to its usual product line, pocket and butcher's knives. Factory closed in 1958 and the business moved to the same address as Saynor, Cooke and Ridal. It is not known if the company name survived this move.

Sheffield Steel Products (SSP) – *circa* 1918 to *circa* 1960s: A consortium of companies; at one time in the 1920s some seventeen firms were involved. Made a wide range of steel products, nuts, bolts tools etc., and although it is known to have made table knives and pocket knives during World War Two the extent of its line of knives is not known.

H. M. Slater – 1858 to present?: 78 Hoyle Street, Sheffield. Founded in 1858 as Slater Bros, manufactured pocket, pen and Bowie knives, dirks and table cutlery. The company went into liquidation in 1901 but was re-established by Herbert Slater in Venture Works, Arundel Street. Made components for many of the major firms and after World War Two had a policy of acquiring many old businesses and their marks. The last family member, Dennis Slater, sold the business in the early 1990s, but the name Herbert M. Slater (1853) Ltd is still listed in the 1997 telephone directory.

Spencer: Some Robbins-style knives have been reported bearing this name.

Staniforths (Severquick): Found on 1949 dated billhook.

J. Stead & Co. – *circa* 1930s to 1960s: The dates are as listed by Levine, but the name is not found in the 1963 directory. A 1940 dated two-piece, moulded bolster knife has been noted bearing the name.

Sutherland & Rhoden: Name found etched on Robbins-style push dagger and on a World War One knuckle knife; possibly a retailer.

Swaine & Aldney: Gentleman's and military outfitters retailed knives, especially those made by George Ibberson, the knives being marked with both their and the Ibberson name. Originally located at 185 Piccadilly, London W1, now renamed Swaine, Aldney and Brigg and located at 10a Old Bond Street, London W1.

Taylor's (Eye Witness) – 1820–1975: Eye Witness Works, Milton Street, Sheffield. Started by a John Taylor in about 1820 and was granted the Eye Witness mark in 1838. Taylor's business was taken over in 1856 by a Thomas Needham who was joined in the 1870s by Veall and Tyzack; the company was henceforth known as Needham, Veall and Tyzack. Made a wide range of cutlery products including razors, table and pocket knives. Used the Taylor's Eye Witness name and trademark extensively on its products. By 1965 the firm was styled as Taylor's Eye Witness, but was taken over by Harrison Fisher in 1975. The Taylor's Eye Witness name does, however, still appear in the 1997 telephone directory.

J. H. Thompson: Made the Electrician's Knife, 1966 dated three-piece stainless steel knife dated 1953, and three-piece moulded bolster knife dated 1950. Despite the 1966 dated knife, name not found in the 1963 directory.

W. Thornhill – *circa* 1880 to early twentieth century: Little information known on this maker, or possibly retailer, of high-quality knives. Listed in some sources as Walter Thornhill and Co., 44 New Bond Street, London.

J. Tidmarsh: Marked on Boer War period knife.

Trafalgar: Noted on 1944 dated three-piece World War Two pocket knife.

Thomas Turner – 1802–1932: Suffolk Works,

Sheffield. Along with Rodgers and Wostenholm, one of the major forces in the cutlery industry. Founded in 1802 and gaining its ENCORE trademark in 1805, the company not only made knives but was a steel and tool maker. Like Rodgers and Wostenholm made a major play for the American market, particularly with large folding knives. The original family connection disappeared in 1893 and the company was bought by Wilfred and Albert Hobson. Turner did not survive the 1930s depression and was bought out by Viner's; their name did, however, still appear in some later directories as Thomas Turner and Co. (Cutlers Sheffield) Ltd with an address at Clarence St.

H. Underwood – *circa* 1820 to World War One ?: 56 Haymarket, London. Little is known. As with Hill and Son could be a maker or retailer, but it is interesting to note that like Hill and Son it was based in the Haymarket.

Walker Hall – 1845–1963: Electro Works, Howard Street, Sheffield. Started by a George Walker in 1845, Hall joined the firm in 1848. The prime business of the company was plated goods, though it increasingly made table cutlery. Combined with Mappin and Webb in 1963 to form British Silverware Ltd, but this closed down in 1971. The name of Walker Hall was, however, revived as a retail arm of Mappin and Webb.

Warriss: There is a Warriss & Co. (Sheffield) Ltd listed in the 1963 directory, their address being given as 19 and 21 Eyre St, Sheffield. Their name has been noted on a 1954 dated two-piece all-metal pocket knife.

W. J. Waterer – *circa* 1939 to 1958: Pughs Place, Carnaby Street, London. Virtually nothing known; certainly made fighting knives during World War Two period.

John Watts – 1853 to *circa* 1995: Lambert Street, Sheffield. John Watts took over a much older firm of clog clasp manufacturers in 1853. By about 1895 the firm had become a cutlery manufacturer and also had a wide range of other products. Was still listed at Lambert St in 1995 but does not appear in the 1997 directory.

Joseph Westby – 1893–1965: Central Works, West Street, Sheffield. Manufactured pen and pocket knives and became one of the first firms to introduce stainless steel cutlery.

George Wostenholm – 1745–1971: Washington Works, Sheffield. Along with Joseph Rodgers one of the pre-eminent names in Sheffield and British cutlery history. Manufacturers of high-quality pocket, pen and Bowie knives and other cutlery products. Their early Bowie knives are highly prized, especially in the US market. Went out of business in its own right in 1971, being bought out by Joseph Rodgers. After a number of other take-overs the famous IXL trademark was obtained by Egginton Brothers.

Wilkinson Sword Co. Ltd – 1772 to present: Brunel Road, Acton, London. Besides being well-known as sword makers, Wilkinson produced some of the most historically important military knives, e.g. the F-S Commando Knife, the RBD Hunting Knife and the Shakespear Knife. Tracing its history back to the gun maker Henry Nock, his son-in-law James Wilkinson inherited the business in 1804. The present name was adopted in 1887. One interesting aside to the company history is that Wilkinson state that they took over Robert Mole and Son in 1920, even though Martindale are also supposed to have taken over Robert Mole.

J. Wilson/I. Wilson – 1750–1903: Sycamore Street, Sheffield. Started as a maker of butcher's knives, skinning knives and Green River Knives were among its chief products. Because of the marking of the J the firm was also known as I. Wilson. The company was sold in 1903 and the name and trademark were then acquired by Elliot.

Wragg: Name found on 1943 dated pocket knife. Although a J. Wragg & Son existed *circa* 1887 to 1900, this does not appear to be the same firm as it was sold to W. R. Humphreys and the J. Wragg name disappeared from the directories.

A.Wright & Son Ltd: Midland Works, 16–18 Sidney St, Sheffield. The maker for many years of the Electrician's Knife.

APPENDIX FIVE
METRIC CONVERSION

As mentioned in the preface, I have used imperial measurements throughout the book, generally for reasons of historical correctness. For those who prefer metric measurements the imperial units can be converted by use of the following data:

1 inch = 25.4 mm; thus a blade of 6.375 inches is in metric terms equivalent to $6.375 \times 25.4 = 161.93$ mm.

BIBLIOGRAPHY

As mentioned in the preface, British and Commonwealth knives have only formed part of many published books on knives, but these books still constitute essential background study. The following are particularly recommended:

Buerlein, Robert A., *Allied Military Fighting Knives and the Men Who Made Them Famous*, The American Historical Foundation, Richmond, Virginia, 1984. Large section on Commando knives.

Cole, M. H., *US Military Knives, Bayonets and Machetes, Books III and IV*, privately published, Birmingham, Alabama, 1979. As the title indicates, these books primarily cover US knives but do include pieces from Australia and New Zealand.

Flook, Ronald E., *A Photographic Primer of Military Knives*, privately published, June 1990. Only a few unusual British and Commonwealth knives shown, the bulk of the material being retained for this publication.

Hughes, Gordon and Barry Jenkins, *A Primer of Military Knives, Parts I and II*, privately published, Brighton, 1991. A good general guide to military knives including British and Commonwealth pieces.

Stephens, Frederick J., *Fighting Knives*, Arms and Armour Press, London, 1980. A good general guide to military knives with a very good section on the Ibberson Gravity Knife. However, a number of the knuckle knives featured are clearly fakes.

Thompson, Leroy, *Commando Dagger*, Paladin Press, Boulder, Colorado, 1985. A general guide, but a number of the illustrations are of presentation or commercial pieces.

Additional reading
Books

Barrie, Alexander, *War Underground*, Frederick Muller Ltd, London, 1962.

Carter, Anthony and John Walter, *The Bayonet – A History of Knife and Sword Bayonets 1850–1970*, Arms and Armour Press, London, 1974.

Chauvet, Maurice, *D-Day 1er B.F.M. Commando*, Amicale des Ancimens Parachutistes SAS and Commandos, Paris, 1974.

Davis, Brian L., *British Army Uniforms and Insignia of World War Two*, Arms and Armour Press, London, 1983.

Fairbairn, W. E., *All in Fighting*, Faber and Faber Ltd, London, 1942.

Foot, M. R. D. and J. M. Langley, *MI9 Escape and Evasion 1939–1945*, Book Club Associates, London, 1979.

Geraghty, Tony, *This Is The SAS*, Arms and Armour Press, London, 1982.

Goins, John E., *Goins' Encyclopedia of Cutlery Markings*, Knife World Publications, Knoxville, Tennessee, 1986.

Henry, Daniel Edward, *Collins Machetes and Bowies 1845–1965*, Krause Publications, Iola, Wisconsin, 1995.

Ladd, James D., *SBS, The Invisible Raiders*, Arms and Armour Press, London, 1983.

— and Keith Melton, *Clandestine Warfare – Weapons and Equipment of the SOE and OSS*, Blandford Press, London, 1988.

Lampe, David, *The Last Ditch*, Cassell and Co. Ltd, London, 1968.

Levine, Bernard, *Levine's Guide to Knives and Their Values*, DBI Books Inc., Northbrook, USA, 1985.

Lorain, Pierre, *Secret Warfare*, Orbis, London, 1984.

Lyle Official Arms and Armour Review, The, Lyle Publications, Galashiels, 1978.

Melton, H. Keith, *OSS Special Weapons and Equipment*, Sterling Publishing Co., New York, 1991.

Messenger, Charles, *The Commandos 1940–1946*, William Kimber, London, 1985.

Silvey, Michael W., *United States Military Knives 1941 to 1991*, privately published, Sacramento, California, 1992.

— and Gary D. Boyd, *United States Military Knives Collector's Guide*, privately published, Sacramento, California, 1989.

Skennerton, Ian D. and Robert Richardson, *British and Commonwealth Bayonets*, privately published, Australia, 1986.

Tweedale, Geoffrey, *The Sheffield Knife Book*, The Hallamshire Press, Broom Hall, Sheffield, 1996.

Washer, Richard, *The Sheffield Bowie and Pocket-knife Makers 1825–1925*, published by T. A. Vinall, 1974.

Wilkinson-Latham, John, *British Cut and Thrust Weapons*, David & Charles, Newton Abbot, 1971.

Magazines/journals etc.

After the Battle
American Blade, The
Antique Arms and Militaria
Blade, The
Canadian Journal of Arms Collecting
Caps and Flints
Combat Handguns
Edges
Fighting Knives
Guns, Weapons and Militaria
Knife World
Military Illustrated, Past and Present
Soldier of Fortune
Tactical Knives
Wilkinson Sword Collectors Society Newsletter

Sales/auction catalogues

Gruenberg, Morris, 'WWII Clandestine Blades of Special Forces', sales catalogue no.3/85

Kent Sales catalogue, August 1981

Manion's Auction 165, February 1995

Melton, H. Keith, 'Sales List of Clandestine Blades', July 1987

Romex International Inc. catalogue no.1/88

Van Dyk, Adrian, 'Catalog No.115. Sale of the personal knife collection of Adrian Van Dyk', 1978

END NOTES

Part One

1. See Stuart Reid, 'John Urquhart' in *Military Illustrated, Past and Present*, no.55, December 1992.
2. Gordon Hughes and Barry Jenkins, *A Primer of Military Knives Part 2*, Knife 128/128A.
3. Ibid. Knife 129/129A.
4. Kent Sales, catalogue for sale held on 26 August 1981, lot 585.
5. See Frederick Stephens, *Fighting Knives*, Chapter 5, pp.47–9; and Hughes and Jenkins, *Primer Part 1*.
6. *The Lyle Official Arms and Armour Review 1978*, p.63.
7. *Primer Part 2*, knife 119/119A.
8. Ibid. knife 141.
9. Ibid. knife 113.
10. *Fighting Knives*, Chapter 7, pp.60–1.
11. Hughes & Jenkins, *A Primer of Military Knives Part 1*, knives 100 to 104 inclusive.
12. 'Per Ardua Libertas, MI9 Technical', War Office, London SW1, 1942.
13. See Robert Wilkinson-Latham, 'The FS Commando Knife' in *Antique Arms and Militaria*, vol. 1, no.5, February 1979.
14. Ibid.
15. See *Primer Part 2*, a note on the marking of square shank FS Commando knives.
16. *Fighting Knives*, knife 515.
17. See *Commando Dagger*, knives 54 and 55.
18. *Fighting Knives*, knife 519.
19. 'Knife Catalog No.115. Sale of the personal knife collection of Adrian Van Dyk', 1978.
20. *Fighting Knives*, knives 496 to 498.
21. *Commando Dagger*, knives 71 and 72.
22. See 'Salvaging the D-Day Beaches' in *After the Battle*, no.34.
23. See Stephens, *Fighting Knives*, knives 506 to 512; and Thompson, *Commando Dagger*, p.73.
24. See 'The Wooden Grip Commando Knife' in *Guns, Weapons and Militaria*, vol. 2, no.1, December 1982.
25. *Commando Dagger*, knives 92 and 93.
26. *Allied Military Knives*, knife 64A.
27. Ibid. knife 70A.
28. See 'Falklands Special Commando Fighting Knife' in *Guns, Weapons and Militaria*, vol. 2, no.2, January/February 1983.
29. See *US Military Knives, Bayonets and Machetes, Book III*, p.172.
30. Leroy Thompson, 'Paratrooper Survival Fighting Knife' in *Soldier of Fortune*, September 1985.
31. Primer Part 2 Knife 120.
32. *Fighting Knives*, knife 537.
33. Primer Part 1 Knife 11.
34. 'Penknives and Pocket Knives', unattributed article on the work of Turner.
35. See *British Army Uniforms and Insignia of World War Two*, p.253.
36. Michael Silvey and Gary Boyd in *United States Military Knives Collector's Guide* (knife 36); and M. H. Cole in *US Military Knives, Bayonets and Machetes, Book IV*, p.112.

Part Two

1. See *US Military Knives, Bayonets and Machetes, Book III*, p.142.
2. *Primer Part 1*, knife 46/46A.
3. *Primer Part 2*, knives 133 and 134.

4. See *United States Military Knives 1941 to 1991*, p.37.
5. See *Primer Part 1*, knife 47; and *Fighting Knives*, knife 253.
6. 'Australian Military Fighting Knives', *Caps and Flints*, vol. 12, December 1990.
7. Manion's Auction 165, February 1995, lot R2007.
8. See *US Military Knives, Bayonets and Machetes, Book IV*, p.100.
9. Ibid. *Book III*, p.178.
10. 'Knife Catalog No.115', knife 268.
11. See Keith Melton, 'Sales List of Clandestine Blades', July 1987; see also Morris Gruenberg, 'WWII Clandestine Blades of Special Forces', Sales Catalog No.3/85.
12. See 'Australian Folders' in *Knife World*, April 1995.
13. See *Levine's Guide to Knives and Their Values*, p.52.

Part Three

1. See 'The Ross Bayonet and Scabbard' in the *Canadian Journal of Arms Collecting*, vol. 9, no.2.
2. *US Military Knives, Bayonets and Machetes, Book III*, p.50.
3. See *Primer Part 2*, knife 111; *Allied Military Fighting Knives*, pp.58–9; and *Commando Dagger*, pp.98–100.
4. 'Arms Sheaths for Fairbairn Sykes Fighting Knife' in *Fighting Knives*, Winter 1992.
5. See *Collins Machetes and Bowies 1845–1965*, p.125.
6. See *Levine's Guide to Knives and Their Values*, p.58.
7. See 'Canadian Military Folders of WWI' in *Knife World*, October 1989.
8. See 'The Special Pocket Knives of W. R. Case and Sons That Your Hardware Store Can't Sell You' in *The American Blade*, May/June 1976.

Part Four

1. 'Military Gurkha Issue Kukris', Army Museum 84.
2. See *US Military Knives, Bayonets and Machetes, Book III*, p.152.
3. See *Primer Part 2*, knife 112; *Commando Dagger*, p.62; and *Fighting Knives*, knife 527.
4. See *Primer Part 2*, knife 114.
5. 'Knife Catalog No.115', knife 168.
6. *Primer Part 2*, knife 143/143A.
7. See *Allied Military Fighting Knives*, pp.46–7.
8. See James Ladd and Keith Melton, *Clandestine Warfare – Weapons and Equipment of the SOE and OSS*, p.120.

Part Five

1. See Tony Geraghty, *This Is The SAS*, illustrations 352 and 361.
2. *US Military Knives, Bayonets and Machetes, Book III*, p.179.

Part Six

1. See *Primer Part 1*, knife 97.
2. 'Knives from Down Under' in *Edges*, Spring 1994.

Part Eight

1. Romex International Inc. Catalog No.1/88, item 16/2.
2. See 'The Swordsman' in the Wilkinson Sword Collector's Society Newsletter, no.2, Summer 1996.
3. See 'Australian Steel and Aluminium', *Knife World*, March 1995.

INDEX